ALSO BY SARAH PHILLIPS

The Healthy Oven Baking Book:
Delicious Bake-from-Scratch Desserts with Less Fat and Lots of Flavor

BAKING 9-1-1

- *Answers to Your Most Frequently Asked Baking Questions*

- *Rescue from Recipe Disasters*

- *40 Recipes for Every Baker*

SARAH PHILLIPS

A FIRESIDE BOOK
Published by Simon & Schuster
New York   London   Toronto   Sydney   Singapore

FIRESIDE
Rockefeller Center
1230 Avenue of the Americas
New York, NY 10020

FIRESIDE and colophon are registered trademarks
of Simon & Schuster, Inc.

For information regarding special discounts for bulk purchases,
please contact Simon & Schuster Special Sales at
1-800-456-6798 or business@simonandschuster.com

Designed by Katy Riegel

Manufactured in the United States of America

1   3   5   7   9   10   8   6   4   2

Library of Congress Cataloging-in-Publication Data is available.

ISBN 0-7432-4682-9

To my family:
My husband Reed and kids Tom and Liz Eswein
and my stepsons, Alex and Zach Phillips.
Thanks for faithfully tasting all of my test recipes!

CONTENTS

ACKNOWLEDGMENTS

❖

It takes a village to write a book and I have a lot of people to thank. First my family, husband Reed, kids Tom and Liz Eswein and Alex and Zach Phillips, for being there for me in such a loving and supportive way. My kids did their best trying to keep quiet when "mom was working," and I applaud them! And my wonderful husband Reed, whom I am so lucky to have married.

I couldn't have done this book without Carol Lloyd, Suzanne Fass, Elizabeth Clark or Tami Smith. Carol Lloyd, a professional food scientist, has been with me through the past 12 years with all of my baking projects and ideas, always lending me her comments and suggestions. I love her down-to-earth philosophy and her no-nonsense approach to food: "good food is good food!" I wish to thank Suzanne Fass, copy editor. Eagle-eyed, she really pulled the final manuscript together while keeping my ideas intact. I am very grateful for her hard work and diligence. Elizabeth Clark, the editor of the first manuscript, is a pleasure. As modern women in an era of computer technology, we worked together very smoothly via e-mail. She is smart and quick. Even though we worked long hours, she was always a pleasure! I enjoyed talking dog-shop in between e-mails. Tami Smith is a professional baker and contributing editor to the "Ask Sarah" Message Board (*www.baking911asksarah.com*) and to my free, bimonthly newsletter, "Sarah's Kitchen." Her information is always practical and sound.

The one and only Doris Cooper, my editor at Simon & Schuster. I have never worked with a more trusting person who supported my ideas, the vision for this book, and the concept of *Baking 9-1-1*. As a creative person, that means a lot to me. Thank you, Doris! And Katie Myers, Doris's assistant, who was always helpful. And my agent, Judith Riven, who believed in the *Baking 9-1-1* concept from the start. Her persistence and support has been incredible.

I wish to thank John Cooper (no relation to Doris) at Chicago Metallic Bakeware Company for giving me the opportunity to create recipes for one of their bakeware lines. His professional, heavy nonstick, and light colored line of pans are some of the best I have ever used.

Thanks also to Tom Payne at Clabber Girl for being the first sponsor of my website, *www.baking911.com*.

Thanks to Barry Marcus, professional chef, who wrote part of the candy section for this book, answering some of the more difficult candy questions I have ever received. And which, because of space limitations, we couldn't fit in. Next time, Barry.

And, cheers to my idols Julia Child, Nick Malgieri, and Jacques Torres with their sound baking and chocolate techniques, from whom I have learned a good foundation of techniques.

To home bakers everywhere, without whom this book would not have been possible.

To my father, Henry Shames, and in-laws, Nancy and Reed Phillips, who always take an active interest in what I do.

And last but not least, to my special mentor, my mother, Priscilla Oaks. I can still remember all of the good times we had in the kitchen together and trolling Los Angeles looking for exotic and ethnic foods. She never worried about whether her cakes or pies were perfect; she taught me to enjoy and cherish whatever I could make with my own two hands—and that, she said, "was good enough!"

INTRODUCTION

Why Baking 9-1-1?
What should I hope to get out of this book?

THIS BOOK IS FOR YOU, the home baker.

As a professional baker, I am a magnet for baking questions. When I made cookies for Manhattan boutiques and stayed to help sell them, customers wanted to know how to make a chocolate chip cookie that was thick *and* chewy. As I distributed gourmet foods to specialty stores in the Northeast, shoppers would constantly stop me just to ask a "quick question" about their cheesecake that would always crack or their bread that wouldn't rise. Inevitably, we'd swap more than a few tidbits of advice. Sometimes when I'm picking up items in the baking section of the grocery store, shoppers ask me about ingredients. They must think that anyone who would fill her cart with fifty pounds each of flour and sugar, or ten boxes of chocolate squares, must know about baking.

Part science, part nuance, and a lot of art, baking leaves people stumped. Yet, there's such an upside—impressive desserts, breads that rise like the summer moon, and pastries as flaky as anything you'd find in Paris—that I understand why people go in search of help as if they were seeking the Holy Grail. In my many incarnations—as baking mix company proprietor, specialty food salesperson, obsessive home baker, and founder of *www.baking911.com*—I have answered more than 75,000 questions. The best questions were the perplexing ones that left me performing kitchen chemistry and testing recipes.

However, when I didn't have time to experiment or couldn't conjure an answer, I didn't know where to direct bakers. Common baking questions such as "When a recipe indicates, '1 cup flour, sifted,' do I sift first and then measure or vice versa?" (page 33), "What is 'room temperature' butter?" (page 14) "Can I use ingredients right from the refrigerator instead of waiting for them to come to room temperature?" "What is the best way to store what I make?" and others confound bakers endlessly because answers to these questions aren't written down anywhere! When I looked in my collection of over 200 cookbooks, sometimes I couldn't find anything more than a recipe with little information for the home baker.

So, I decided to create my own source. I wanted to give you something that would fit on your kitchen counter, a manageable tome you could depend on for easy reference, that you would reach for as quickly as your favorite pan. I believed answers to more than 130 questions I was asked most frequently would assist any baker, from novice to professional. To accompany my answers I developed forty recipes for the baked goods people most like to make, because I discovered that many recipes aren't tailored toward getting you the result you want. My recipes are designed to help you circumvent the problems that leave you with disappointing outcomes. Some recipes took months to develop and refine, and don't appear on my website—this book is their debut!

My favorite saying is "the recipe rules!" A recipe is a blueprint, ensuring you will get a specific outcome. In essence, you can't get thick chocolate chip cookie unless you have a recipe written to make one. Yes, techniques help, such as chilling the dough or avoiding placing cookie dough on a warm baking sheet, but the ultimate DNA of a cookie comes from its recipe.

My goal in solving problems was to keep the baked goods as close as possible to the color, texture, smell, and other qualities people most adore. I also explain why things happen the way they do so you can predict and avoid disappointment when baking other recipes.

MY PROMISES TO YOU

There's nothing more frustrating than hearing someone make empty promises about baking, which, again, is all about the odd combination of science, nuance, and art, which are ethereal and unpredictable. When I sat down to write this book, I vowed the following:

- **To never say "It is quick and easy," because baking isn't:** especially when you're learning how to bake or making a recipe for the first time. Baking becomes easier with practice (and with this book, even if you just bake for the holidays), but it isn't automatically a breeze.
- **To never use the word "perfect."** Baking is a creative process in which there are hundreds of variables at play at once. It is not a realm in which you should strive for perfection. However, I will show you tips and tricks that will minimize mishaps.

- **To always *explain* why something happened the way it did.** Recipes leave out explanations and can simply say: "Prepare pan;" "Cream butter with sugar;" "Whip egg whites;" "Take it from the oven when done." If you know why to do something you can apply that knowledge to all areas of baking and cooking.
- **To *avoid* funny-sounding or obscure ingredients.** I worked hard to develop recipes that use common ingredients, with familiar mixing and baking techniques.
- **To *avoid* recipe variables** that make you play chemist: Recipes that suggest "If you add two tablespoons of flour you will get a puffy cookie" or "More chocolate makes for a fudgier brownie" are vague and invite disappointment.
- **To *not* be vague:** If you understand what you are doing, baking will make much more sense and become easier. I have set out to give ample and detailed explanations throughout the book.

PERFECTION IS HIGHLY OVERRATED

The most common question I get is, "What did I do wrong?" Perfection is the theme of all the e-mail I receive: "I want my recipe to turn out flawlessly because the relatives are coming for Christmas, and I haven't baked all year!" "I want to surprise my new husband with a cheesecake, but I've never made one before." "I want to make cupcakes that are richer than anyone has ever had for my son's birthday."

My answers and recipes will help anxiety-ridden bakers, but the best advice I give is simple: Worrying is a waste of time. Be yourself and do what you can do—and always pat yourself on the back for trying to make something homemade. The thought, effort, and love you put into your recipes are always revealed at the table.

If you do end up with something subpar, do what I do: serve it as is or have an extra dessert on hand, either from the store or one you baked from a cake mix and stored in the freezer for emergencies. Don't say a word; cover it with whipped cream. I always say: "Whipped cream hides most baking sins!" Or serve a bowl of ice cream and some fresh fruit.

TAKE MY SUGGESTIONS BUT TRUST YOURSELF

The suggestions in *Baking 9-1-1* reflect my observations, what I have learned from others, and what I have gleaned from experimentation. My family always jokes that as long as I'm baking and cooking, they'll *never* eat anything twice. If you have a way to bake that works for you, then stick with it (as long as safety concerns are followed) and see if my tips help you to improve upon what you know.

WHAT'S THE BEST WAY TO USE THIS BOOK?

Whether you're a novice or experienced, an everyday baker or holidays-only, I think you will find ideas and recipes here that will work their way into your baking practice and canon of favorite things to make. Of course you can use this book in any way that suits you, but here's what I recommend:

- Explore the first three chapters, either skimming if you're experienced or reading intently if you're a novice. You'll find essential background on some of what you'll be doing as you bake, whether with my recipes or with others.
- Move on to the chapters that have baked goods that interest you—cakes, cookies, pastry, pies, chocolate, breads, and quick breads. Each chapter explains the interplay of ingredients, essential methods, and tips. Avoid making substitutions, unless you've fully considered their impact and compensated for it.

WHAT IF I STILL HAVE QUESTIONS?

You can ask me baking questions any time. Just go to *www.baking911.com,* click on "Ask Sarah," and post your question.

I hope these questions, answers, and recipes help make you a supremely confident baker, and a successful one. Enjoy the fruits of your labor of love!

Happy Baking!

1

SARAH'S KITCHEN PANTRY

So, what's in your kitchen, Sarah?
. . . the inside story on equipment I can't live
(or at least bake) without.

THE BAKER MUST WORK within the parameters of a recipe to produce a baked good that will rise, set, and taste the way he or she intends. Important in your ability to achieve that is having the right equipment and an accurate oven, and by avoiding overmixing or overbaking. Recipes don't have to be followed dead on, but if you stray by more than about 20 percent, you risk disappointment. Keep in mind, too, that not all recipes work in the first place, and it's hard to tell that in advance!

WHAT EVERY BAKER SHOULD HAVE

Nested metal dry measuring cups: Measure dry ingredients, solid fats, brown sugar, peanut butter, honey, molasses, corn syrup, sour cream, yogurt, applesauce, and flaked coconut. I use them in sets in $\frac{1}{8}$, $\frac{1}{4}$, $\frac{1}{3}$, $\frac{1}{2}$ and 1 cup sizes.

Heatproof glass measuring cups for liquid ingredients: Measure all liquids such as water, milk, buttermilk, and oil, in amounts at or above $\frac{1}{4}$ cup; for less than $\frac{1}{4}$ cup use measuring spoons. I have the basic 1-, 4-, and 8-cup sizes. Larger sizes (4-cup or more) are perfect to use as mixing bowls as well.

Measuring spoons: They come in different sizes. They are used to measure both dry and liquid ingredients. Don't try to measure with spoons meant for table use.

Ruler and tape measure: I always keep a ruler and a tape measure in my kitchen drawer and use them all the time. They measure the size of pans and parchment paper, cookie dough, pie crusts, ready-made pastry, etc. A ruler is handy when scor-

Welcome to my kitchen:

"It's an avalanche," I yelled on a hot summer day many years ago as I opened the door to my large closet-like pantry. As the shelf inside gave way, out came bags and boxes of ingredients and pots and pans galore and things that I didn't even remember owning. It was then I decided to make some changes. It was either remodel the kitchen or clean out the closet. Luckily for my marriage I chose the latter.

My goal was to keep only the essentials I needed for cooking and baking so that I would not have to wear a bicycle helmet every time I opened that door. I share with you my findings.

Because I bake (and cook) all the time not only for my family but also to develop recipes, I have several sets of everything listed here, especially measuring cups and spoons. I have been collecting kitchen stuff for years. My kitchen is small by suburban standards, but everything is within reach, making it extremely efficient.

This is a small sampling of what I have on hand to bake almost anything. Of course, I occasionally go to the store for something special.

Happy baking,
Sarah

ing dough; place it on the dough as a guide for the knife. A recipe will bake more evenly if divided equally.

Scale: When more than doubling a recipe, I recommend weighing dry ingredients to ensure accuracy. Make sure the scale measures up to several pounds in $\frac{1}{4}$-ounce (5-gram) increments.

Thermometers: These come in different types for different purposes. They are essential to accurate baking and chocolate work. When you get a new thermometer, always place in it boiling water for about five minutes to test whether or not it reads 212 degrees F (100 degrees C) at the boiling point. This way you will know your exact thermometer reading, and you can make adjustments if necessary or return it.

- Instant read thermometer: A small and thin thermometer with a gauge or digital readout on top. I use mine all the time to check the doneness of breads, temperature of ingredients, and the temperature of the warm water used to dissolve yeast. You'll notice that chefs have them clipped on their jackets all the time.
- Candy or deep-fat thermometer: A handy kitchen gadget necessary for testing temperature when making candy, syrups, jams, jellies, and when deep-frying, in order to get the food to exactly the right temperature.

- Mercury-gauge chocolate thermometer: Used when melting and tempering chocolate; is the most accurate thermometer for these purposes. Don't use a candy thermometer because the temperature gauge does not register low enough.
- Oven thermometer: Essential to baking. Ovens can be off by as much as 50 degrees F and the thermometer helps you to adjust the heat for proper baking.

Sarah Says: Every baker has—or develops—preferences about specific makes of equipment. But if you're just beginning to bake, I recommend trying out equipment that seems solid and well made, but is not necessarily the most expensive.

Timer: This is essential to help you keep track of baking times. I also use mine to keep track of mixing times. You can use the timer from the microwave or stove or get a freestanding one.

WOULDN'T-WANT-TO-BAKE-WITHOUT-IT EQUIPMENT

BAKING PANS

Always use the size and type specified in a recipe. If you don't have the correct pan size, you can substitute one for another, but the ideal pan substitution is one that keeps close to the same batter volume and depth of the original. Heavyweight, dull aluminum pans with straight edges are the best to use. If your budget is limited, here is one place to splurge for a really good set.

For pies, I prefer heatproof glass pie plates. They distribute the heat better than metal ones, and you can look underneath to see how the crust is browning. I also prefer heatproof glass pans for fruit-based desserts, but you can use nonstick metal ones, too.

QUESTION: *I just purchased a set of nonstick pans. Do I have to grease them?*

ANSWER: Yes. Think of nonstick pans as "less-stick," as baking recipes still stick to them. Spray with vegetable oil or grease with butter or shortening. For cakes that are hard to unmold such as Bundt cakes, flour the pan as well. Or, if you want to apply an extra thick layer of grease in the pan, grease the pan as you normally would, pop it in the freezer for 5 to 10 minutes to set, and then apply a second coating. Let it sit at room temperature before filling.

To verify the size you have:

- Check the bottom of the pan and see if the manufacturer has marked it for you.
- If it is a baking pan such as cake pan, measure the length and width at the inside edges across the top.
- To find the volume measure tap water in a measuring cup and pour into the pan. Fill it to the brim. Note how much water you used.
- Saucepans and skillets should be measured from outside edges across the top.
- Depth is always measured on the outside, vertically from the bottom of the pan to the top edge.

BAKING (COOKIE) SHEETS

When I was invited to tour Land O'Lakes Headquarters in Minneapolis, I witnessed the making of chocolate chip cookies in their test kitchen. The goal was to test three different types of cookie sheets. The winner: non-insulated, nonstick, shiny aluminum pans with rims. The cookies were lightly and evenly browned around the edges, with a hint of browning on top. They spread the least and baked the fastest. Insulated sheets were far inferior for baking cookies evenly.

If you like to use insulated ones and can't buy them, double up your current pans: put one on top of another to create "padding" against the oven heat. Be careful when taking the top sheet out of the oven—leave the bottom one in the oven and just take out the top one holding the cookies.

Sarah Says: Using a metal spatula, always scrape the crumbs from your baking sheets between batches. Or, line with parchment if you prefer a quick and easy clean-up.

BOWLS

You've just got to have them. What kind and how many:

- Mixing bowls: I prefer nested metal ones because they are light and can be banged around more without getting hurt, but heatproof glass bowls work well, too.

- Heatproof glass custard cups: great for melting butter and chocolate in the microwave and for holding premeasured ingredients.

CUTTING BOARDS

I use plastic cutting boards, separated by the food types I cut on them. Wooden boards can hold oils and odors that food will absorb.

DOUBLE BOILERS

Used as an indirect heating method, a double boiler is basically two pots that stack one on top of the other, where the bottom pot holds boiling water and the top one holds the food. The steam from the hot water beneath gently heats the contents in the pot above with a cushion of air in between. It is used when making delicate custards, melting chocolate (page 166) or cooking meringue icing (page 55), to provide gentle cooking heat.

If you don't have a double boiler, you can take a heavy-bottomed saucepan and fit a stainless steel or heatproof glass bowl tightly over it. I prefer a glass bowl because it retains the heat more evenly, which is good for chocolate work.

Never let the top of your double boiler touch the water below. Boiling water is 212 degrees F; that's too hot and is considered direct heat.

ELECTRIC MIXERS

These can be either stand or handheld. I have both a KitchenAid Heavy Duty stand and Cuisinart handheld mixers. If you are a beginner, start with a handheld mixer.

Stand mixers are more powerful and quicker than handheld, so be sure not to overmix your dough or batter.

MIXING SPOONS

I recommend both wooden and heatproof spoons for hot mixtures. Stainless steel cooks' spoons work well for all others. Do not use wooden when melting chocolate (page 166); it absorbs moisture and may cause chocolate to seize.

MUFFIN TINS

Muffin tin measurements will vary. Use a size closest to the ones listed. They come in 6- or 12-muffin sizes. Fill about ½ to ¾ full depending on the recipe. Muffin *top* tins are filled to the rim:

- Standard muffin cup is approximately 2½ inches in diameter and holds ¼ to ⅓ cup of batter.
- Giant, jumbo, or Texas-size muffin cup is approximately 3½ inches in diameter and holds 1 cup of batter.
- Miniature muffin cup is approximately 1½ to 2 inches in diameter and holds about 1 tablespoon batter.
- Muffin *top* cup is approximately 4 inches in diameter but only ½ inch deep. Holds ½ cup batter.

PAPERS AND FOIL

- Parchment paper: I use parchment paper, also called baking paper, frequently because it is nonstick and allows me to remove the baked recipe from its pan more easily.
- Waxed paper: Waxed paper is essentially tissue paper that's coated with paraffin on both sides, supposedly making it greaseproof and moisture proof. It lets liquids soak through eventually, tears easily, and the wax will start to melt unless it's completely covered and protected from the heat. Many bakers use it to line the bottom of a batter-filled cake or brownie pan, but I prefer parchment.
- Aluminum foil: There is no difference between the shiny and dull sides—I called the manufacturer and asked. It doesn't matter "which side is up."

PIE AND TART PANS

Standard pie pans are 8 or 9 inches in diameter and 1¼ inches deep. The two sizes are interchangeable. Deep-dish pies are baked in larger pans with deeper sides or baking pans or casserole dishes. Larger or deeper pans require additional dough and filling.

Standard tart pans are round, with a 9- or 10-inch diameter and 1-inch deep fluted sides and a removable bottom. I prefer tin-plated tart pans to black steel ones; they are easier to maintain and do not rust. Tarts are also baked in metal rings placed directly on a baking sheet.

ROLLING PINS

Both straight wooden and straight stainless steel pins are highly recommended. Never wash your hardwood pin; wipe it thoroughly with a damp cloth after each use.

SHEET (JELLY ROLL) PANS

There are two types of sheet pans, one for commercial use, and the other that can fit in a home oven. You'll see both types for sale. Home sizes:

$10\frac{1}{2}$- by $15\frac{1}{2}$- by 1-inch
$12\frac{1}{2}$- by $17\frac{1}{2}$- by 1-inch

SPATULAS AND SCRAPERS

- Rubber spatula: I have them in multiple sizes. I mostly use them to scrape ingredients off the sides of bowls during mixing, for folding ingredients into a dough or spreading batter evenly in a pan.
- Offset spatula: the true spatula. A long metal blade with a rounded tip and straight edges, bent at an angle to be lower than but parallel to the handle; used to flip and transfer foods, lift edges to look underneath, and level dry ingredients for proper measuring. I also use it to loosen the sides of baked goods from the pan because it's thin and relatively sharp.
- Icing spatula: I like to use a 10-inch spatula for icing cakes. An icing spatula can be straight or offset, and only about 1 inch wide.
- Metal Spatula. A versatile utensil for flipping pancakes, removing cookies or corn bread from baking pans, and serving cake squares. The sharper the edge, the better.
- Bench or dough scraper: Used to scrape and lift dough from flat surfaces, for example pastry or cookie dough. A bench scraper is a small, rectangular (3 by 6-inch or 4 by 6-inch) stainless steel somewhat dull blade with a handle, available in cookware stores. If you can't find one, go to any paint or hardware store and pick up a 5- or 6-inch wide Sheetrock broad knife.

STRAINERS

Strainers and sieves are bowl-shaped utensils with a perforated or mesh bottom and sometimes a handle, used to separate solids from liquids and to sift dry ingredients. I have from small to large.

WHISKS

A whisk has strands of looped wire attached to a long handle. I use a flat, straight whisk for making smooth sauces or cooked fillings because it can get into the corners of the pan. Balloon whisks are used for whipping and folding delicate ingredients by hand. I also have piano whisks in several sizes that I use to mix sauces or light batters as well as to do quick whisking.

WIRE CAKE OR COOLING RACKS

Essential. They are used to cool baked goods. Mine have a 3-inch clearance between the rack and the countertop; it prevents condensation from forming. The general rule is to remove the pan with its contents to the wire cake rack for 10 minutes before unmolding. This will help prevent the recipe from cracking or breaking because it's too hot. However, if you leave most baked goods in the pan too long after baking, they will sweat on the bottom and become nearly impossible to remove neatly from the pan.

For glazing baked goods I use a ¾-inch-high rack set in a parchment- or waxed paper–lined sheet pan.

2

INGREDIENTS

What do ingredients contribute to your recipe?

A RECIPE IS ONLY AS GOOD as the ingredients that are used to make it. If you put top quality ingredients into your recipe, you'll get a top quality baked good. Use only the freshest and best that you can buy. Use real chocolate when making chocolate confections. Those chocolate-flavored morsels may be cheaper, but that's exactly how they taste. The same is true for almost every ingredient. This is the place to splurge.

Wheat flour, sugar, fat, eggs, liquid, leavening, and salt are the basic ingredients used in batters and doughs. The quality of home-baked products depends on the proportions of ingredients, how they are measured, mixed, at what temperature, and in which type of pan and for how long they are baked. These relationships affect the color, flavor, texture, shape, and volume of the finished product.

Use the ingredients your recipe specifies. I'm taking a strong position in making this statement. Remember, baking a recipe successfully is all about the balance among ingredients. If you substitute beyond what the recipe calls for, you can throw off its delicate balance. Even a seemingly simple substitution of a different kind of flour, sugar, or fat can do that.

In general, ingredients can be divided into two types, sometimes overlapping: "tougheners/strengtheners" (flour, whole eggs, egg whites, and milk) are essentially what hold the recipe together, while "tenderizers/weakeners" (fat, sugar, egg yolks, and acid such as lemon juice or cream of tartar), do the opposite: they actually soften the structure. In order for a recipe to bake with all of the qualities we like—creamy, moist, chewy, dense—there needs to be a balance between the two types. If one is increased, decreased, or substituted for, the other must be adjusted to compensate.

Having the right types and proportions of flour, eggs, sugar, and fat makes all the difference.

THE TEMPERATURE OF INGREDIENTS

Old-fashioned recipes were hand-mixed, hence the need for warmer ingredients so they'd mix faster. Today, we use electric mixers most of the time and they warm the ingredients. This may sound blasphemous, but I think the whole room temperature thing is old-fashioned. I usually use ingredients cold from the refrigerator except for temperature-sensitive ingredients such as chocolate. In the case of creaming butter and sugar, cold butter will take longer to get to the right consistency before you can add the sugar, but it will get there. You may have some textural differences in your final product, but with electric mixers these differences are minimized.

For recipes other than chocolate ones, I seldom have time to let my eggs and dairy come to room temperature; I always use them right from the refrigerator. I always thought I was doing something wrong and "breaking the rules," but I didn't see any difference in how recipes came out. I've decided to "come out of the pantry" and share my experience with you. In my recipes, I indicate room temperature to avoid confusion.

Here is my spiel on temperature: Unless a recipe says "chilled," "cold," or "warm," or specifies a temperature in degrees, the implication is to use room temperature ingredients.

METHODS FOR ROOM TEMPERATURE INGREDIENTS (68 TO 70 DEGREES F)

BUTTER

Don't let butter get too soft or melt (unless specified). If it does, get another cold stick from the refrigerator. It warms as you work with it.

Your butter is at room temperature when:

1. you hold the wrapped butter in your hand and press it gently between your thumb and index finger, they leave an indentation. The butter should still be firm;
2. you can bend a stick of butter slightly with your hands. Again, it should still feel firm;
3. the butter has a shiny surface but doesn't appear greasy;
4. an instant read thermometer inserted in the center of the stick of butter reads 65 to 68 degrees F. This is the most accurate test.

You can melt butter in a microwave. Unwrap, cut, and place it in a microwave-safe container such as a custard cup, and microwave 1 stick (8 tablespoons or ½ cup) at 100 percent power for one minute. Use less time for smaller amounts such as 30 to 45 seconds when melting 3 to 4 tablespoons (¼ cup or ½ stick butter). Watch carefully so it doesn't burn! (Note: lower wattage ovens may need more time.) If you melt butter on top of the stove use low heat and watch carefully while stirring frequently. Remove from the heat immediately when just melted.

> **Sarah Says:** If you want to use room temperature ingredients, let them sit out, well covered on a countertop, until they reach 65 to 68 degrees F, which is considered to be fine for room temperature. Nothing that is usually refrigerated (eggs, milk, butter) should stay out for more than two hours.

EGGS

Put whole, uncracked eggs in their shells in a bowl of medium-warm tap water for ten to fifteen minutes only. Set a kitchen timer to help you keep track of the time. Turn the eggs in the water with a spoon during that time. If the egg shells are still cold to the touch, repeat for two minutes. Dry them with a towel before cracking.

CREAM CHEESE

You can soften Philadelphia Brand cream cheese by letting it stand for no more than 1 to 2 hours at room temperature. If you can't wait, place a single unwrapped package on a microwavable plate. Microwave on HIGH for 15 seconds. Add 15 seconds for each additional package of cream cheese. Or beat the cream cheese in a stand mixer on low speed with the paddle attachment.

MILK

For 1½ cups, microwave in a microwave-safe bowl at 50 percent power for 1 minute.

STORING INGREDIENTS

Once you've invested in those top quality ingredients, you need to ensure they remain in top form by storing them properly. Here are three basic guidelines to storage:

• Items that must be refrigerated, such as eggs and dairy products, should be kept cold throughout storage, and used quickly.

• Items that don't require refrigeration, such as spices, white flour, and baking powder, are still perishable.
• Even non-refrigerated items should be kept away from heat.

Flour doesn't keep forever and is more susceptible to spoilage than you might think. If flour is stored improperly or for too long—especially whole-wheat flour—it can develop a rancid flavor. The fat from the germ in whole grain flour can rot over time, and you can tell by smelling it. Store white flours in a dark, cool pantry in an airtight container; don't refrigerate or freeze. Whole-wheat flour can also be stored this way, but I like to freeze mine for a longer shelf life.

Leaveners such as baking powder and baking soda should be stored in a cool, dry place; the pantry is fine. Refrigerating them is not a good idea, since they can absorb moisture and odors. Store dehydrated yeast in a cool, dark pantry or in the freezer (it keeps longer frozen, sometimes a year after its expiration date). Store fresh yeast in the refrigerator.

Fats go rancid easily if they are not stored properly. Keep butter in the refrigerator, and oils in a cool, dark pantry. Solid shortening, which is hydrogenated to give it a longer shelf life, can be stored at room temperature. If you have an excess of butter, it freezes nicely.

Store sweeteners, whether crystalline or liquid, in airtight containers in a cool, dark pantry. This is especially important for brown sugar, which dries out quickly and hardens. Salt should be stored in a cool, dark, dry place.

Eggs should be stored in their original carton in the coldest part of the refrigerator. All other dairy products should be kept refrigerated, although unopened cans of evaporated or condensed milk may be kept in the pantry. Cream cheese can pick up odors easily if not in its original closed package, so wrap it tightly in plastic wrap.

Store chocolate and cocoa powder in a cool, dry place. In very hot weather, or if your kitchen is always warm, you can keep chocolate in the freezer. Make sure it is well-wrapped.

Store nuts in the freezer, so they won't turn rancid quickly.

Check expiration or "use by" dates on ingredients, and discard expired ones. Make it a practice to check the dates on leavening, such as yeast, baking powder, and baking soda, and anything perishable such as dairy. Make sure any fats, such as butter or oils, are not rancid; smell, and discard if any are. I always say, "When in doubt, throw it out."

INGREDIENTS ❖

16

EXPLORING INGREDIENTS IN DEPTH

Each ingredient in a recipe contributes something important to the final baked good, and works in conjunction with every other.

WHEAT FLOUR

Wheat flour provides the structure in baked goods from both its gluten-forming proteins, glutenin and gliadin, and its starches. Wheat is the only grain that contains significant amounts of gluten-forming proteins and for that reason is the only type of

QUESTION: *What's the difference between unbleached flour and bleached?*

ANSWER: One main difference between unbleached and bleached flour is the color; flour is off-white and becomes pure white when the carotenoid (yellow) pigments are bleached. If a recipe doesn't specify, you can use either one, but where a whiter color is desired, use the bleached one. For those looking for *untreated* flour, note that unbleached flour can still be treated with maturing agents and chemical dough improvers. See page 181 for more on flours in bread.

QUESTION: *Which grains can I consider using in a bread recipe? How much should I add?*

ANSWER: "Whole grain flours" come from many sources in addition to grains; legumes, starchy vegetables, nuts, and carob. I like barley flour (gives breads a cake-like texture and pleasant sweetness), potato flour (mild potato taste; softness and tenderness), kamut (nutty flavor), amaranth (smooth textured breads), spelt (exceptional protein and fiber profile), soy (slightly sweet, pleasant flavor), millet (nut-like, slightly sweet flavor), rice (brown rice flour gives bread a moist, smooth texture), plus triticale, oat flour, sweet chestnut, teff—the list goes on and on. They all contain some protein, but not enough to develop gluten for a bread loaf, so they must be mixed with wheat flour except for special baking, where other ingredients are added. Generally, I recommend adding no more than 25 percent of the weight of the flour in whole grains unless there are special instructions that go along with using a particular grain.

BAKING 9-1-1

❖

17

flour that can be truly leavened. When wheat flour is stirred, mixed, beaten, kneaded, or otherwise manipulated with moisture, the glutenin and gliadin proteins hydrate and form gluten strands, much like rubber bands, that connect and cross-connect. Gluten gives dough elasticity, strength, structure, and gas-retaining properties. Baking "sets" this framework. Starches begin to gelatinize (absorb water and set from the heat of the oven) between 140 and 158 degrees F (the exact temperature depends on the specific starch). During baking, the stretched gluten becomes rigid as the moisture evaporates from the heat, and sets the structure. Other ingredients also play a role.

There are many types of wheat flour. The primary determinant of outcome is the amount of gluten, protein, and fiber the flour has. If the recipe just says "flour" or "white flour," it means all-purpose, the most common type. I like to use unbleached all-purpose flour, but you can substitute bleached.

Flour is measured by spooning flour into a dry measuring cup, filling it, and leveling to top.

LEAVENERS

Leaveners contribute airiness, color, texture, and flavor.

BAKING SODA AND BAKING POWDER

Chemical leaveners create carbon dioxide (CO_2) when activated. They expand the air bubbles beaten into the batter; they do not create new ones. Double acting baking powder is a blend of acid (aluminum pyrophosphate), baking soda (sodium or potassium bicarbonate, both alkaline) and a carrier (cornstarch). Baking soda (sodium bicarbonate) is generally used when there is an acidic ingredient in the recipe such as vinegar, lemon juice, sour milk, or buttermilk. The acid might be hidden in honey or molasses. When baking soda comes in contact with an acidic ingredient and is moistened, the alkali-acid combination creates carbon dioxide.

Self-rising flour has the salt and leavening agent already added: 1 cup of self-rising flour equals 1 cup of cake or all-purpose flour plus 1¼ teaspoons baking powder and a pinch of salt.

YEAST

Yeast is a living microorganism that is destroyed by heat. As yeast grows and multiplies, it releases carbon dioxide gas, which causes the dough to rise. Its action is affected by the addition or deletion of other ingredients such as salt and sugar. (See information on yeast in bread baking, page 185). Packaged or baker's yeast: Active dry yeast, instant active dry, and bread machine yeast are available as dehydrated granules in packets. Fresh yeast is found in the refrigerator section of your supermarket.

STARTERS

Before this yeast was available, bakers developed a wild or natural leaven called a **sourdough** from a highly fermented mixture of water and wheat flour. Now, with added yeast this is called a sponge, page 205.

FATS

Fat, in the form of solid shortening, or butter, or in the liquid form of vegetable or olive oil, contributes tenderness, the perception of moistness, and a smooth feel on

QUESTION: *There are so many types of yeast in the grocery store. I often don't know what to choose. Please help.*

ANSWER: For homemade yeast bread recipes I recommend using active dry yeast because it's reliable, easy to find, and easy to use. Fresh yeast gives the strongest yeast taste, but it expires quickly. A newer product, instant active dry yeast, is blended in with the flour. I use it with my bread machine recipes, not my loaves made by hand; it doesn't impart as much flavor.

QUESTION: *How do I substitute one kind of yeast for another?*

ANSWER: Here is a guideline, but equivalencies may vary, so follow the package instructions:

One (1/4-ounce) packet of active dry yeast, or one (0.6-ounce) compressed fresh yeast cake equals 2¼ teaspoons dry yeast (active dry, instant active dry, bread machine).

QUESTION: *Does yeast expire?*

ANSWER: Yes, packaged yeast will literally expire because it is a living organism. It has an expiration date printed on its package. Fresh yeast has a shelf life of 2 to 3 weeks in the refrigerator. If you store dry yeast in the freezer, it will keep well beyond its expiration date, for about a year if unopened. But if you keep it that long or are unsure if it's still active, I suggest testing it before use.

1. Fill a 1-cup measure to the 1/2 cup level with warm water at 100 to 110 degrees F as measured with an instant read thermometer. (If you place a few drops of water on the inside of your wrist, it should feel comfortable.)
2. Stir in 1 teaspoon sugar (whether called for in the recipe or not) and sprinkle the yeast evenly over the surface. After a few minutes, whisk in the yeast until it has fully absorbed the water.
3. Let the yeast mixture sit for another 2 or 3 minutes. Tiny bubbles should begin to appear on the surface and it should smell yeasty. At the end of 10 minutes, it should bubble to the top of the cup and have a rounded crown. The froth will deflate when stirred. Adjust the recipe for the yeast, water, and sugar used in the test.

the palate to baked goods. Butter is 81 percent fat and 19 percent water. Fats such as butter and oil enhance the flavors of other ingredients, too. When creamed with sugar, solid fat plays a role in leavening. Fats can go rancid easily, so smell them before using.

Shortening is 100 percent fat and is solid at room temperature. It is hydrogenated to give it a longer shelf life. The process of hydrogenation also raises the melting point somewhat. Shortening comes in both cans and sticks.

In baked goods such as muffins, reducing the amount of fat in a recipe results in a

QUESTION: *I have only salted butter and my recipe calls for unsalted. Can I use it?*

ANSWER: Yes. Salted butter has only ⅛ teaspoon salt per stick (½ cup), which won't have an impact on your recipe. Do not use the soft butter in tubs. Unsalted butter tends to be fresher than salted; salt is a preservative.

tougher product because gluten develops more freely. Another tenderizing agent such as sugar can be added or increased to tenderize in place of the fat.

SWEETENERS

In addition to providing sweetness, sugar:

- tenderizes;
- helps attract and retain moisture;
- can cause spreading during baking (as with cookies);
- in large amounts, slows yeast fermentation; in very sweet dough the rising time is longer. It can also kill the yeast by taking water away from it;
- helps with browning.

Crystalline sugars such as granulated (regular or superfine), brown sugar, and confectioners' (also known as powdered or 10X), and liquid sugars such as honey, corn

QUESTION: *During storage my brown sugar turned hard as a rock. Can it be saved?*

ANSWER: Yes. Air hardens brown sugar by evaporating the water from it. To soften: Place what you need in a microwave-safe container. Cover loosely with a damp paper towel. Microwave on HIGH, checking the sugar every 30 seconds, and cool. Caution: It gets really hot. Then measure.

To keep sugar from hardening in the first place place it in a resealable plastic bag, place the filled bag in an airtight container, and store in a cool, dry place or freeze. To use frozen sugar thaw it at room temperature. Gently stir immediately when thawed.

❖

syrup, and molasses, are staples in just about everyone's kitchen. Knowing which type to use can be confusing. When a recipe calls simply for "sugar," it is safe to assume that granulated table sugar is intended.

A crystalline sugar cannot be easily exchanged for a liquid one, although superfine may be substituted for regular white sugar.

Fructose, such as honey, attracts more water than sugar; therefore, fructose-sweetened products tend to be moist. Honey, brown sugar, and molasses are acidic so the leaveners may need to be adjusted.

EGGS

When a recipe says "eggs" it means fresh large Grade A eggs that have been refrigerated. Make sure they aren't cracked. If they have to be separated first (page 37), a

QUESTION: *I have read in recipes that I can use egg white powder and meringue powder. What are they, and how do I use them?*

ANSWER: Egg white powder is just that: dried egg whites. Meringue powder is dried egg whites with sugar, cream of tartar, and cornstarch, so you may not need to add the sugar called for in a meringue recipe. Both dried egg whites and meringue powder are pasteurized and completely safe from harmful bacteria (Salmonella). I store opened meringue powder in the refrigerator. Opened egg white powder can be stored in the pantry. They can be used in any recipe calling for raw egg whites such as foam cakes (page 64), meringue (page 36), and royal icing. To figure out how much you need, look on the container: it should direct you as to how much to use to equal the amount of raw egg whites. The usual measurements are: two teaspoons of *egg white powder* mixed with two tablespoons of warm water equals one large egg white; two teaspoons of *meringue powder* mixed with two tablespoons of warm water equals one large egg white.

These powders often clump when you dissolve them. To avoid clumping, put the appropriate amount of *warm* water in a bowl, sprinkle the powder over the surface of the water, and let it sit for about 5 minutes, stirring once. Break up any clumps with your fingertips. Then whisk to combine.

Refrigerate any unused rehydrated powder. If it has clumped you'll have to break up the clumps before using it. If the clumps won't break up, unfortunately you'll have to start over again because they won't dissolve during baking!

QUESTION: *Sometimes I find recipes which call only for egg whites, such as an angel food cake. I really don't know what to do with the left over egg yolks and I don't like to waste. Any suggestions?*

ANSWER: I hate to throw anything out myself. You can freeze yolks for later use. Beat the egg yolks lightly, then add sugar or salt, depending on whether you intend to use them in a sweet or savory recipe. Per $\frac{1}{4}$ cup egg yolks, about 3 to 4 yolks (1 egg yolk equals 1 tablespoon), mix in $1\frac{1}{2}$ teaspoons of sugar or corn syrup or $\frac{1}{8}$ teaspoon of salt. Store the extra egg yolks in the freezer in an airtight plastic container, clearly marked with the date and number of yolks. Some cooks freeze one egg yolk per cavity in an ice cube tray, and then transfer these to a plastic, airtight bag where they will keep for one year. To use, thaw in the refrigerator, then mix well. Use within three days. They will not look the same as fresh egg yolks, but they work just as well.

Egg whites and whole eggs can be frozen in the same manner as yolks except that there's no need to add anything.

recipe should specify that in the ingredients list—for example "xx large egg whites" or "xx large egg yolks" or "xx separated eggs."

See page 54 for help on dividing whole eggs when cutting a recipe.

Safe food handling alert: Before you start handling eggs, always wash your hands thoroughly with hot, soapy water. After contact with raw eggs, wash your hands, cooking utensils, and countertops immediately with hot, soapy water. The American Egg Board (*www.aeb.org*) recommends briefly rinsing eggs and drying before cracking them.

DAIRY

Milk contains proteins (as do eggs and flour) that contribute to the structure of baked goods by setting or coagulating from the oven's heat. Dairy also adds moisture. Some dairy products, such as buttermilk, sour cream, or cream cheese, add richness and flavor; cakes made with them keep well. The acid in buttermilk and sour cream tenderizes the gluten in the recipe, producing a fine crumb. Sour cream and cream cheese add richness, making recipes that call for them super moist, almost springy. Cream is the high-fat component of milk; the more fat a recipe contains, the richer the outcome.

Evaporated and sweetened condensed milks are made by removing about 50 to 60 percent of the water from fresh milk. Sweetened condensed milk is thicker and sweeter; more water has been removed and sugar added than in evaporated milk.

They cannot be substituted for each other. Store in a dark, cool pantry for 6 months to a year or more. Once opened, refrigerate.

Freshly whipped cream adds volume and velvety texture to mousses and batters. When lightly flavored with sugar, liqueur, extracts, or citrus zest, whipped cream adds a rich, snowy blanket to fresh fruit, pies, cakes, and tarts.

OTHER LIQUIDS

Liquid is necessary in baked goods for hydrating flour proteins, starch, and ingredients and, not surprisingly, for contributing to moistness. When water vaporizes in a batter or dough during baking, the steam expands the air cells, increasing the final volume of the recipe.

If a recipe calls for hot water, use the hottest water from the tap. If it says boiling water, then it must be boiled before using because hot water isn't hot enough.

QUESTION: *How do I whip cream?*

ANSWER: Believe it or not I get lots of questions on how to whip cream. A recipe will indicate either "1 cup heavy cream, whipped to stiff peaks," meaning take 1 cup of heavy cream and whip it to stiff peaks, or will indicate "2 cups whipped cream," meaning that you take 1 cup of liquid cream and whip it, which results in 2 cups of whipped cream. Here's a recipe:

WHIPPED CREAM RECIPE

2 cups heavy cream (36 to 40% butterfat), chilled
2 to 3 tablespoons confectioners', superfine, or regular sugar
2 teaspoons vanilla extract or 1 tablespoon dark rum or flavored liqueur

1. Chill the cream in the refrigerator, preferably overnight. It must be well chilled. Place the bowl and whisk or beaters in the freezer for a good 20 minutes before using. Use a bowl that's deep and narrow with at least a 3-quart capacity as the cream will double in volume when whipped.

2. Using a handheld electric mixer, beat on low speed until small bubbles form, about 30 seconds, and then increase the speed to medium and then to high. Slowly add the sugar and flavorings to the cream at the side of the bowl. Continue to whip as you do. Move the beaters up, down, and around the side of the bowl while whipping. With a rubber spatula, scrape down the side of the bowl often.

3. Stop whipping when the cream has doubled in volume, is smooth, thick, and is billowy when the beaters are raised.

4. Serve immediately—it is best made the day of use. Cover and refrigerate for up to 24 hours. If the cream separates in the refrigerator, whisk the cream again until it has come back together (do not beat).

Notes: Don't whip the cream too long or it will turn to butter. At the beginning of turning, it will look like it is curdling, and takes on a very light yellow color. To salvage: put a little more cream into the mixing bowl. Then whisk it by hand to incorporate. If whipped cream has gone to the butter stage, it's too late to correct it, but use it as butter instead.

Most often overlooked, the room where you beat the cream must also be on the cool side. If the kitchen is always warm, make sure you place the mixing bowl in a larger bowl filled with ice water as you whip.

QUESTION: *My recipe calls for beating egg whites with cream of tartar. I haven't been able to find any. Is there a substitute?*

ANSWER: Cream of tartar is not easy to find, and can be quite expensive. See online sources, page 243. You can generally substitute $\frac{1}{4}$ teaspoon of lemon juice for $\frac{1}{8}$ teaspoon of cream of tartar. But I've found that you can whip egg whites just fine without it. While the acid speeds up the coagulation (denaturation) of the egg whites, making them easier to beat into a foam, it also makes it easy to overbeat them, and the acidity in meringue works as a destabilizer over time.

CHOCOLATE AND COCOA POWDER

For everything about chocolate, see Chapter 9 (page 160). Chocolate comes in 1-ounce squares.

ACIDIC INGREDIENTS

Buttermilk, cream of tartar, lemon juice, and other acidic juices tenderize and add flavor. They are best used in a recipe containing baking soda. To get more juice out of your citrus fruit, microwave it on HIGH power for 10 seconds. Remove it from the microwave and roll the fruit on the counter, pressing lightly.

SALT

In my recipes, salt means table salt. Do not eliminate it from a recipe because it enhances flavor, and in yeast bread recipes it keeps the yeast producing carbon dioxide gas at a steady rate. You can use table salt, sea salt, or kosher salt, but each one has to be used in a different measure because their crystal size differs. Here are equivalents: 1 teaspoon table salt equals $1\frac{3}{4}$ teaspoons Kosher salt equals $1\frac{1}{2}$ teaspoons sea salt.

NUTS

When a recipe says "$\frac{1}{2}$ cup walnuts, chopped," measure first and then chop. When it says "$\frac{1}{2}$ cup chopped walnuts," chop before you measure. Cut until the pieces are a uniform size, about $\frac{1}{16}$- to $\frac{3}{8}$-inch in diameter. When the recipe says "finely chopped" the pieces should be about half that size. You can do this with a chef's knife or with a small hand-turned nut chopper, which I prefer.

Take note also of when the recipe tells you to toast the nuts: "¼ cup pecans, chopped and toasted" will be measured, then chopped, and finally the chopped bits should be toasted. I recommend toasting chopped nuts in the oven at 350 degrees F for about 7 to 15 minutes, stirring them frequently so they don't burn. Cool thoroughly before adding to the recipe.

3

TECHNIQUES

Baking is the technique of applying dry heat to a recipe in a closed environment such as an oven.

HAVE YOU EVER WONDERED how a few simple ingredients become a loaf of bread or a luscious layer cake? Although many think of baking as an art, a great deal of science helps along the way. When you bake, you'll always start with a recipe. A recipe is really a scientific formula, listing ingredients and their measurements, including step-by-step directions to reach a desired result. Sometimes serving and storage suggestions are included.

Many recipes, however, are vague, and many cookbooks don't adequately explain the nuances of baking. I believe that's why home bakers have so many problems. I learned to bake standing next to my mother. I'm able to bake her recipes because I learned all of the techniques by watching and practicing at her side and supplemented that knowledge with classes and my own experience of baking. I know when a batter "looks right," but that comes through lots of experience. Today, though, many of us don't have the family baker—a mother, father, grandmother, or aunt—near us to bake with and turn to with questions.

Let's look at the steps—all easily mastered—that help guarantee success in the kitchen.

STEP #1: READ THROUGH THE RECIPE

The very first step with any baking recipe is to read the title of the recipe and the number of servings. Make sure you are going to bake what you want and that you will have enough servings. Read the recipe all the way through, from beginning to end. At this point, look up terms you don't understand.

After you have read the recipe, gather all the ingredients, pots, pans, bowls, and measuring utensils you'll need. See if you can substitute anything if you're missing something.

STEP #2: ALWAYS MEASURE INGREDIENTS IN ADVANCE

Recipes start with the ingredients list and corresponding measurements, listed in the order they are to be used.

Mise en place is a French term for assembling your ingredients. It means "put in

QUESTION: *How do I measure ingredients?*

ANSWER: When you're baking, dry ingredients and liquid ingredients are measured using different sets of utensils: nested measuring cups for dry, heatproof glass cups for liquid, and measuring spoons for both.

Common Abbreviations & Measurement Terms:

Abbreviations and baking-specific measurement terms are frequently found in the lists of ingredients. Don't confuse the ounce of weight with the fluid ounce (a measure of volume) because they are *not* the same; there is no standard conversion between weight and volume unless you know the density of the ingredient. If ingredients are listed without a measurement amount, have small amounts available for use.

Common Abbreviations of Measurements

t or tsp	teaspoon
T or Tbsp	tablespoon
oz	ounce
c	cup
pt	pint
Q or qt	quart
gal	gallon
lb or #	pound
deg or °	degrees
F	Fahrenheit, the temperature measurement system we use

Measurement Equivalents

dash or pinch	equals	$\frac{1}{8}$ teaspoon		
3 teaspoons	equals	1 tablespoon		
4 tablespoons	equals	$\frac{1}{4}$ cup		
5 tablespoons plus 1 teaspoon	equals	$\frac{1}{3}$ cup		
8 tablespoons	equals	$\frac{1}{2}$ cup		
1 fluid ounce	equals	2 tablespoons	equals	$\frac{1}{8}$ cup
1 cup	equals	$\frac{1}{2}$ pint		

2 cups	equals	1 pint		
4 cups	equals	2 pints	equals	1 quart
1 cup	equals	8 fluid ounces		
1 pint	equals	16 fluid ounces		
2 pints	equals	1 quart		
4 quarts	equals	1 gallon		
16 ounces (weight)	equals	1 pound		
1 square of chocolate	equals	1 ounce (weight)		

place;" this is done so that recipes can be assembled quickly and easily, and it helps prevent accidentally leaving something out.

Recipes indicate butter measurements in different ways—by sticks, weight (pounds or ounces), or cups, and sometimes by tablespoons. Measure stick butter in tablespoons using the guidelines on the wrapper. Stick margarine is measured the same way. However, oil is always measured in a glass measuring cup, or with measuring spoons if a small amount.

Stick Butter Measurements

4 sticks	equals	1 pound	equals	16 ounces	equals	2 cups		
2 sticks	equals	½ pound	equals	8 ounces	equals	1 cup	equals	16 tablespoons
1 stick	equals	¼ pound	equals	4 ounces	equals	½ cup	equals	8 tablespoons
½ stick	equals	⅛ pound	equals	2 ounces	equals	¼ cup	equals	4 tablespoons
¼ stick			equals	1 ounce	equals	⅛ cup	equals	2 tablespoons
						⅓ cup	equals	5 tablespoons plus 1 teaspoon

MEASURING DRY AND LIQUID INGREDIENTS

Dry ingredients (flour, sugar, cocoa powder, salt, bread or cookie crumbs, and most leaveners) are measured with dry measuring cups or measuring spoons. Unless there are special instructions, measure level amounts: Fluff up the ingredient in its container and spoon it into the appropriate size cup or scoop with a measuring spoon, filling it completely; use the long straight edge of a spatula or the back of a knife to level to top (wipe away the excess even with the top edge of the cup or spoon). Do not scoop the flour or cocoa powder or you'll end up with too much. White sugars can be scooped.

Measure liquids (oil, milk and buttermilk, water, and juice) in glass measuring cups, or with measuring spoons if only a small amount (less than one-quarter cup). On a level surface pour the liquid into the cup to the level required. Before measuring buttermilk, be sure to shake the container well to recombine it thoroughly. Check by looking at the marking on the side of the cup at eye level, not from above. Liquid sweeteners such as honey, corn syrup, or molasses are measured in dry measuring cups filled to the rim. Other ingredients such as applesauce, sour cream, and yogurt are spooned into the dry measuring cup and leveled to top.

SPECIAL INSTRUCTIONS

You will sometimes encounter additional instructions for measuring the correct amount of an ingredient. A recipe might require "1 cup brown sugar, packed," or "2 heaping cups flour." If you encounter one of these special requests, consult the information below.

FIRMLY PACKED

With a spatula, a spoon, or your hand, firmly press the ingredient, such as brown sugar or shortening, into the measuring cup and level. It should keep its shape when dumped out.

LIGHTLY PACKED

Press the ingredient into the measuring cup lightly.

ROUNDED

Allow ingredient to pile up above the rim slightly, into a soft, rounded shape.

QUESTION: *How do I measure chocolate? Some recipes use ounces and some refer to squares. Do they mean the same thing?*

ANSWER: Recipes specify chocolate by weight. Baking chocolate generally comes individually wrapped in 1-ounce squares, or in bars that are scored to break apart easily into 1-ounce portions. If you are using a solid chunk of block chocolate, measure the desired amount on a scale. Chocolate chips, however, are measured in dry measuring cups (6 ounces equal 1 cup; one 12-ounce package equals 2 cups). Cocoa powder should be spooned into a dry measuring cup and leveled at the top, while chocolate syrup is measured in a dry measuring cup filled to the rim.

HEAPING

Pile as much of the ingredient above the rim of the measure as you can.

SIFTED

If a recipe says to measure "1 cup sifted flour," sift before measuring to ensure ingredient is not compacted. If it says "1 cup flour, sifted," measure first and then sift. Confectioners' sugar and cocoa powder should be sifted after measuring.

STEP #3: ADJUST THE OVEN SHELVES, IF NECESSARY, AND PREHEAT THE OVEN

Adjust the placement of the shelves in the oven, according to the recipe. Usually certain recipes are baked on certain shelves:

- Middle shelf: most baking recipes, such as cakes, quick breads, cookies, and pan breads
- Lower third: pies
- Lowest shelf: pizza and some artisan breads

Hang an oven thermometer so that you can double check the temperature. Allow at least 20 minutes for your oven to get hot. Turn on the oven to the temperature called for in the recipe. However, if you are using a dark, nonstick pan or heatproof glass pan, reduce the temperature setting by 25 degrees F.

QUESTION: *When a recipe says to use a prepared pan, what does that mean?*

ANSWER: "Prepare a pan" means to put a coating inside it so the batter or dough won't stick when baked, to make it easy to remove the baked good. There are different types of coatings depending on the recipe: butter, shortening, parchment paper, flour, or baker's grease (equal parts of shortening, oil, and flour that you make yourself). Some recipes, such as foam cakes, use ungreased pans because fat deflates their delicate structure. After greasing, the inside of the pan can be dusted with all-purpose flour. Alternatively, you can grease a pan lightly, line it with parchment paper, and then grease the paper.

Type of Baking	Degree of Difficulty in Unmolding from Pan	Solution: Preferred Method for Preparing Pan
cakes baked in fluted or Bundt pans or cake molds	difficult	baker's grease, butter, or shortening and optionally flour dusting or vegetable oil cooking spray
buttercakes, genoise, or cake mixes, as well as quick breads and muffins	medium	baker's grease, butter, vegetable oil cooking spray, or shortening and optionally flour dusting; for a chocolate cake, use sifted cocoa powder instead of flour
sponge, angel food, chiffon, and other foam cakes, as well as pie and optionally tart pans	not applicable	ungreased
cookie sheets can be greased or ungreased; follow the recipe	depends on the recipe	ungreased or greased sheets can be lined with parchment paper or sprayed with vegetable oil cooking spray

STEP #4: PREPARE THE PANS AND SET ASIDE

Pans are prepared in different ways depending upon the recipe. Generally, I don't recommend using paper muffin liners as some batters stick to them no matter what you do. But if you choose to use them, spray the insides of the liners with cooking oil spray.

STEP #5: CAREFULLY FOLLOW EACH MIXING STEP IN THE RECIPE BEFORE YOU PUT YOUR BATTER OR DOUGH IN THE PAN

Each step has a purpose. Use a kitchen timer to help you keep track of mixing as well as baking times. Combine the ingredients in the order given. Mix only for the time and at the mixer speed specified in the recipe; don't overmix. Overmixing leads to dryness by creating too much gluten that can't be tenderized by the sugar in the recipe. To avoid overmixing I like to add in nuts, raisins, and fruits after the batter or dough is almost mixed, with a large spatula, moving in a gentle folding motion rather than stirring, even if the recipe specifies otherwise.

If you see some unblended flour in the batter after mixing, remove the bowl from the mixer and finish mixing by hand with a spatula in a gentle folding motion until *just* incorporated.

Each mixing method gives a different texture and character to the baked good. The implements used, such as blades, whisks, or spoons and even bowl size used have a great impact on what happens during mixing. General objectives of mixing batters and doughs are: uniform distribution of ingredients; prevention of too much gluten forming; minimum loss of the leavening agent; and creation of air bubbles. Mixing techniques include:

- **Beating** is the vigorous combining of ingredients with a spoon, fork, whisk, handheld or stand electric mixer until you achieve a smooth and uniform consistency.
- **Blending** is less vigorous blending of ingredients than beating. It is usually done by combining ingredients until smooth with a spoon, whisk, rubber spatula, blender or electric mixer.
- **Creaming** is a mixing method specifically for combining a solid fat such as butter or shortening with crystalline sugar, to introduce air into the mixture and make it light and fluffy. See page 39 for a complete description.
- **Cutting in** is the process of introducing a solid fat such as shortening into dry ingredients to create flaky layers of pastry. The fat is literally cut into smaller and smaller pieces. At the same time the bits of fat are tossed and coated with the dry

ingredients. You're done cutting in when the desired size of the particles has been achieved. See page 130.

- **Folding** is the gentle combining of ingredients or two batters using care not to introduce air into your mix. This is done with a rubber spatula, balloon whisk or large spoon, very gently bringing the ingredients up from the bottom of the bowl, through, and over the other ingredients in a circular motion. See page 40.
- **Kneading** is a mixing method you use specifically with breads. It is pushing, folding, and turning the dough to develop the gluten for elasticity. Kneading may be done by hand, using a stand mixer with a dough hook attachment, in a bread machine or food processor. See page 190.
- **Processing** is the use of a food processor or chopper to chop, blend, or grind ingredients.
- **Stirring** is done to put or keep ingredients in motion. You may be called on to stir occasionally, frequently, or continuously.
- **Whipping** is done to add air to increase the volume until the mixture is light and fluffy. It may be done by hand with a whisk, or with an electric mixer.

MIXING EGG WHITES AND YOLKS AND MERINGUE FOAMS

BEATING EGG WHITES

Egg whites go through four stages of foam when beaten, depending upon the result needed. Do not stop the mixer in between any of the stages. When you reach your desired stage, use the eggs immediately. Foams typically act as part or all of the leavening in baked goods. Egg whites have a great ability to hold air and increase in volume—about eight times—when beaten and baked. Beaten egg yolks (see page 39) hold air too, but not as effectively as whites.

The real issue, however, is the egg's freshness. Newer fresh eggs have thicker

Sarah Says: Sugar serves as a whipping aid to stabilize beaten egg foams, which are essentially a delicate protein network. Sugar pulls the water from the structure and allows the structure to set better. Therefore, meringues made from beaten egg whites and sugar can sit longer and hold their shape longer than foams without sugar. If a whipped egg white recipe does not include sugar, and the egg whites will eventually be folded into a base, I recommend adding in a couple of tablespoons of white sugar to stabilize the whites.

QUESTION: *When a recipe indicates to "separate eggs," how do I do it?*

ANSWER: The goal in separating eggs is to have the whites in one bowl and the yolks in another. If a speck of grease or yolk remains in the egg white bowl, and you can't get it out with the edge of a paper towel, start again with fresh whites.

Eggs separate more easily when they are cold, right from the refrigerator.

1. You'll need two clean, dry bowls: one for the whites and the other for the yolks.
2. With one hand, give a firm tap across the circumference of the egg's shell against the flat work surface (not the rim of a bowl).
3. Open the two sides and quickly drop the whole egg into the hollow of your other hand over a bowl designated for whites. Pass the egg back and forth between your hands, letting the white run between your fingers into the bowl below. Place the yolk in the second bowl. The trick is to leave some of the white with the yolk so you don't pop the yolk.
4. You can also toss the egg between the two halves of the egg shell, letting the white fall into a bowl beneath, but I find the jagged edge of the shell frequently pierces the yolk, ruining the whole batch of whites for beating.

Sometimes whites have twisted strands known as the *chalazae* attached to the yolk. This is just thickened albumen that will be pulverized by the beaters when you whip the whites or yolks. Remove the larger strands before cooking, or they will harden when heated. (In addition, I always recommend straining a stovetop egg custard or filling before using.)

whites. They reach more volume and have greater stability when beaten than older eggs, although they require more beating.

Egg whites beaten for a recipe hold air bubbles. When sugar is added, often with another stabilizer such as salt or cream of tartar or its substitute lemon juice, its ability to hold air bubbles is increased. This results in stiffer, higher, and more stable foam. Sugar also makes the resulting foam smoother. When using a copper bowl or making meringue for a pie topping, do not use cream of tartar.

Place room temperature or cold egg whites in a stand mixer fitted with the whisk attachment or in a medium-size bowl for a handheld mixer fitted with beaters. Turn mixer on medium.

Stage 1: Egg whites will start to foam. Add cream of tartar and salt. Beat until they are white and opaque and starting to hold a shape.

Stage 2: Soft Peak: Increase mixer speed to high. Add sugar slowly at the side of the bowl. Egg whites will become light and fluffy. You can pull the whites into a soft "peak" but they won't hold it when the mixer is stopped and the beaters lifted.

Note: For a crisp and dry meringue add four tablespoons of sugar per egg white. For a meringue topping on a pie use two tablespoons of sugar per egg white.

Stage 3: Firm Peak: Keep mixer speed on high. Whites become glossy, firm, and smooth. When mixer is stopped and beaters lifted, you can pull whites into a peak that will curl but not stand.

Stage 4: Stiff Peak: Keep mixer speed on high. Whites will be glossy and very stiff. When the mixer is stopped and the beaters lifted, the egg whites form a pointed peak that holds its shape. Egg whites are beaten enough, if, when cut with a knife, the cut remains visible.

Ruined stage: The foam separates and is dry and lumpy. The whites are overbeaten and not usable in recipes. Start over.

Sarah Says: Think of egg white foam as those soap bubbles kids blow out of a bubble pipe. As you blow the soap solution, the mass grows quite large. If you blow harder and faster, the air bubbles become smaller and stronger, similar to when egg whites are beaten on a high speed with a mixer. (Small bubbles are stronger than big bubbles.) However, the soap foam, delicate like egg white foam, breaks very easily when handled. If left to sit out on its own, over time the bubbles will break and join together with a neighboring bubble to create a larger weaker bubble.

Although yolks can't incorporate as much air as whites, beating them does create a foam that expands four times and is important to airy concoctions such as sponge or chiffon cakes. A foam can be created by beating egg yolks with or without sugar with a whisk or a handheld or stand mixer on high speed. Always add the sugar slowly. In recipes you will often see instructions such as "beat the egg yolks and sugar until thick and lemon-colored," typically for 3 to 5 minutes. The instructions should also include "and forms a ribbon." The action of the beaters denatures the protein in the yolks, allowing them to trap air while the sugar absorbs the water in the yolks, eventually forming a thick, pale

Sarah Says: If a recipe calls for separately beaten egg yolks and whites, beat the yolks first because they don't deflate as easily. They can sit for ten minutes. If they dehydrate, add a teaspoon of water and give a few quick turns of the beater or whisk.

yellow syrup with air bubbles trapped within its protein structure. When the whisk or mixer's beaters are lifted no more than 4 inches from the surface of the foam, the mixture should fall into a thick stream that folds upon itself into the bowl below, called "ribboning."

BEATING SOLID FAT AND CRYSTALLINE SUGAR: CREAMING

1. With the paddle attachment of a stand mixer or the beaters of a handheld mixer, soften the cold or room temperature fat on low speed for about 1 minute. When softened, the fat will fan out in the bowl with ridges. If

QUESTION: *When a recipe says to "beat the butter and sugar until light in color and fluffy," what does that mean?*

ANSWER: It means you need to cream them. The volume of the butter increases from aerating (whipping air into it) so it becomes fluffy. If you touch it, it feels like cold cream, and it's a pale yellow. The texture becomes soft but the butter still retains its shape; it is not melted or greasy. The butter–sugar mixture has numerous ridges in it from the beaters and is sticky when the beaters are lifted.

using both butter and shortening, soften the shortening first and then add the butter. If the butter is cold, straight out of the refrigerator, the process takes a bit longer.

2. Add crystalline sugar in a steady stream at the side of the bowl. After adding the sugar, increase the speed to medium and beat for 5 minutes. Throughout the process of creaming, stop the mixer often and thoroughly scrape the beaters and the side and bottom of the bowl. This is especially important if the mixer's beaters do not reach the bottom of the bowl.

3. Finally, as most recipes say, beat until "the mixture is light in color and fluffy." Note: In reduced-fat recipes the mixture will be like coarse bread crumbs.

4. The creamed mixture should be used immediately: do not let it sit, especially in a warm room.

MIXING LIGHT WITH HEAVIER: FOLDING

Folding is a gentle mixing method used to combine a light mixture such as an egg white foam into batters or ribboned egg yolks, or to combine dry ingredients into foams. Folding is also useful when adding raisins, nuts, or even melted chocolate or butter to a batter; it helps to avoid too much stirring, which toughens a recipe.

The cardinal rule is that the airy mixture is placed on top of the heavier one, so it does not deflate. I often fold in increments, adding the lighter mixture in thirds. It is important to work delicately so the egg whites and batter retain as much of their volume as possible. In some recipes, large air pockets need to be eliminated by running a small metal spatula or knife through the batter in an "S" shape before baking. And if you fold too much, your cake won't rise as high because the delicate air bubbles have popped during the process.

When folding egg whites into a heavy thick batter (as when making Priscilla's Orange Sponge Cake, page 69) use a large rubber spatula—my favorite is a 13-inch heavy spatula—and a glass bowl so that you can easily see that all ingredients are folded together. Scrape the side of the bowl a few times during the folding process to make sure you get everything.

THE FOLDING TECHNIQUE

1. Imagine the bowl is a clock face with 12 o'clock on the far side of the bowl and 6 o'clock at the bottom nearest you. The clock never moves even if the bowl rotates.

2. Place the heavier batter in a large bowl, add a big spoonful of egg white foam (about one-third of the total) into the batter and stir lightly with a few strokes of your rubber spatula. This will help "lighten" the batter, bringing the consistency of the batter closer to that of the foam, so the rest of the egg whites fold in more easily.

> **Sarah Says:** Make sure you turn the bowl a few degrees before you deposit the batter and beaten egg whites. If you don't, you are really only stirring as opposed to folding, and over time the batter will begin to liquefy.

3. With the rubber spatula, place one-third of the egg whites in the middle on top of the heavier mixture. Cut down with the thin edge of the spatula, from the dead center of the mixture to the bottom of the bowl reaching into the heavier mixture as you do when rowing. Draw the spatula against the edge toward you to 8 o'clock. Exit with a scoopful of the mixtures attached and hold over the bowl. Turn the bowl a few degrees.

4. Turn your hand over at the wrist so the bottom of the spatula and your inner wrist face up, and deposit the spatula's contents at 2 o'clock, in essence folding the batter.

5. Repeat steps 3 and 4, folding in only one-third of the egg whites at a time until both mixtures are thoroughly combined into a light, airy mixture. You should not see streaks of the different mixtures; if you do, keep on folding! Just do not overdo it.

FOLDING FLOUR INTO AN EGG WHITE–BATTER MIXTURE

Sift one-third of the flour mixture over the whites, and follow the technique above. Repeat with the remaining two-thirds.

Place the melted butter or chocolate in a medium bowl. Let it cool to tepid. Gently stir in one cup of batter until almost combined. Add in the rest of the batter and fold as above until both are *thoroughly* combined.

STEP #6—GET YOUR RECIPE INTO THE PREHEATED OVEN RIGHT AWAY!

Don't forget to preheat your oven as the first step in the recipe. Baking at the correct temperature is crucial to the success of the recipe. Allow at least 20 minutes for the oven to heat to the proper temperature.

As soon as you are done mixing, get the batter or dough into the prepared pans, page 34. If I'm making a recipe that requires more than one pan, I use a soup ladle to measure the batter evenly. I alternate between the two pans, making sure I put the same number of scoops in each. It works every time! Another way is to weigh each filled pan to determine if they hold equal amounts; you can move some batter from one to the other if they don't.

Make sure you get all the batter or dough into the pans, using a rubber spatula. You'll be surprised how much can be left behind if you only pour and don't scrape. Place the filled pans immediately into the preheated oven, on the shelf specified. If your recipe waits too long, the leaveners will start to lose their power: carbon dioxide produced by chemical leaveners will dissipate; beaten eggs will deflate; and yeast will cause the dough to rise too much and collapse.

STEP #7—BAKE FOR THE TIME SPECIFIED IN THE RECIPE

Begin checking your recipe at the shortest listed cooking time. But also let your nose, eyes, and ears serve as guides. Watch through the oven window until the top is lightly browned. Cakes and breads sound hollow when tapped. When it's done, remove the baked good from the oven promptly.

STEP #8—CAREFULLY FOLLOW THE UNMOLDING AND COOLING INSTRUCTIONS

Each type of recipe has its own instructions, but some general principles apply. Some baked goods are meant to be eaten right out of the pan, and can be cooled in the pan

QUESTION: *My cakes have too many air bubbles. After I trim the top, it looks like an ant farm inside. How do I get rid of the air bubbles?*

ANSWER: To get rid of excess bubbles in your cake, bang the pans on their bottoms against the countertop. Do it once or twice, but no more. You can also swirl a table knife a couple of times through the batter. Do not do this with cakes with a lot of fruit or nuts in them.

on a wire cake rack. For recipes that require unmolding, place the pans on a wire cake rack and let them stand for 10 to 15 minutes first. If a baked good is unmolded right after it comes out of the oven, chances are it will fall apart or stick to the pan. See pages 49–50 for more on unmolding and cooling.

4

CAKES

*Why aren't my made-from-scratch cakes as light
and fluffy as the kind I make from a mix? . . .
and other cake crises you can avoid.*

TECHNICALLY, A CAKE IS A LEAVENED, sweet foodstuff, prepared
by baking a wheat flour–based dough or batter in a pan into a compact form. Cakes
come in myriad varieties: one or more layers, filled, unfilled, frosted, adorned,
plain—and made in a rich array of flavors. We all have our favorites. Cakes are an in-
tegral part of celebrating life's milestones—birthdays, weddings, showers, engage-
ments—or they can be enjoyed simply as a dessert or snack. When I make a cake, it
is usually for a special event. From the questions and feedback I've heard from all
kinds of bakers, novices and experienced, that's the case for most of us, making us
all occasional bakers of cakes. This can lead to being less practiced in the techniques
that are so important to making a cake from scratch.

THE ALCHEMY OF CAKES

There is a special kind of alchemy to all cakes. Ingredients I thought I knew—almost
relied upon like old friends—didn't behave the same way when I put them together
in new combinations.

The two types of cakes are called *shortened,* also known as buttercakes, and *unshortened,* also known as foam cakes. These types are distinguished by the way they
are leavened and the way air is introduced into the batter.

Shortened (butter) cakes include buttercakes, Bundt cakes, and pound cakes.
They are rich and buttery with textures ranging from fine to dense, containing tiny
evenly spaced and sized air holes. Buttercakes are primarily leavened by chemical

leaveners—baking powder and/or baking soda—whose carbon dioxide expands the air bubbles previously created by creaming and mixing. Their structure comes from proteins in wheat flour and its starches, and to a lesser degree those found in milk and eggs. A flour structure is very sturdy. Buttercakes' cellular structure comes primarily from the starches and gluten proteins in flour, which are by nature stronger than egg protein structures.

You know you're getting ready to make a shortened cake when the recipe begins with: "Cream the butter and sugar until light and fluffy." This involves taking solid fat, such as shortening or butter, and beating it with crystalline sugar, whose crystals literally cut into the fat. This creates thousands of tiny air bubbles held in by the fat. Because of the semisolid nature of the fat, buttercake batters tend to be stable over time.

The next mixing step incorporates the other ingredients into the batter without destroying the creamed fat structure. The tiny air bubbles in the creamed fat will be released only when the fat melts during baking. These air bubbles will grow in size when the leavening gas from baking powder or baking soda is released during baking. This leavens the product until the starch in the flour gelatinizes (absorbs water) and forms a rigid structure.

Unshortened (foam) cakes include angel food, sponge, chiffon, and genoise cakes. They are leavened primarily by air beaten into whole or separated eggs—usually lots of beaten egg whites and sugar—and to a less extent by chemical leaven-

---

QUESTION: *How do I get my made-from-scratch buttercakes as light and fluffy as those I make from a store-bought boxed mix?*

ANSWER: This is by far the most frequently asked cake question I receive. We all expect that if we go to all the trouble of making a cake from scratch, we'll be rewarded with a cake that's moister, richer, lighter, fluffier—just better than what we'd get from a box. But it is hard to duplicate the texture found in boxed cakes in made-from-scratch cakes. The key is in choosing the right recipe. Look for one with a creaming step, ingredients like sour cream or buttermilk, lots of butter, eggs (especially yolks), chocolate (not cocoa powder), and sugar.

Boxed cake mixes contain chemical emulsifiers, found naturally in egg yolks, which make them creamy and moist. Emulsifiers give cakes what is known as *tolerance,* the ability to keep their texture despite human error. Cake mixes also contain special leavening ingredients, which help them become fluffy regardless of the mixing technique used.

ers. Steam from the liquid ingredients also plays a role in expanding the air bubbles, as does heat from the oven. These cakes have little or no fat; when they do, it's usually egg yolks, melted butter, or oil which won't hold air, but will tenderize and moisturize. When baked, egg proteins coagulate and form the structure, along with a small amount of wheat flour protein. This makes these cakes light and airy, sometimes sponge-like, with excellent volume and the larger air holes so characteristic of foam cakes.

Low-fat cakes such as apple, banana, carrot, and pumpkin are commonly made with vegetable oil. (See Applesauce Cake Squares, page 218.) Oil makes the moistest cakes because it does an excellent job at coating the flour proteins to prevent the formation of gluten and gives the perception of moistness. Because of this, dense cakes made with fruit purees, fruit, and oil stay moist and tender—the fruit adds pectin and forms a film around the air bubbles, similar to what occurs when you cream solid shortenings with sugar, but not as effectively.

BUTTERCAKES: POINTERS, QUESTIONS, AND RECIPES

Buttercakes are what most of us think of when we think of cake; they're the old faithful and reliable members of everyone's recipe collection. Nine times out of ten, if you're making a birthday cake or cupcakes you'll use a buttercake recipe, baked with common ingredients that you already have or can find easily. The texture is sturdy—especially the pound cake's, whose denseness is perfect for making Bundt or character cakes that are easily removed from the pan without cracking or disturbing delicate impressions and designs. A buttercake's fluid batter allows you to bake it in practically any shape of pan imaginable.

The ideal buttercake should have a level or slightly rounded top after baking, an evenly browned crust, and a fine-grained crumb (inside texture) that is soft, smooth, and resilient when touched. The cake should be somewhat sweet, light, tender, and slightly moist.

When you cut cakes to serve, they should be completely cooled first to prevent breaking. To cut a buttercake, use a knife with a sharp, straight edge and a thin blade. Cut with a light, even motion. Foam cakes are best sliced with a sharp serrated knife moved in a sawing motion.

QUESTION: *Why do some cake recipes have you add in the dry ingredients in three equal parts, alternating with the liquid one, in two equal parts, beginning and ending with the dry ingredients (dry-wet-dry-wet-dry)?*

ANSWER: Let's start at the beginning of a recipe: This alternating way of adding ingredients is done with the creaming method (page 39). These steps prevent the fat in the batter from separating from the liquids, breaking the emulsion and releasing the air bubbles so essential to a cake's good taste and texture. Emulsions, which are essentially what a cake batter is, have a much better chance of forming and staying that way if the elements are brought together slowly.

Here's what you do:
1. Begin by adding about ⅓ of the blended dry ingredients to the creamed butter–sugar–egg mixture. Flour helps cement the emulsion formed by the creamed fat and eggs (yolks) which would otherwise break, causing the batter to separate and the air bubbles to be lost.
2. Add ½ of the liquid. Because the flour proteins have already been coated with fat in the first step, you can mix them with liquids and not form much gluten.
3. Quickly add the second ⅓ of the dry ingredients. This time, the flour addition isn't protected by a "fat raincoat" so you must mix in a short amount of time. Recipes never seem to tell us this, and it can lead us to take our time with mixing—which leads to a tough cake.
4. Add the remaining ½ of the liquid and the last ⅓ of the dry ingredients. These should be easy to mix in; just as above, you'll want to mix them quickly.

Cakes are stored according to their fillings and frostings. If the filling or frosting is perishable, such as whipped cream or a cream cheese mixture, the cake must be refrigerated. Otherwise, store frosted cakes at room temperature in a dark, cool place for up to three days. They can be stored under a domed cake keeper, an inverted bowl, or an aluminum foil tent kept loose to prevent moisture from accumulating under the wrapping. Once completely cooled, unfrosted cake layers should be wrapped well in plastic wrap and then aluminum foil. They can be kept at room temperature for up to three days, or frozen for about one month.

QUESTION: *I have the hardest time deciding when my cake is done baking. I either overbake it and it becomes dry, or underbake it causing it to collapse. I'm so frustrated. When should I start checking and how do I do it?*

ANSWER: The rule I follow is: for small cakes, such as one layer, check after 20 minutes of baking; for larger ones, 30 minutes; pound cakes, about 40 minutes. Your cake isn't likely to be done before that unless your oven is working improperly. This is why it is important to make sure your oven is working correctly and that it is well preheated.

The classic tests for doneness for buttercakes are "when touched with a finger, it springs back" or "a toothpick inserted in the center comes out clean." I find these definitions cause many to overbake their cakes. When you take your cake from the oven, it will continue to bake in the pan, so you want to take it out right before it's done. It just takes some practice to get it right.

Don't pull the cake out of the oven to test for doneness because if it isn't set, it will likely fall in on itself or dip in the middle where the batter isn't as baked—and you can't save it from there. Don't open the door all the way: when the oven door is opened, the rush of cooler air lowers the temperature by approximately 20 percent. When you open the door, do so just enough so you can reach in and lightly touch the cake surface with your palm. Be careful not to burn yourself. If the cake needs more baking time, close the door immediately.

To check for doneness:

1. The cake should be lightly browned all over, flat or gently rounded, and may shrink a little from the side of the pan; it should also *smell* done. Close the door if the cake doesn't look done and its center sinks slightly.

2. Touch the top of the cake with your palm, not a fingertip, otherwise you'll make a dent. The top should feel firm and give slightly when a small amount of pressure is applied; it will not spring back.
3. You should still hear a few tiny air bubbles popping on the top of the cake when you remove it from the oven.
4. If you place a cake tester in the middle of the cake and remove it, it should come out with a few moist crumbs—not batter—attached.

As soon as your cake is done, take the pans out of the oven and place them on a wire cake rack to begin to cool.

QUESTION: *I am having a terrible time frosting my layer cakes. The top layer slides off the bottom, the icing melts, and the cake crumbles. I need lots of help!*

ANSWER: You are not alone. The very idea of frosting a layer cake can send many of us running out of the kitchen!

UNMOLD

Here are hints to help you once your cake is out of the oven. Some cakes are cooled, frosted, and cut directly in the pan. Others are unmolded to cool on a wire cake rack. Wait 10 minutes after removing the pans from the oven and placing them on a wire cake rack before unmolding (15 minutes for Bundt and pound cakes). If the cake needs loosening, gently run a thin knife blade or an offset icing spatula around the side of the pan. Center a second wire cake rack over the rim of the pan and flip the "sandwich" over. Hold the pan's side, lift it slowly, no more than $\frac{1}{4}$ inch above the wire cake rack, and jiggle it. The cake should come out easily, but if it doesn't, keep one hand under the cake and tap the bottom of the pan with the other, or use a metal one-cup measure to tap it. If it still doesn't come out, let it sit a few more minutes on the wire cake rack (it may still be too hot), turn it back over, and run the knife around it again.

As soon as the cake is unmolded, peel off any parchment paper, if used. Turn it upright to cool completely. If a cake layer is delicate or large, you may need help: place a second rack on the exposed bottom of the upside down cake. The inverted cake is now sandwiched between two wire racks; flip both racks and the cake over together. Remove the top rack and the cake should be sitting right side up.

COOL THOROUGHLY

Be sure your cake is cooled completely to room temperature before you try to cut, frost, or store it. Otherwise the icing will slip off or melt into the cake, or the condensation formed inside the wrapping will ruin it. It may also crack. Cupcakes liners tend to stick like glue if the cupcake is even slightly warm when you try to take them off.

ASSEMBLE CAKE LAYERS

I prefer to frost and fill cake layers right on the cake plate, if it's flat, but a turntable works well as does the flat side of the removable bottom of a 9- or 10-inch spring-form pan.

Some cakes crumb easily when freshly baked. To avoid a crumb-speckled icing, put the wrapped layer in the freezer for a couple of hours, which tightens the crumb. After thawing the cake in the wrappers at room temperature, apply a thin layer of icing ("crumb coat"). Let it set for 10 minutes. Proceed with icing the top and side of the cake. Use even strokes without lifting the spatula from the cake.

1. If the tops aren't level, slice off any "hump" with a serrated knife.
2. Tear off four strips of waxed paper and place them in a square on your flat surface, leaving an open space in the middle.
3. Place a dab of icing in the middle of the surface and center one cake layer, bottom side down, over it. Press lightly so that the layer adheres to the icing and won't move around while you're working.
4. Using an icing spatula (see page 11) or a table knife, spread $\frac{1}{3}$ of the icing over the top surface of the cake layer.
5. Set the second layer, bottom up, on top of the first and frost first the top and then the side of the cake. Use even strokes without lifting the spatula from the cake.
6. Carefully ease out the waxed paper strips, and you will see why you used them: your serving platter is perfectly clean!

QUESTION: *My cake is dense and didn't rise very much. What happened?*

ANSWER: There are lots of possible reasons. Check to see if your chemical leaveners (baking powder or baking soda) have expired (page 19), a common problem. Too much flour or too little liquid due to inaccurate measuring (page 32) causes a dense cake that won't rise as well. The butter and sugar may not have been creamed enough or creamed too much, or the butter may have been too warm and therefore unable to hold air bubbles. If the recipe called for cake flour and you used a higher gluten flour, such as all-purpose, this can cause the cake to be denser, making it harder to rise. Perhaps the eggs were not mixed in thoroughly after each addition to form a proper emulsion. There could have been a long delay in baking the batter after mixing, or it was refrigerated for some time and the batter lost air bubbles. Also, if the flour was beaten too long, the cake becomes tough and less elastic. Finally, if your oven was not preheated or its temperature was off, it may not have been hot enough to get a good rise out of the cake.

QUESTION: *How do I prevent my cake from doming?*

ANSWER: My experience with doming is that generally there is too much liquid in proportion to flour in the recipe, or the cake has been overmixed (easy to do if there is too much liquid). However, as a preventive measure, you can use damp cloth strips wrapped around the pan to insulate the sides so the batter bakes evenly. Cut an old bath towel into strips a little narrower than the height of your pan. Wet with cold water, squeeze out the excess, and wrap around the outside of the pan; pin or tuck in place. Then fill with batter and bake as usual. Also, there are cake strips you can buy that do the same thing (see Online Sources, page 243). No doubt this method will decrease doming once it is baking, but if this is a consistent problem, look at the recipe. Sugar and fat reduce the problems of doming, so a lean cake recipe is more susceptible.

QUESTION: *My pound cake always cracks on top. Why?*

ANSWER: I have never seen a pound cake NOT crack. During baking, the center doesn't set as quickly as the sides, and the top gets pulled apart as the middle rises. Think of how an earthquake fault line works with tectonic plates moving in opposite directions, while the earth pushes up from below.

Cracking may also be due to underbaking or unmolding too early, while the cake is too hot (page 50).

QUESTION: *Can I double my buttercake recipe? What oven temperature should I use and how long will it take?*

ANSWER: Generally, all buttercakes can be doubled, cut in half or made into cupcakes. The temperature stays the same (because it is still the same recipe) but the baking time may vary by ten minutes or less. When substituting a baking pan, size does matter (see page 7). If you end up using two or more pans, be sure to place them in the oven about an inch apart (and away from the sides of the oven) or stagger them on two shelves near the center of the oven, so air can circulate freely. If you lack room, don't double the recipe. It's not a good idea to mix batter in advance because the leaveners may lose potency. Instead prepare the recipe twice.

If you're making cupcakes, follow these guidelines. From a recipe for two 8-inch layers or one 11- by 7-inch cake, you'll get 24 standard-size cupcakes ($2\frac{1}{2}$-inch diameter). A $\frac{1}{4}$-cup dry measuring cup is perfect to measure batter with and fill a standard muffin tin cup. (It should be filled one-half to two-thirds full.) I find large metal measuring spoons even easier to use. They come in $\frac{1}{8}$-, $\frac{1}{4}$- and $\frac{1}{2}$-cup sizes. If you don't have enough batter to fill all the individual cups in a muffin pan, fill the empty ones halfway with water so they won't smoke during baking.

QUESTION: *My buttercakes always end in disaster. Do you have tips that will help? My mother always bakes them just right and I'd like to do the same.*

ANSWER: You can't go wrong with my Ultimate Buttercake with Seven-Minute Vanilla Bean Icing (recipe follows). Carefully review the directions in this chapter for a better understanding how to make this or any buttercake.

ULTIMATE BUTTERCAKE
WITH SEVEN-MINUTE
VANILLA BEAN ICING

MAKES TWO 9 X 2-INCH ROUND LAYERS OR 36 CUPCAKES

To me, this is the ultimate buttercake: moist, buttery, and tender. It is a good basic cake that I can dress up for special celebrations or down for an everyday snack cake for my family. I must have gone through 30 pounds of butter fine-tuning my Ultimate Buttercake over and over again until I couldn't imagine looking at another piece (and wouldn't think of stepping on a scale)! But eventually I got it right, and it has become a favorite part of my repertoire.

The cake lends itself to many fillings and icings, but my favorite is the Seven-Minute Vanilla Bean Icing on page 55 because it complements the cake's lightness: together they literally melt in your mouth! If you're rushed for time, you can use cold eggs and dairy ingredients right from the refrigerator.

INGREDIENTS

4 cups unbleached all-purpose flour; spoon into dry measuring cup and level to top; don't use cake flour
3 teaspoons baking powder
1 teaspoon salt
2 cups (4 sticks) unsalted butter, room temperature
2 cups sugar or superfine sugar
3 large eggs, room temperature
1½ cups whole or 2% milk, room temperature; measure in liquid measuring cup
1 tablespoon vanilla extract plus ½ teaspoon almond extract, or 1 teaspoon orange or lemon extract, or 1 tablespoon grated orange or 1 to 2 teaspoons lemon peel, or ¼ teaspoon citrus oil

1. Position a rack in the center of the oven and preheat the oven to 350 degrees F. Generously grease two 9-inch pans. Or lightly grease the pans, line them with parchment paper, and then grease the paper lightly.

2. In a medium bowl, combine the flour, baking powder, and salt; set aside. Be sure your baking powder is evenly distributed throughout the flour so that the cake doesn't develop holes as it bakes.

3. In the bowl of a stand mixer, beat the butter with the paddle attachment on low

speed until soft. Add sugar in a steady stream at the side of the bowl. Increase speed to medium and beat for 5 minutes until light yellow and fluffy. For more on creaming, see page 39.

4. With the mixer on low, add the eggs one at a time and beat for 20 seconds after each addition. Without turning off the mixer, add the flour in 3 equal portions, alternating with the milk in 2 equal portions, beginning and ending with the flour mixture in a steady stream at the side of the bowl (see page 47). Add in extracts. Beat for 1 minute or until smooth. The batter should be thick and fluffy. Divide the batter evenly between the prepared pans; lightly smooth the tops.

5. Bake for 40 to 45 minutes or until the top feels firm and gives slightly when touched with a cupped palm. If you insert a toothpick in the middle and remove, it should have a few moist crumbs attached, but not batter. The cake should be lightly browned all over and will shrink a little from the side of the pan; it will also smell done. You will still hear a few air bubbles popping.

6. Remove the pans to a wire cake rack, let cool for 10 minutes, and unmold. Turn the layers upright to cool completely. Be careful, this cake is delicate when warm. Meanwhile, make the icing (page 55).

Assembly: page 50

Storage: Because the 7-minute icing is meringue-based, the frosted cake is best served within 24 hours, but can be stored, covered, at room temperature for 2 to 3 days. Freezing the frosted cake is not recommended.

Variation: When baking cupcakes, grease the muffin tins and fit them with paper liners. I don't like to grease the inside of the liners, because with buttercakes I find they fall off too easily. For best results, fill paper liners ¾ full. Bake at 350 degrees F for about 30 minutes or until the tops are golden brown. When done, cool in the tins for 10 minutes, then remove to a wire cake rack to finish cooling.

QUESTION: *I want to cut this recipe in half and make only one cake layer. How do I halve the 3 whole eggs called for in the full recipe?*

ANSWER: When you cut a recipe in half and you need a number of eggs such as one and a half, you don't usually halve the second one but add it in as a whole egg. But in this recipe, it works best if you halve one of the eggs. Each egg is approximately 4 tablespoons. To halve 3 eggs, use 1 egg plus 2 tablespoons of a second egg; thoroughly beat the second egg before measuring. It may be hard to measure because eggs are slippery. Save the rest in the refrigerator.

SEVEN-MINUTE
VANILLA BEAN ICING

MAKES ABOUT 7 CUPS;
FROSTS TWO 9-INCH ROUND LAYERS OR 24 TO 36 CUPCAKES

This heavenly icing tastes like whipped marshmallow and has a thick, fluffy consistency. The name of this classic refers to the length of time that the ingredients must be beaten continuously over simmering water. If the icing gets too soft, refrigerate it for 30 minutes and beat again. This icing is best used the day it is made. It does not need refrigeration; the sugar acts as a preservative.

INGREDIENTS

3 large egg whites, room temperature
1½ cups sugar, preferably superfine
¼ cup cold water
½ teaspoon cream of tartar (optional)
1 tablespoon light corn syrup
Seeds from 1 Tahitian vanilla bean, or 2 teaspoons vanilla extract,
*   or 1 tablespoon grated orange or lemon peel (see Note, page 56)*

1. Place the egg whites, sugar, water, and cream of tartar in the top part of a double boiler. For a marshmallow-like texture, add the corn syrup now. With a handheld mixer, beat 30 seconds on low speed to combine. Let sit for 10 minutes, beating frequently on medium to partially dissolve sugar crystals, until the mixture feels like fine sand when rubbed between your thumb and forefinger. When there are a couple of minutes left, fill the bottom of the double boiler half full with water. Make sure the bottom of the top bowl does not touch the water beneath. If it does, reduce the water to no less than 2 inches. Bring rapidly to a boil, and then reduce the heat to maintain a simmer.

2. Set the top over the bottom of the double boiler, cover, and cook for 1 minute. Remove the lid and stir briefly. Using a pastry brush, wipe the side of the saucepan with water to prevent crystals from forming. Cover and cook 30 seconds longer.

3. Using a handheld mixer, beat at high speed over the simmering water for a minimum of 7 minutes until thick, fluffy, and forming soft peaks when the beaters are lifted. The mixture does not start to thicken until well into the cooking time. The more you beat after 7 minutes, the more marshmallow-like the icing becomes. Remove from the heat when thick enough.

4. If you want a fluffier texture and did not add the corn syrup in Step 1, add it now. Add the vanilla seeds and beat on medium speed for 30 seconds to combine.

Variations: Caramel Icing: Substitute 1 cup sugar and ½ cup light brown sugar for the sugar. Omit the vanilla seeds.

Coconut Icing: Press one 7-ounce package of coconut all over the outside of the cake right after icing. Allow it to set before serving. (To tint coconut first, place the coconut in a large bowl and sprinkle it with a few drops of food coloring. Don't overdo it, you can always add more. Wearing gloves, toss the mixture until uniform in color.)

Note: Since this recipe contains no fat, extracts won't flavor it as strongly as the vanilla bean will.

QUESTION: *Why is my Seven-Minute Icing always gritty? My mother made it all the time and hers never was.*

ANSWER: Grittiness is caused by undissolved sugar crystals in the mixture, or by any sugar crystals left on the side of the bowl "seeding" the whole batch to crystallize. You can use regular table sugar, but superfine or confectioners' sugar are better because they dissolve faster with their smaller crystal size. I also take some extra steps to prevent crystallization:

1. Partially dissolve the sugar in the mixture by beating with a mixer on medium-low every couple of minutes, taking up to 10 minutes in total (usually necessary when using table sugar); the mixture will feel slightly gritty when ready to be used.
2. "Wash down" the crystals left on the side of the pan at the beginning of cooking by creating steam from a lid and washing with a wet pastry brush;
3. Don't scrape the bowl. Hardened icing makes the batch gritty.

QUESTION: *I've been baking cakes for a long time. I have tried a new cake recipe several times and have yet to make it work. I am really frustrated. Please help!*

ANSWER: I'd try a different recipe. Believe it or not, sometimes recipes (even published ones) are not balanced properly or include mistakes. Or the recipe may be too advanced for your skill level at the time. Start smaller, with buttercake cupcakes and then advance to layer cakes, and much later to foam cakes, such as angel food. Of course, brush up on your cake-making tips because they always help no matter how much experience you have. Here is a tried-and-true recipe that I use again and again: Almond Bundt Cake.

ALMOND BUNDT CAKE

❖

MAKES ONE 12-CUP BUNDT CAKE, OR TWO 8- OR 9-INCH LAYERS

This has a delicate almond fragrance making it one of my favorites. Don't use an intricately designed decorative Bundt pan but rather use one with a simple design as this cake is too soft and won't show the design or unmold easily. Buttermilk in the recipe makes for a tender, moist cake.

INGREDIENTS
CAKE
3 cups unbleached all-purpose flour; spoon into dry measuring cup and level to top
1½ teaspoons baking powder
½ teaspoon baking soda
½ teaspoon salt
1½ cups buttermilk, well shaken; measure in liquid measuring cup
1 teaspoon vanilla extract
¼ teaspoon almond extract
¾ cup (1½ sticks) unsalted butter, room temperature
2 cups sugar or superfine sugar
3 large eggs, room temperature

POURABLE ICING
2 tablespoons (¼ stick) unsalted butter, softened
⅛ teaspoon almond extract
1 cup (¼ pound) confectioners' sugar
2 to 3 teaspoons milk
¼ cup almond slices

1. Position a rack in the center of the oven and preheat the oven to 350 degrees F. Generously grease a 12-cup Bundt pan. If baking in layers, lightly grease the pans. Optionally, line them with paper, and then grease the paper lightly.

2. In a medium bowl, combine the flour, baking powder, baking soda, and salt with a spoon. Set aside. In a separate bowl combine the buttermilk, vanilla extract, and almond extract. Set aside.

3. In the bowl of a stand mixer, beat the butter with the paddle attachment on low speed until soft. Add the sugar in a steady stream at the side of the bowl. Increase the speed to medium and beat for 5 minutes until light and creamy. Stop the mixer and scrape the bowl often. For more on creaming, see page 39.

4. With the mixer on low, add the eggs one at a time and beat 20 seconds after each addition or until the mixture is smooth. With the mixer still on low speed, add the flour mixture in 3 equal portions, alternating with the buttermilk, combined with the extracts, in 2, starting and ending with the flour mixture (page 47). At the end, beat 1 minute or until smooth. The batter should be thick and fluffy. Pour the batter into the prepared pan and lightly smooth the top (page 42).

5. Bake for 60 minutes or until the top feels firm and gives slightly when touched with a cupped palm. For cake layers, bake 30 to 40 minutes. If you insert a toothpick in the middle and remove, it should have a few moist crumbs attached, but not bat-

QUESTION: *No matter what I do, my cake sticks to my Bundt pan making it hard to get out of the pan without breaking.*

ANSWER: Bundt cakes are notorious for sticking to the pan, so use a pastry brush to grease every nook and cranny with shortening, making sure every area is evenly covered. With a paper towel, lightly smooth any pockets of shortening. Some recipes say to also flour the pan, but I find it ruins the design because the flour collects in the cracks. Not every cake recipe will unmold well from a Bundt pan. Be sure you are using a recipe that is designed for one, such as a pound cake. It's perfect because it's richer than a regular buttercake, with more sugar and fat. Its texture is dense and not so fluffy.

ter. The cake should be lightly browned all over and will shrink a little from the side of the pan; it will also smell done. You will still hear a few air bubbles popping.

6. Remove the pan to a wire cake rack, let cool for 10 minutes, and unmold. Turn the cake upright to cool completely.

7. Prepare the Icing: The icing can be made in advance and sit, covered with plastic wrap, at room temperature. The sugar acts as a preservative. With a mixer on low, beat the butter and almond extract until well-mixed but not creamed. Slowly add the confectioners' sugar. Add enough milk to make a thick yet pourable icing. Cover. Icing keeps for two weeks at room temperature, but is best used when freshly made. Whip before using, and adjust the consistency by adding milk 1 teaspoon at a time if it is too thick, or sugar 1 tablespoon at a time if too thin.

Assembly: When the Bundt cake has cooled, put on a wire cake rack set over a piece of waxed or parchment paper. Pour the icing over the top. Sprinkle with the almond slices. Let the icing set for 10 to 15 minutes and serve. To assemble the cake layers, see page 50.

Storage: page 48

QUESTION: *How much red food coloring should I use in my Red Velvet Cake? Mine always turn out dark pink, and I want my cake red.*

ANSWER: For a really red cake I like to use 2 ounces of food coloring per 2 to 2 ½ cups flour and cocoa powder; I found that adding only 1 ounce makes the cake dark pink. See my Red Velvet Layer Cake (recipe follows).

RED VELVET LAYER CAKE
WITH CREAM CHEESE ICING

❖

MAKES TWO 9 x 2-INCH ROUND LAYERS, OR TWO 8 x 2-INCH
ROUND LAYERS, OR 24 TO 36 CUPCAKES

Red Velvet Cake is a favorite throughout the South. No one is quite sure why you add red food coloring to chocolate cake, but coloring does make its naturally light brown color more appealing. The addition of buttermilk helps with leavening and makes for a very fine, tender cake. Keep the cake refrigerated if filling and frosting it with the Cream Cheese Icing.

INGREDIENTS
CAKE
2 cups unbleached all-purpose flour; spoon into dry measuring cup and level to top
½ cup cocoa powder, sifted; spoon into dry measuring cup, level to top, and then sift
2 teaspoons baking powder
½ teaspoon baking soda
1 teaspoon salt
1 cup buttermilk, room temperature, well shaken; measure in liquid measuring cup
1 tablespoon vanilla extract
4 tablespoons (2 ounces) red food coloring
1 cup (2 sticks) unsalted butter, room temperature
1½ cups sugar
4 large eggs, room temperature

ICING
One 8-ounce package cream cheese, cold
½ cup (1 stick) butter, cold
1 teaspoon vanilla extract
4 cups (1 pound) confectioners' sugar, sifted after measuring

1. Position a rack in the center of the oven and preheat the oven to 350 degrees F. Generously grease two 9-inch pans. Or lightly grease the pans, line them with parchment paper, and then grease the paper lightly.

2. In a medium bowl, combine the flour, cocoa powder, baking powder, baking

soda, and salt with a spoon, mixing well; set aside. Measure the buttermilk and stir in the vanilla and red food coloring; set aside.

3. In the bowl of a stand mixer, beat the butter with the paddle attachment on low speed until soft. Add the sugar in a steady stream at the side of the bowl. Increase the speed to medium and beat for 5 minutes until light yellow and fluffy. For more on creaming, see page 39.

4. With the mixer on low, add the eggs one at a time and beat for 20 seconds after each addition. Without turning off the mixer, add flour in 3 equal portions, alternately with the buttermilk mixture in 2 equal portions, beginning and ending with the flour mixture in a steady stream at the side of the bowl. (See page 47.) At the end, beat for 1 minute or until smooth. The batter should be thick and fluffy. Scrape the bowl and divide evenly into the prepared pans; lightly smooth the tops (page 42).

5. Bake for 20 to 30 minutes or until the top feels firm and gives slightly when touched with a cupped palm. If you insert a toothpick in the middle and remove, it should have a few moist crumbs attached, but not batter. The cake will shrink a little from the side of the pan; it will also smell done. You will still hear a few air bubbles popping.

6. Remove the pans to a wire cake rack, let cool for 10 minutes, and unmold. Turn the cake upright to cool completely. Meanwhile, make the icing.

7. The icing can be made in advance, but must be refrigerated at all times. In a medium bowl, with a handheld mixer on medium, beat the cream cheese and butter to soften. Add the vanilla extract. With the mixer running on low, slowly add the confectioners' sugar and beat until light and fluffy. Correct with milk or sugar if it is too stiff or soft.

Assemble: page 50

Storage: Store the frosted cake in the refrigerator; cream cheese is perishable.

QUESTION: *I'd like to make a buttercake with honey instead of sugar. Do I just substitute one for the other?*

ANSWER: You can use honey to flavor and sweeten a buttercake. But honey does not cream with a solid fat such as butter or shortening to create the air bubbles so necessary for the delicate structure of a buttercake. Instead it is mixed much like a quick bread (page 215). Most honey cakes tend to be dense with an overpowering honey flavor. The recipe that follows isn't.

ORANGE-HONEY FROSTED
LAYER CAKE

MAKES TWO 8- OR 9-INCH ROUND LAYERS

This cake has a nice subtle flavor of honey. It's delicious with a cup of hot tea and lemon.

INGREDIENTS
CAKE
2¼ cups cake flour, not self-rising; spoon into dry measuring cup and level to top
1½ teaspoons baking powder
½ teaspoon baking soda
1 teaspoon salt
½ cup (1 stick) butter, room temperature
¾ cup sugar
¼ cup orange-flavored honey, or any delicately flavored variety; to measure,
    pour into dry measuring cup to the rim
2 large eggs, room temperature
2 teaspoons vanilla extract
½ cup buttermilk, well shaken; measure in liquid measuring cup
1 tablespoon grated orange peel (from 1 large orange)

FROSTING
½ cup (1 stick) butter
2 tablespoons orange-flavored honey, or any delicately flavored variety
4 cups (1 pound) confectioners' sugar
¼ cup milk plus more if needed; measure in liquid measuring cup
1 teaspoon vanilla extract
1 tablespoon grated orange peel (from 1 large orange)

1. Position a rack in the center of the oven and preheat the oven to 350 degrees F. Generously grease two 8- or 9-inch pans. Or lightly grease the pans, line them with parchment paper, and then grease the paper lightly.

2. In a medium bowl, combine the flour, baking powder, baking soda and salt; set aside.

3. In the bowl of a stand mixer, beat the butter with the paddle attachment on low

speed until soft. Add the sugar in a steady stream at the side of the bowl. Increase the speed to medium and beat for 5 minutes until light yellow and fluffy. For more on creaming, see page 39. Add the honey and beat for 1 minute more.

4. With the mixer on low, add the eggs one at a time and beat for 20 seconds after each addition. Add the vanilla. Without turning off the mixer, add the flour in 3 equal portions, alternately with the milk, beginning and ending with the flour mixture (see page 47). Add the orange peel. At the end, beat for 1 minute or until smooth. The batter should be thick and fluffy. Scrape the bowl and divide evenly into the prepared pans; lightly smooth the top (page 42).

5. Bake for 25 to 30 minutes or until the top feels firm and gives slightly when touched with a cupped palm. If you insert a toothpick in the middle and remove, it should have a few moist crumbs attached, but not batter. The cake should be lightly browned all over and will shrink a little from the side of the pan; it will also smell done. You will still hear a few air bubbles popping.

6. Remove the pans to a wire cake rack, let cool for 10 minutes, and unmold. Turn the cake upright to cool completely. Meanwhile, make the icing.

7. The icing can be made in advance and sit, covered with plastic wrap, at room temperature. The sugar acts as a preservative. In a medium bowl, with a handheld mixer on medium speed, beat the butter and honey until fluffy. Gradually add in 2 cups confectioners' sugar. Beat well. Add ¼ cup of the milk, the vanilla, and orange peel and beat until well combined. Slowly beat in the remaining confectioners' sugar until spreadable. Fix with 1 teaspoon of milk and 1 tablespoon of confectioners' sugar, if necessary to correct the texture.

Assemble: page 50
Storage: page 48

FOAM CAKES: POINTERS, QUESTIONS, AND RECIPES

The texture of foam cakes is light, spongy, and airy, very different from compact buttercakes. Foams made from separated, beaten eggs represent a very large portion of this type of cake. Up to 11 or 12 egg whites are beaten with sugar to stabilize, and then folded with flour (usually cake flour) that supplies some structure. Egg foam is the main source of leavening and its proteins are responsible for the cake's structure, as in soufflés and meringues.

When foam cakes are baked, the air bubbles beaten into the eggs expand from the heat and steam, and the protein structure sets. Baking essentially dries out the egg white or meringue base. Some foam cakes contain oil or melted butter which don't hold air but do act as tenderizers, though not as effectively as solid fat.

Foam cakes are the nemesis even of many experienced bakers. If you understand the techniques, you should have a head start on the process.

- Separating eggs (page 37)
- Room temperature eggs (page 15)
- Beating egg whites with sugar to make meringue (page 36)
- Beating egg yolks so they "ribbon" (page 39)
- Folding ingredients (page 40)

TIPS BEFORE YOU START: PREPARING THE PAN

Pans for angel food, sponge, and chiffon cakes aren't prepared by greasing. These types of batter literally climb up the pan's side to rise and fat deflates their foam. Only genoise cake needs a greased pan. (See Table, page 34.)

WATCHING YOUR CAKE BAKE (THROUGH THE OVEN WINDOW)

Foam cakes increase much more in size, proportionately, than do buttercakes. That's because when you whipped the eggs, you trapped a great deal of air in the batter. That air expands from the heat of the oven, producing a very dramatic "before and after" effect.

CHECKING FOR DONENESS

When the minimum time is up on a foam cake, open the oven door a crack just to hear if the cake is done. As long as a sponge or angel food cake is "singing" in the oven, the sound of the eggs releasing steam, it hasn't finished baking. When the singing almost stops and the cake is a deep golden brown, it is done. Press the top lightly—it should spring back. If it sounds hollow when tapped on the pan, it is

Sarah Says: When an angel food or chiffon cake is done, proper cooling is just as important as baking. The cake is inverted to cool in its pan, which prevents its delicate egg protein structure from shrinking or falling, and maintains the open texture characteristic of these cakes. If placed on a rack to cool, it would deflate much of that hard-earned volume.

My favorite way to cool an angel food or chiffon cake is to place the pan upside down in a colander. The holes allow the cake to cool properly, and it is certainly more stable than trying to balance it over the neck of a bottle or a funnel, the traditional cooling method. Another way is to rest the pan upside down on the little feet around the rim of the pan, but that brings it too close to the countertop, allowing condensation to form and making the cake damp. Once cool, your cake can be unmolded and served.

done. If not, close the oven door and continue to bake, checking at 5-minute intervals. Timing is especially critical with foam cakes: overbaking makes them dry and flavorless, but significant underbaking makes them collapse.

CITRUS ANGEL FOOD CAKE

MAKES ONE 10-INCH TUBE PAN CAKE, 4 TO 5 INCHES HIGH

This is a classic angel food cake, which is highly adaptable; just add different extracts and citrus peels. However, do not add any flavored oils to the batter; fat deflates its delicate foam. It's delicious served as is, drizzled with my Chocolate Ganache Fudge Sauce (page 175) or accompanied by a fresh fruit salad.

INGREDIENTS

CAKE

12 large egg whites or 8 tablespoons ($\frac{1}{2}$ cup) egg white powder dissolved in
   1 $\frac{1}{2}$ cups warm water (page 22); eggs may be cold or room temperature
$\frac{1}{4}$ teaspoon salt
1 $\frac{1}{2}$ teaspoons cream of tartar or 1 teaspoon lemon juice
1 $\frac{1}{4}$ cups sugar or superfine sugar
1 tablespoon fresh orange juice or water
Grated peels of 1 orange and 1 lemon
1 cup cake flour, not self-rising; spoon into measuring cup and level to top

OPTIONAL GARNISH
About $\frac{1}{8}$ cup confectioners' sugar

1. Position a rack in the center of the oven and preheat the oven to 325 degrees F. Do not grease the pan.

2. In a dry, clean mixer bowl, with the mixer on medium-low speed, beat the egg whites until foamy. Add the salt and cream of tartar or lemon juice. Continue whipping until the foam is white and opaque. Increase mixer speed to high and add the sugar at the side of the bowl. Beat until the egg whites are glossy and form stiff peaks (page 38). Beat in the orange juice and grated peels in the final moments of whipping.

3. Sift one-third of the flour mixture over the whites, and with a large rubber spatula, fold it into the whites (page 41). Repeat this process with the remaining flour mixture, folding in only one-third at a time. Gently scrape the batter into an ungreased 10-inch tube pan. Run a table knife in a zig-zag pattern through the batter to get rid of any large air pockets.

4. Bake 40 to 50 minutes, until the top of the cake is golden brown and springs back when gently pressed in the center, and a toothpick inserted in the center comes out clean. It will not shrink from the side of the pan.

5. To cool, invert the cake pan onto the neck of a bottle or funnel (if the cake tilts a little, that's fine) or place it upside down in a colander for more stability. Cool completely in the pan, 1 to 2 hours.

6. To remove the cake from the pan, slip a flexible metal spatula carefully down the side of the pan. Slowly trace around the perimeter to release the cake, pressing the spatula against the side of the pan so you don't mar the cake. When the side is free, push up on the removable bottom. Holding the central core, remove the cake from the side. Free the cake from the base the same way, turn it over on a plate and carefully remove the base. Place upright on a serving platter.

7. To serve, sift confectioners' sugar over the top of the cake and slice with a serrated knife using a sawing action.

Variation: Cocoa-Orange: Substitute ¾ cup cake flour and ¼ cup cocoa powder for 1 cup cake flour. After measuring, sift the flour and cocoa together several times (cocoa powder lumps). Omit the lemon peel and add 1 teaspoon vanilla extract with the orange juice.

Storage: Keeps well at room temperature for up to 5 days well wrapped in plastic wrap. Can be frozen for 2 to 3 months.

ANGEL FOOD CAKES

Angel food cakes are foam cakes with no shortening. They use only flour, sweetener, salt, flavoring, and beaten egg whites—as many as 10 or 12 (about one and a half cups) in a recipe! Rather than crack open a dozen fresh eggs and be left with a lot of yolks, I prefer to use egg white powder (page 22).

QUESTION: *I baked my angel food cake. It rose in the oven and then fell when almost done baking. What happened?*

ANSWER: This can happen from under- or over-whipped egg whites, not folding the flour thoroughly into the foam, not preheating the oven, or its temperature being off. Another cause for this is baking your recipe in a nonstick angel food pan or greasing the pan. If the pan's side is too slippery, the cake can't hold on to climb and will eventually collapse. How do I know? I learned the hard way with one of my recipes!

SPONGE CAKES

Sponge cake (not to be confused with a butter sponge cake or genoise) is sometimes used to refer to the whole category of foam cakes. It is an airy cake similar to an angel food cake except that it is made with beaten egg yolks or with whole eggs. The texture and flavor of sponge cake are so delightful that it is usually eaten without adornment. Place the batter in the oven and shut the door immediately after mixing, before the air cells have had a chance to break down or coalesce. Don't open the oven until the batter is almost baked. During baking, the air bubbles expand from the heat and steam and, if the ingredients are beaten and folded properly and the oven temperature is accurate, your cake will rise quite high. Remove your cake from the oven at the correct time.

Sponge cake is versatile. It can be baked in a regular cake pan, springform pan, or jelly roll pan. It can be filled with whipped cream and spread with jam and tightly rolled to create a jelly roll cake. It can be cut into rounds with scissors to serve as a base for cheesecake or baked with different colors to decorate and wrap around the sides of a cake. Sponge cakes can include hot milk, which makes them richer and more cake-like and which is sturdier, making a nice base for a Boston cream pie. Genoise cakes, French classic sponge cakes, are made by beating warm whole eggs with sugar until the mixture more than triples in volume, then folding in the flour and sometimes melted butter, too. Passover sponge cakes are made with matzoh flour.

PRISCILLA'S ORANGE SPONGE CAKE

MAKES ONE 9-INCH SPRINGFORM OR ROUND CAKE PAN

This was my mother Priscilla's all-purpose party cake, handed down from my grandmother. The texture and flavor of this sponge cake is delightful and delicate and goes well with a fresh fruit salad of orange and grapefruit segments and some whipped cream. Once cooled, cut it with a serrated knife; otherwise you'll squish it.

INGREDIENTS

CAKE

1 cup cake flour (not self-rising); spoon into dry measuring cup, level to top

5 large eggs, separated (separate when cold, cover, and let come to room
    temperature, about 20 minutes)

1 cup sugar or superfine sugar

5 tablespoons orange juice or water

1 teaspoon vanilla extract

1 teaspoon orange extract or 1 tablespoon orange peel, finely chopped
    (from 1 large orange)

1 teaspoon cream of tartar or 1 teaspoon lemon juice

½ teaspoon salt

GLAZE

1½ cups confectioners' sugar

¼ cup orange juice or water

1 tablespoon grated orange peel (from 1 large orange)

1. Position a rack in the center of the oven and preheat the oven to 325 degrees F. Grease only the bottom of a 9-inch springform or cake pan, line it with parchment paper, and grease the paper. Make sure you don't grease the side. (This type of cake is easier to remove from a springform pan.)

2. Sift cake flour 3 times into a small bowl or onto a large piece of parchment or waxed paper. Set aside.

3. In a large bowl, whisk the egg yolks to break them up and then add ½ cup of the sugar, the orange juice, and vanilla and orange extracts. Vigorously whisk for a couple of minutes until the yolks are light in color and ribbon when you lift the

whisk (page 39). (You can also use a mixer.) Whisk in the flour to make a smooth batter; don't beat in a mixer. Cover and set aside.

4. In the dry, clean bowl of a stand mixer, with the mixer on medium-low speed, beat the egg whites until foamy. Add the cream of tartar and salt. Continue whipping until the foam is white and opaque. Increase mixer speed to high and add the remaining $\frac{1}{2}$ cup of sugar at the side of the bowl. Beat until the egg white foam is light and fluffy. When you stop the mixer and lift its beaters, the whites should form a soft peak and then have its tip droop and fold over (page 38).

5. Add a small amount of the whites to the batter and stir with your whisk to lighten. Place the rest of the beaten egg whites on the surface of the batter. Fold very carefully so the whites don't lose their volume (page 41). The batter should be homogenous. Scrape into the prepared pan.

6. Bake for 40 minutes or until the cake is well risen, firm, and sounds hollow when lightly tapped on the pan with the handle of a wooden spoon. It should also be golden brown on top. It will not shrink from the side of the pan. The cake will form a slight dome.

7. Cool the cake in the pan on a wire rack for ten minutes.

8. To remove the cake from the pan, slip a flexible metal spatula carefully down the side of the pan. Slowly trace around the perimeter, unlatch the clamp and slip off the pan side. When the side is free, turn it over on a plate, slip a flexible metal spatula between the cake and the pan's bottom to loosen, and remove. Place cake upright on a wire cake rack to cool.

9. Make the confectioners' sugar glaze: Beat together the confectioners' sugar, orange juice, and orange peel. Add more juice 1 teaspoon at a time if the glaze is not pourable, or add confectioners' sugar 1 tablespoon at a time to stiffen.

Assembly: When the cake has cooled, and been unmolded, place it on a wire cake rack set over a piece of waxed or parchment paper set on a rimmed cookie sheet or pan. Pour the icing over the top. Let the icing set 10 to 15 minutes, and serve.

QUESTION: *My sponge cake has a thick layer of baked cake on the bottom. How can I fix this in the future?*

ANSWER: Undermixed batter will form a thick layer on the bottom of the cake, and it will be streaked from the egg mixture. You need to master two important techniques and your sponge cake will be light as a cloud: beating the egg whites to a stable foam (page 38), and folding dry ingredients into the egg white foam (page 41).

QUESTION: *When the sponge cake is still warm, it is quite soft. But after keeping it wrapped on the countertop, it is hard two days later. Why?*

ANSWER: I'm sorry to say, but that's the nature of sponge cakes. They quickly begin to stale after being removed from the oven. An unfrosted sponge cake will keep, tightly wrapped, for a day or two. If you want to keep it longer, store it in the freezer. A frosted cake, however, will stay moist longer, depending on the wetness of the icing. Remember to keep it covered or refrigerated if it contains perishable ingredients.

To serve, cut thin slices with a sharp serrated knife and serve with fruit salad or ice cream and berries.

Storage: Store the frosted cake at room temperature under an inverted glass bowl or cake keeper for a day or two. If you want to keep your unfrosted cake layer longer, freeze it wrapped first in plastic wrap, then in foil, and finally in an airtight container. It will keep for 2 to 3 months.

5

CHEESECAKES

*How can I keep my cheesecake from cracking? . . .
and other secrets to achieving cheesecake greatness.*

OH, THE COOL, CREAMY (and maddening) cheesecake! It takes on count-less flavors: in its filling, swirled throughout with chocolate, pumpkin, or strawberry preserves; in its crust, from the classic graham cracker to crumbled Oreo cookies to brownie or cake layers, or no crust at all; in its topping, from sour cream mixed with sugar and vanilla, to mixed berries, to a chocolate ganache glaze, to vanilla butter-cream, to sometimes just plain. Even the cheesecake's texture can vary greatly, from light and airy, to dense and rich, to smooth and creamy—it's all a matter of preference, bringing up much debate among connoisseurs about what makes a true cheesecake.

Cheesecake is an absolute favorite of many, including my husband Reed. This lus-cious dessert takes on countless variations: no-bake cheesecakes, essentially mousses held with gelatin that sets in the refrigerator; curd cheesecakes made with ricotta, farmer, or cottage cheese; and cheesecakes made with cream cheese. Only the cream cheese variety has almost driven most bakers, including me, over the edge.

THE ALCHEMY OF CREAM CHEESE CHEESECAKES

Cheesecake is essentially a sweetened custard filling, layered on top of a bottom crust; the two are baked together. There may be an optional topping added after the cheese-cake has been baked. The filling becomes a gel, composed mainly of eggs, cream cheese, heavy or sour cream, sweetener, sometimes starch, and flavorings. A cheese-cake is typically baked until it partially gels and then is chilled until it fully gels.

Even many experienced bakers have convinced themselves that if they can just get their techniques perfect, and if they can prepare to bake in a really organized way, they'll be able to conquer the most consistently frustrating problems. However, there are other variables at play and as a result, you may encounter some recurring disappointments unless you understand how the ingredients come together to make cheesecake magic.

Eggs are the primary structural and strengthening ingredient of a cheesecake's filling. Egg yolks contribute to creaminess because of their fat content and lecithin (a natural emulsifier). The more eggs, the creamier and more mousse-like the filling. Egg whites beaten alone result in an airy and fluffy filling. Sometimes there are four or five eggs or more in a filling. At the same time, more eggs make the cake more susceptible to overbaking and cracking.

When heated, eggs coagulate—that is, change from a fluid to a gel or thickened mass. Basically, cracks and other problems in the finished cake happen when the eggs' proteins over-coagulate from baking at too high a temperature or for too long, and later shrink when cooled. If eggs overcook, their proteins bind together so tightly that they become thick and curdled, and they squeeze out all the moisture they'd previously trapped from other ingredients. This phenomenon is called *syneresis,* whereby serum (water plus dissolved components) can be seen weeping from tiny tunnels in the custard.

Cream cheese, although not as structurally important as eggs, is high in milk proteins and fat, giving a smooth and creamy texture. Its milk proteins contribute to the viscosity and gel strength of the filling. Cream cheese melts easily, even at low temperatures; this is ideal for cheesecakes that need to bake "low and slow."

Most brands contain carrageen, gums, and added emulsifiers; these give the cheese its creamy consistency and help make a cheesecake more stable. The high moisture content allows it to combine well with other ingredients. Neufchatel (reduced-fat cream cheese) can be used, although full-fat works best. Do not use low-fat or no-fat. I have found that Philadelphia Brand cream cheese in bricks gives the most reliable results. It has a thick, creamy, even texture.

Heavy (whipping) cream, another form of protein and fat (the higher the fat content, the creamier, richer, and more flavorful), not only gives a velvety smooth texture, but also makes the cheesecake puff more from the steam created from its liquid content. Sour cream often contains gelatin, rennin, and vegetable enzymes. The acid in it gives it a pleasant tang. The gelatin in sour cream is useful for its stabilizing and textural properties. Note that heavy cream and sour cream also contain gums that contribute to the cheesecake's gel structure.

Sugar, typically white table sugar, adds sweetness, softness, and a mousse-like texture. Sugar is also important to the gel strength (viscosity) of the custard. Sugar raises the temperature of coagulation, allowing time for the rest of the ingredients to set. However, if too much is used, the cheesecake won't gel at all.

Starch, such as cornstarch or flour, features in more and more recipes. It makes the cake less likely to crack. The starch molecules prevent the egg proteins from over-coagulating: no over-coagulation, no cracks. Two to four tablespoons of cornstarch should be enough for two pounds of cream cheese. The flavor won't be affected, but the texture will be firmer and slightly less custard-like. Leaner cheesecakes need more starch than higher fat ones. Too much, however, will render your cake tough. Those with flour and two or three eggs will be slightly firmer, since the flour absorbs excess moisture. It is often said that cheesecakes without starch need a water bath, while those with some form of starch can be baked at a moderate temperature without one because the starch renders them less susceptible to over-baking. However, I like to use a water bath or steam in both cases, because the added humidity in the oven prevents cracking by maintaining a lower heat and more even baking.

Lemon juice adds flavor to a cheesecake but it also adds acid, a structure weakener. Acid tends to accelerate the denaturation of the egg proteins, slowing down coagulation. In other words, while encouraging an egg to cook and form a solid, it keeps the solid moist and creamy. Different acids have different degrees of ability to alter the egg's proteins.

Crusts for cheesecakes can be made from cookie crumbs, cake, or pastry. If you're using a crumb crust, make it in the pan but don't prebake it; that will make it too hard. Instead, just pack it down firmly. If the kitchen is warm, I refrigerate a crumb crust while I make the filling; the refrigeration keeps it firm when I pour in the filling. To use a sponge or buttercake crust, cut a thin layer and fit it in the bottom of the pan. You can also pour in half of the cheesecake batter, place a thin cake layer over it and fill with the remaining batter. (Make sure your pan is tall enough to accommodate the extra cake layer.) Bake for the same time and temperature as the recipe states. To cut cake to use as a crust, place the cake on a work surface with a cake pan the next size up from the cheesecake pan on top as a guide; run a sharp knife around the pan's edge.

Toppings add another level of flavor to your cheesecake. One commonly used topping is prepared from a mixture of sour cream, sugar, and vanilla extract spread on the filling immediately after baking, and then baked briefly at a high temperature. Many toppings, such as fruit compote or fresh berries glazed with melted preserves, are put on after the cheesecake has cooled. (Fruit is better used as a topping rather than as part of the filling, as its moisture will ruin a cheesecake's creamy interior.) The possibilities are almost endless. You can use whipped cream, shaved chocolate curls, candy bar pieces, or assorted nuts. I have seen frosted cheesecakes as well as cakes glazed in chocolate ganache or simply dusted with confectioners' sugar or cocoa powder.

CHEESECAKES: POINTERS, QUESTIONS, AND RECIPES

You've got a good sense for the way ingredients work in a cheesecake; now, let's move on to some tips on preparation.

CHOOSE YOUR PAN CAREFULLY

Use a springform or regular cake pan. You can substitute a two- to three-inch deep round cake pan—three-inch is better—with the same diameter for the springform in

QUESTION: *I am making a graham cracker crust. Shouldn't the number of crackers to make 1¼ cups be 18 to 20, not 9 as my recipe indicates?*

ANSWER: When you open a box of graham crackers, you see three separately wrapped packages of 9 full-size crackers each. When you grind one package—9 full-size, which equal 18 individual squares—you get about 1¼ cups of crumbs.

most recipes. Because a cake pan is heavier than a springform, it maintains a more even temperature and protects the cake against direct heat from the oven, so the cheesecake bakes better. I prefer cake pans.

Make sure you have enough room for the batter. A solid cake pan often ends up being filled right up to the rim. Check that your springform base is attached tightly and evenly to the sides. Generously grease the bottom and sides of the pan with melted butter or cooking spray, and optionally place a round of greased parchment or waxed paper in the bottom. For how to unmold a cheesecake from both regular and springform pans, see page 79.

BAKE THE CHEESECAKE IN A HUMID OVEN

Some cooks simply bake their cheesecake in the oven with no water bath or steam. The result depends solely upon the ingredients (fewer eggs, more fat from heavy cream, smaller and less thick cheesecake recipe) and techniques used in the recipe. However, if the eggs are overbeaten or the batter overmixed, cracks will certainly result.

As the cheesecake bakes, it loses a considerable amount of moisture. If it loses too much too fast, the cake will crack. One solution to this problem is to increase the humidity in the oven. Choose whether you'll use the water bath or steam method. I decide based on whether or not any starch is present, and how many eggs are in the recipe. With starch, if there are three eggs or less, I use the steam method; for four or more eggs, I use a water bath. Without starch, it is best to use a water bath every time.

WATER BATH METHOD

The water bath (*bain marie* in French) is used for custards, cheesecakes, and similar recipes. The method consists of placing a filled pan in a large, shallow pan of warm water for even, slow cooking. Foods may be cooked in this manner either in an oven or on a range top (though for cheesecakes you will always be cooking in an oven). The water surrounds and protects the delicate batter from direct heat, allowing it to

QUESTION: *If I use a water bath and place my springform pan in it, water usually leaks into it ruining the crust and the cheesecake. What do you recommend?*

ANSWER: Springform pans are notorious for water leaking into them from the water bath. To prevent seepage I gather a 15 x 17-inch Reynolds Hot Foil Bag around the sides of the pan. It shouldn't be closed over the top of the cake.

bake "low and slow." The lower temperature prevents the egg proteins from over-cooking and over-coagulating, the classic cause of cracked cheesecakes. The steam generated also prevents crust formation on the top and rapid expansion, which can also lead to cracks.

The water bath pan (I like to use a broiler pan, but roasting pans—metal or disposable—work well too) should be at least 1 inch wider than the cheesecake pan so that the moat of hot water can circulate and no less than $1\frac{1}{2}$ inches deep. This tempers the cooking significantly, because no matter how hot the oven is, the temperature of the water cannot rise above 212 degrees F.

Place the filled cheesecake pan in the empty bath pan and pour in hot water one inch up the side of the cheesecake pan (I use my tea kettle with its long, thin spout).

Steam Method

Another way to produce humidity in the oven is by placing a large pan, such as a 9- by 13-inch pan, on the rack immediately below the one that will hold the cake. Preheat the oven with an empty pan, place the cake on the shelf above, and then pour in boiling water to a depth of about one inch. Quickly shut the oven door. It creates a moist environment and cuts down on surface cracks (don't feel badly if you still get some though. It even happens to me!). The eggs in the cheesecake gently cook and set without too much browning or drying out on top.

TEMPERATURE

Cheesecake recipe temperatures should be in the moderate range; they should bake "low and slow." Most recipes call for 325 degrees F; 300 degrees F is too low, creating microbiological concerns. I put my cheesecake in a preheated 350 degree F oven to set its structure, and immediately reduce the temperature to 325 degrees F. I've seen recipes for more compact cakes with the oven temperature as high as 375 degrees F. The higher heat will brown the top, while lower heat will give it a nice, slow bake for an amazingly creamy texture.

QUESTION: *How do you get a browned top on a regular cheesecake, like in those Italian bakeries?*

ANSWER: Bake the cheesecake in a very hot oven (25 degrees F higher than the recipe states). After 10 minutes, reduce the heat to the recipe temperature. The intense heat will brown the top.

QUESTION: *How can I tell when my cheesecake is done baking?*

ANSWER: The idea is to bake the cheesecake just long enough to make it solid and creamy. If it is overbaked, it will crack, shrink, and weep. The problem with a cheesecake is that when it is done, it doesn't look done. The best way to tell if it is done is to bake it the exact time specified in the recipe.

When a cheesecake is just about ready, the surface turns from shiny to dull. The side should be raised and just barely beginning to brown. Another way to test if it has finished baking is to partially open the oven door and tap it on its side with a long-handled wooden spoon. Don't remove it from the oven to test or pull it out on the oven shelf. The top of the cake should move as one semisolid piece rather than as a liquid with the edge more set. Never use a toothpick or cake tester to check a cheesecake for doneness because you could start a hole from which a crack could form.

QUESTION: *How do I keep my cheesecake from cracking?*

ANSWER: This is the second most frequently asked of all baking questions I receive, so I decided to find out myself what causes cracking, and to create cheesecake recipes that are less susceptible. After about 50 pounds of cream cheese my family almost went on strike.

The very basis of a cheesecake's batter—cream cheese (about two pounds per 9-inch cheesecake), eggs (sometimes up to 5), and heavy cream—are all high in protein. It's these high-protein ingredients that coagulate into a custard-like filling, forming delicate, web-like protein bonds that hold the cheesecake's ingredients together.

However, this protein-rich structure tends to be highly susceptible to overbaking, cracking, weeping (syneresis), curdling, and not setting properly. Sometimes a cheesecake will crack no matter what you do, because its perfection is tied to many variables: ingredients, measuring, mixing, moisture, baking, cooling, and unmolding. Most cake recipes and other flour-based baked goods are not as sensitive to heat and thus less susceptible to cracking than cheesecakes.

COOLING

Although cheesecakes are soft when warm and freshly baked, they become firm as they cool, and even firmer after being refrigerated. A cheesecake will set properly and improve in taste and texture when chilled overnight.

Don't put a hot or very warm cheesecake in the refrigerator to cool. Condensation can cause the cake to become soggy. Let the cake sit for two hours to cool at room temperature on a wire cake rack before refrigerating. It is not safe to leave it out any longer. Even if it is still slightly warm after two hours, place it uncovered in a refrigerator. When it is cold, cover with plastic wrap. Once it is completely chilled (at least 12 hours, preferably 24) the cheesecake is ready to be unmolded.

UNMOLDING

These steps are for cheesecakes with no toppings. If your cheesecake is frozen, don't defrost it. A frozen cheesecake unmolds the best.

FROM A SPRINGFORM PAN

About an hour before serving:

1. Gently run a paring knife between the side of the cake and the pan while touching the bottom. Take care not to cut into the cake. Unlatch the springform clasp and slip off the pan side.
2. Place a foil-covered cardboard round or plate on top and flip the whole pan over onto it. You are now holding an inverted cake pan on the cardboard or plate.
3. If you lined the springform pan with a greased round of parchment paper before baking, this may not be necessary: To help the crust loosen from the

pan take a kitchen towel, soak it briefly in hot water, and wring it out. (Be careful because it's hot.) Place it on the pan's bottom only and count to ten. Repeat as many times as necessary. (If the pan's bottom is stubborn, I often heat it for 10 to 15 seconds on the stove's burner on low while rotating before removing the pan's side.) Take a thin, large knife or large icing spatula and carefully loosen the crust from the pan's bottom.

4. Once loose, remove the pan, and immediately put a second cardboard or serving plate on the newly revealed, crusted side (the bottom of the cake). Holding both plates, flip the cake right side up. If desired, the side can be smoothed with a knife or offset spatula, warmed by dipping it in hot water and then drying it. Cover and refrigerate before serving.

FROM A SOLID CAKE PAN

1. When the cake is done, remove it from the water bath and place it on a wire cake rack. Allow the cake to cool completely, then chill it at least overnight, preferably for 24 hours. You want the cake to be solid. You can also freeze it for 2 hours after refrigeration to make it really stiff.

2. When it is time to remove the cake from the pan, have one flat serving plate and a foil-wrapped cardboard round, or two flat plates, ready.

3. Run a thin knife around the sides all the way to the bottom. Gently heat the bottom of the pan on the stove, rotating the pan every 10 to 15 seconds so it heats evenly. You want to warm the bottom just barely. When you feel the bottom and the side of the pan beginning to warm, hold the pan with both hands, firmly rap the bottom of the pan across the edge of a countertop to release the cheesecake. (If you have trouble getting the cake out, do this a few more times.) Place the cardboard round or plate on top and flip the whole pan over onto it. You are now holding an inverted cake pan on the cardboard or plate.

4. Firmly tap the edge of the pan all the way around with a wooden spoon or one-cup metal measuring cup to release the cheesecake. When you feel the cake give way, remove the cake pan. If it sticks, re-warm the bottom.

5. Once loose, remove the pan, and immediately put the second cardboard or serving plate on the newly revealed, crusted side (the bottom of the cake) and, holding both plates, flip the cake right side up. If desired, the side can be smoothed with a warm knife or offset spatula. Cover and refrigerate before serving.

QUESTION: *I recently baked a couple of cheesecakes that came out fairly well. My problem was in trying to slice them; they were very mousse-like and creamy, made with lots of eggs. Do you have any suggestions on how to get a clean slice?*

ANSWER: I am convinced that cutting a frozen cheesecake yields the very best slices no matter what type of texture. Put yours in the freezer unwrapped until the cheesecake hardens (unless it has a sour cream topping). Wrap and freeze for a couple of hours, preferably overnight so it gets really hard. Take it out and don't let the cake thaw. Use a very sharp knife with a long blade to cut it. Do so with one stroke, pressing straight down. If you have an electric knife, use that. I also use a bench scraper, my favorite tool. You can cut straight down with it, leaving less chance for torn cake or uneven slices. Put the cut cake in the refrigerator to finish thawing, or serve frozen. Frozen cheesecake is out of this world!

WITHOUT INVERTING

When a cheesecake is topped with sour cream, fruit, or anything else you can neither flip it over to remove it from the pan nor can you unmold it from a solid pan. Before baking grease the pan and line it with a piece of greased parchment paper two inches larger than the diameter of the pan. When you clamp on the side part, the extra parchment should stick out at the bottom. When unmolding, hold down one corner of the parchment paper and gently push on the bottom of the cheesecake so it slides off onto a flat serving platter. Make sure the platter is positioned at the same level as the cheesecake. This way you don't have to remove the paper on the bottom. If the cheesecake starts to crack when removing it, chill it in the freezer (15 to 20 minutes) until it becomes hard enough to safely take out of the pan. It works really well.

STORING

Store the cheesecake in the refrigerator for up to five days, tightly covered with plastic wrap. Even though you can't freeze cream cheese, you can freeze cream cheese cheesecakes, as long as they don't have sour cream topping (which won't freeze well). They can be frozen for two to three months. To thaw place the whole cake, still wrapped, in the refrigerator overnight.

NO CRACK NEW YORK DENSE AND CREAMY CHEESECAKE

A cheesecake's soul is its filling; this one is creamy and rich. It is simply flavored with vanilla extract and baked with a graham cracker crust—that's it. I wanted to develop a cheesecake that had less of a chance of cracking than a typical recipe—to get this right, I stopped counting at 30 pounds of cream cheese.

I found that baking it in the oven with steam from a pan beneath sets the middle better than using a water bath. You shouldn't get any major cracks from this recipe because it contains cornstarch. However, tiny ones are typical on any cheesecake.

This recipe is best made with ingredients right from the refrigerator. Keep the mixer on low speed at all times to avoid mixing too much air into the batter. If you don't, the cheesecake puffs up and falls during baking, causing cracking. Stop the mixer frequently and scrape the bowl and beaters with a rubber spatula. Make sure you get the bottom of the bowl.

The initial high temperature gives the cheesecake its characteristic browned top and helps to set its structure, and the subsequent lower temperature keeps the eggs from overcooking, which makes for a tough, dry filling. Don't reduce the temperature by 25 degrees F if using a dark or nonstick pan. This bakes best in a dull solid pan, or a springform pan.

INGREDIENTS

CRUST

Vegetable oil cooking spray

1¼ cups graham cracker crumbs, from 9 full-size crackers (18 squares total)

¼ cup sugar

⅓ cup (5 tablespoons plus 1 teaspoon) unsalted butter, melted

FILLING

2 cups sugar

¼ cup cornstarch

32 ounces (four 8-ounce packages) cream cheese, cold

1 tablespoon vanilla extract

¾ cup heavy cream, cold

3 large eggs, cold

QUESTION: *I have lots of guests coming for Thanksgiving. Can I double my cheesecake recipe?*

ANSWER: The bigger the better? Not for cheesecake! Generally a 9-inch cake can serve 10 to 12 people. I would definitely recommend that you bake many small cheesecakes rather than one large one. Smaller, less thick cheesecakes seem to crack less. The larger and thicker cheesecakes that result from doubling a recipe tend to overbake at the edge before the center has reached the temperature necessary to coagulate the eggs. If the cake isn't properly baked, it will form deep cracks upon cooling and will be tough. For your next special occasion, you may want to try my Dulce de Leche Swirled Cheesecake (page 85)—your company will be blown away!

1. Position one oven rack in the middle, and another one rung down. Place a 9- by 13-inch pan on the shelf below the middle rack. (You will later fill it with boiling water.) Preheat the oven to 350 degrees F.

2. Generously spray the bottom and side of the pan with vegetable oil spray. Optionally, put a disk of parchment paper in the bottom and grease that. Mix the graham cracker crumbs and sugar right in the pan. Drizzle the melted butter over the crumbs and mix until moistened. Press into the bottom of the pan. Set aside in the refrigerator.

3. Blend the sugar and cornstarch together. Place one 8-ounce package of the cream cheese and ½ cup of the sugar-cornstarch mixture in the bowl of a stand mixer. Beat with the paddle attachment on low speed until creamy, about 1 minute. Beat in the remaining 3 packages of cream cheese and the vanilla.

4. With the mixer still on low, beat in the remaining sugar-cornstarch mixture. Add the heavy cream in a steady drizzle at the side of the bowl. Blend in the eggs one at a time, until completely mixed after each one. Be careful not to overmix. Stop the mixer and remove the bowl. Scrape and mix in any unblended ingredients. (If the batter has tiny lumps, it is okay.) Tap the bowl's bottom on the countertop about six times to get rid of large air bubbles.

5. Gently pour the filling into the graham cracker crust. (If using a solid pan, the batter will come to the rim.) Tap the pan on its side with the handle of a wooden spoon about a dozen times to get rid of large air bubbles. Smooth the top.

6. Place the cheesecake on a foil-lined baking sheet and put it in the oven. Immediately pour about an inch of boiling water in the heated pan below and shut the door. After 10 minutes, reduce the heat to 325 degrees F. Bake the cheesecake about an hour. (See page 78 for testing for doneness.)

7. When the cake is done, remove the pan to a wire cake rack for 1 to 2 hours to cool. Remove the pan of water from the oven once the water has cooled. The cake will come from the oven slightly puffed and will fall back down and flatten as it cools. Cover with plastic wrap and chill it for at least 12 hours, preferably for 24 hours if using a cake pan.

8. Unmold (page 79) and serve or store (page 81).

DULCE DE LECHE
SWIRLED CHEESECAKE

This one is a show-stopper and a cheesecake that's less apt to crack because it contains only two eggs and cornstarch. I first tasted a cheesecake with dulce de leche *(DOOL-say duh LAY-chay) at a restaurant in California and I flipped! It means "sweet milk" and is a thick, rich, and creamy caramel syrup made by combining milk with sugar and baking soda and cooking it until it is reduced to a thick amber syrup. When swirled into a cheesecake, it adds a lot of flavor and color. Dulce de leche is a traditional dairy product from Latin America. I decided to create my own dulce de leche recipe when I got home. It adds some work, but for a special treat, you may want to try it at least once. Make dulce de leche up to a week ahead; it needs to be made at least 2 hours ahead. It takes an hour to cool before swirling into the cheesecake. I pour mine into a large heatproof glass pan so it cools faster. It can also be purchased in Latino markets, some grocery stores, and online (page 243). Don't reduce the oven temperature by 25 degrees F if using a dark or nonstick pan. This bakes best in a dull solid pan, or a springform pan.*

INGREDIENTS
DULCE DE LECHE
2 cups whole milk, cold; measure in liquid measuring cup
1 cup sugar
½ teaspoon baking soda
½ teaspoon vanilla extract

CRUST
Vegetable oil cooking spray
1¼ cups graham cracker crumbs, from 9 full-size crackers (18 squares total)
¼ cup sugar
*¼ cup pecans, chopped and toasted, optional; measure, chop, and toast for
    5 minutes at 350 degrees F, turn often. Cool before using.*
1 tablespoon grated orange peel, optional (from 1 orange)
⅓ cup (5 tablespoons plus 1 teaspoon) unsalted butter, melted

1¾ cups sugar
¼ cup cornstarch
32 ounces (four 8-ounce packages) cream cheese, cold
1 tablespoon vanilla extract
¾ cup heavy cream, cold
2 large eggs, cold

1. Make dulce de leche at least 2 hours in advance: In a heavy 5- or 6-quart saucepan with at least 4½- to 5-inch sides, stir the milk and sugar over medium heat until the sugar is dissolved and the mixture is boiling. Remove the pan from the heat. Stir in the baking soda. Be aware that the mixture will bubble and rise to the top of the pan, but will eventually fall back down. Reduce the heat to low to medium-low and simmer, stirring frequently with a heatproof spatula. Don't scrape the side of the pan. The pot will look like a mess, but will clean easily if soaked. Cook about 1 to 1½ hours, until the mixture is amber colored and syrupy, but thinner than maple syrup, and is reduced to about 1 cup. It should coat the back of a spoon. Pour through a fine strainer into a heatproof glass bowl; discard residue. Stir in the vanilla. Let the mixture cool about a half hour before using. It will thicken as it cools. For long-term storage, store it in an airtight container at room temperature for 2 to 3 days.

2. Position one oven rack in the middle, and another one rung down. Place a 9- by 13-inch pan on the lower shelf. (You will later fill it with boiling water.) Preheat the oven to 350 degrees F.

3. Generously spray the bottom and side of the pan with vegetable oil spray. Optionally, put a disk of parchment paper in the bottom and grease that. Mix the graham cracker crumbs, sugar, pecans, if using, and orange peel right in the pan. Drizzle the melted butter over the crumbs and mix until moistened. Press into the bottom of the pan. Set aside.

4. Blend the sugar and cornstarch together. Place one 8-ounce package of the cream cheese and ½ cup of the sugar-cornstarch mixture in the bowl of a stand mixer. Beat with the paddle attachment on low speed until creamy, about 1 minute. Beat in the remaining 3 packages of cream cheese and the vanilla.

5. With the mixer still on low, beat in the remaining sugar-cornstarch mixture. Add the heavy cream in a steady drizzle at the side of the bowl. Blend in the eggs one at a time, until completely mixed after each one. Be careful not to overmix. Stop the mixer and remove the bowl. Scrape and mix in any unblended ingredients. (If the batter has tiny lumps, it is okay.) Tap the bowl's bottom on the countertop about six times to get rid of large air bubbles.

6. Gently pour half of the cream cheese filling into the unbaked graham cracker crust. With a spoon, drizzle a third of the dulce de leche syrup in squiggles evenly over the batter, avoiding the sides. Swirl in with the spoon, taking care not to dis-

turb the graham cracker crust. Do not overdo it; you want to see well-defined swirls of the syrup and batter. Repeat with the remainder of the batter and syrup. If using a solid pan, the batter will come to the rim. Tap the pan on its side with the handle of a wooden spoon about a dozen times to get rid of large air bubbles. Some will remain from the dulce de leche sugar. Smooth the top.

7. Place the cheesecake on a foil-lined baking sheet and put it in the oven. Immediately pour about an inch of boiling water in the heated pan below and shut the door. After 10 minutes, reduce the heat to 325 degrees F. Bake the cheesecake about an hour. (See page 78 for testing for doneness.)

8. When the cake is done, remove the pan to a wire cake rack for 1 to 2 hours to cool. Remove the pan of water from the oven once the water has cooled. The cake will come from the oven slightly puffed and will fall back down and flatten as it cools. Cover with plastic wrap and chill it for at least 12 hours, preferably for 24 hours if using a cake pan.

9. Unmold (page 79) and serve or store (page 81).

QUESTION: *Is it possible to make a low-fat cheesecake?*

ANSWER: Yes it is and in the recipe that follows I have devised a way to remove the fat without altering the texture and flavor.

CHOCOLATE PEANUT BUTTER CUP CHEESECAKE

MAKES ONE 9-INCH SPRINGFORM CAKE

I lightened this recipe with a meringue and Neufchatel cheese. Beaten egg whites incorporate air and therefore lightness in the cake. This cake does not need a water bath or steam because the filling is more of a meringue than a custard. Do not make it in a regular cake pan.

INGREDIENTS

CRUST

Vegetable oil cooking spray

1¼ *cups chocolate graham cracker crumbs, from 9 full-size crackers (18 squares total); or use Oreo or other cookie crumbs*

¼ *cup sugar*

⅓ *cup (5 tablespoons plus 1 teaspoon) unsalted butter, melted*

PEANUT BUTTER CHUNKS

⅓ *cup confectioners' sugar*

2 tablespoons dark brown sugar, packed

⅓ *cup chunky peanut butter*

FILLING

1 ounce semisweet or bittersweet chocolate (1 square)

12 ounces (1½ packages, 8 ounces each) Neufchatel cheese, cold

¼ *cup Dutch-process cocoa powder; spoon into dry measuring cup and level to top; sift after measuring if lumpy*

1 teaspoon instant espresso powder or instant coffee granules

1 teaspoon vanilla extract

4 large egg whites, room temperature

1 cup sugar

1. Position a rack in the middle of the oven and preheat the oven to 350 degrees F. Lightly spray a 9-inch springform pan with cooking oil spray.

2. To make the crust in the pan, stir the crumbs, sugar, and butter until well com-

bined. Press the mixture evenly and firmly over the bottom of the prepared pan. Set the crust aside.

3. To make the peanut butter chunks, in a small bowl combine the confectioners' sugar and brown sugar. Add the peanut butter. Using your fingertips, rub the mixture until it forms small crumbs. Sprinkle evenly over the crust.

4. Melt the chocolate according to the directions on page 166. Set it aside and let it cool until tepid (close to body temperature) but still liquid.

5. In the bowl of a stand mixer fitted with the paddle attachment, mix the Neufchatel on low speed until smooth, scraping down the side of the bowl with a rubber spatula. Add the cooled chocolate, the cocoa, espresso powder, and vanilla and mix on low speed until combined.

6. In a grease-free medium bowl, using a handheld electric mixer set at low speed, beat the egg whites until foamy. Increase the speed to high and beat until soft peaks begin to form. Gradually beat in the sugar until the mixture forms stiff, shiny peaks (page 38).

7. Add the egg whites to the cream cheese mixture and beat on low speed until just combined. Don't overmix; it should take no longer than 10 seconds. Turn into the crust and smooth the top.

8. Bake for about 25 minutes, until the edge of the cake is slightly puffed and very lightly browned. The center will seem somewhat unset, but will firm when chilled. When the cake is done, remove it to a wire cake rack for 1 to 2 hours to cool. Cover with plastic wrap and chill for at least 12 hours, preferably for 24 hours.

9. Unmold without inverting (page 81) and serve or store (page 81).

6

COOKIES AND BARS

*How can I make my chocolate chip cookies puffy
and chewy instead of flat and crispy? . . .
and other cookie conundrums.*

COOKIES, TO ALMOST EVERYONE who cooks—even if they don't think of themselves as bakers—seem like equal opportunity baking. It's the one thing we feel we ought to be able to master. I guess that's why it seems so unexpected—or worse, downright unfair—when cookies don't turn out the way we want them to. I mean, for goodness sake, they're cookies—are you telling me I can't even make cookies?!?

That's the feeling we all get when our cookies go wrong. If it's any consolation, it's happened to me too. It took me dozens of experiments to come up with the just-right chocolate chip cookie recipe, and a range of brownie recipes for every taste. But in any case, that frustration is a feeling you are about to be able to say goodbye to, forever! And just as in other types of baking—and cooking in general—it's the ingredients and the way they work together, and the mixing and baking techniques that dictate whether your brownies turn out cakey or fudgy, and your cookies turn out puffy and chewy or flat and crispy.

COOKIES AND BAR-TYPE COOKIES

I love cookies—I've never met anyone who doesn't love them too. Cookies, technically, are little handheld sweet flat cakes that come in a wide variety of shape, texture, and flavor. Cookies are part of our culture. Some of us bake cookies from our family's heritage, or bake certain types every year for Christmas. Cookies appear at special occasions such as weddings, birthdays, and family get-togethers, and as an everyday afternoon snack. Cookies are a perfect blank canvas for decorating, and can be dipped in chocolate, glazed, sandwiched together, or dusted with confectioner's sugar. Cookie baking is such a great project to do with children that it was the introduction to baking for many of us.

Cookies are usually distinguished by the way they are formed on the baking sheet or in the pan. There's a lot of variety in method and results in each group.

Cookies include drop cookies such as chocolate chip, oatmeal, and peanut butter, for which the ingredients are mixed in one bowl and the resulting soft dough is dropped by the spoonful onto a cookie sheet. Rolled and cut cookies are made from stiff dough that's usually chilled in a disk or block shape, rolled out into a thin layer with a rolling pin, and cut into shapes—cut-out sugar cookies are the type we tend to be most familiar with. Refrigerated dough cookies, such as vanilla sugar cookies or vanilla-and-chocolate pinwheel cookies, are called "slice and bake." Molded dough cookies include biscotti and ladyfingers, plus cookies baked in a mold. Filled cookies such as Linzer cookies are either baked with a filling in the dough, or baked in two parts and then sandwiched together around fillings. There are also fried cookies such as *churros, timbales,* and *cannolis,* and cake mix, reduced-fat, and no-bake cookies.

Bar cookies include brownies of all varieties, as well as blondies and lemon or lime bars. Bar cookies are usually made by spreading a thick, cake-type batter in a shallow pan, baking, cooling, and cutting into bars. Bar cookies may also be more complex, such as those layered in the pan, with an unbaked or baked crust and a soft layer baked on top.

THE ALCHEMY OF COOKIE TEXTURES

Whether gourmet, soft, or bite-sized cookies, new concoctions are always cropping up. No one book could hold the recipes for all of the various types. Different types of cookies are made from ingredients combined in different proportions, with various mixing and baking methods. We all love them: Chocolate Chip (page 98), Oatmeal Raisin (page 104), Fudge Brownies (page 108), Cake Brownies (page 110), Sugar Cookies (page 100), and Biscotti (page 102). They are chewy, crispy, flat, thick, cake-like, fudgy, and more.

However, we all get frustrated when a supposedly puffy and thick cookie flattens or a fudge brownie turns out cake-like. It's because of the recipe: if a recipe is written to produce a puffy or thin cookie, that's what you'll get. Outside factors such as humidity, greased, ungreased, or warm baking sheets also have an influence, but nothing is as powerful as the recipe.

Cookies are formulated similarly to cake: with flour, sugar, butter, eggs, leavening and salt, and sometimes milk, sour cream, buttermilk, flavorings, spices, and add-ins such as nuts and chocolate chips. Except that in a cookie, there is less liquid (eggs and milk), allowing them to be baked on cookie sheets because the batter is thicker and doesn't need to be contained.

Cookie recipes are especially sensitive: relatively small additions or deletions of ingredients, such as one tablespoon of flour or butter, can make the difference between a slightly puffy cookie or one that spreads too much. I know because I have developed lots of cookie recipes, including reduced-fat ones, and have seen the results.

I'm frequently asked about variations in results even when using the same recipe. Sometimes tried-and-true recipes produce cookies that look like little mountains, while other times the cookies are puffy and chewy and spread out perfectly. I feel that the result has to do with lots of variables acting in concert with one another. There may be temperature differences in the oven that are out of your control. The humidity level also has an effect. Bakeries and baking companies use controlled environments to make their products exactly the same over and over again. Home bakers can't exert such rigid control over their environments—and after all, it's a batch of cookies, it's not your whole life! But the result is that one batch may differ from the next. This is just my own theory, but try to keep in mind that the whole

QUESTION: *How do I get puffy, chewy cookies?*

ANSWER: Those attributes are opposites when talking about cookies. Puffy equals more flour; chewy equals more eggs, fat, and sugar. You need a fine balance to achieve both qualities, unless you're making a bar cookie. My Chocolate Chip Cookie recipe (page 98) is a recipe that almost produces both: puffy with a slight chew.

baking process is based on an interaction of ingredients, time, temperature, and moisture.

INGREDIENTS INFLUENCE TEXTURE

FLOUR

Even one or two tablespoons less or more can make a difference in whether a cookie spreads or puffs more.

FAT

Cookies made with butter have an outstanding taste, but those made with shortening hold their shape better by the nature of their composition. By combining part butter and part shortening you can get some buttery flavor while controlling the spread.

SUGAR

Whether granulated white, brown, or honey, sugar also has a key role to play. White sugar will make a cookie crisp, while brown adds sweetness, chewiness, and flavor. Like honey, brown sugar actually absorbs moisture, helping to insure that the cookies stay moist and chewy. But ones with honey often become too soft.

EGGS

Eggs help cookies puff from steam created from their liquid and egg whites, especially if beaten, hold air. Recipes that rely on only egg whites usually counteract their drying effect with more sugar, thus making them very sweet.

LEAVENING

Chemical leaveners such as baking soda and baking powder are common agents in cookies, but separated and beaten eggs also leaven. A little-known fact is that baking powder and baking soda also contribute to flavor, texture, spread, and color. Baking soda makes a cookie spread and brown more, as in my Classic Crispy Sugar Cookie recipe (page 100), giving it more flavor; but too much makes the cookie bitter. Baking powder, on the other hand, produces lighter-colored and puffier cookies. Other leaveners include steam (created from liquids such as water, milk, or cream) which causes the cookie to puff. With too much liquid, you'll have a "pancake-y" batter that will puff but then fall from the lack of gluten structure, and won't bake like a cookie at all!

MIXING METHODS INFLUENCE TEXTURE

Cookies are mixed in different ways, each making a difference to the texture.

- Creaming (page 39) is the way most cookies are mixed. The same as for cakes, fat and sugar beaten together incorporate air, making the cookie tender. Examples are chocolate chip or peanut butter cookies.
- One bowl mixing does not aerate the dough. Molded cookies such as biscotti and batter cookies (*pizzelle*) are mixed this way.
- Cutting fat into flour (page 35) produces a flaky or crumbly cookie, such as the base of lemon squares.
- Folding the dry ingredients into beaten egg whites (page 41) for a sponge makes light, airy cookies, such as meringue kisses or ladyfingers.

FORMATION, PAN PREPARATION, AND BAKING INFLUENCE TEXTURE

Drop cookies, such as chocolate chip or oatmeal, require you to "drop" the dough on your cookie sheet in equal size mounds. You want to try to get all your cookies the same size and weight so they bake evenly. Otherwise, you'll

Sarah Says: Don't allow cookie dough to sit at room temperature for more than one hour. The eggs and dairy products the dough contains are perishable. Always refrigerate if there is a long delay.

QUESTION: *Why do some recipes indicate to grease the pan, others not to grease the pan, to put down parchment or waxed paper? What's the difference? And what are Silpat baking mats?*

ANSWER: Cookies can require that you grease pans, not grease them, or use parchment or Silpat baking mats (a reusable woven mat made of silicone, useful for its nonstick properties). Waxed paper is not recommended when making cookies because it burns easily. So, follow your recipe. If cookie sheets are greased, the cookies will spread more than if not, but greasing may be essential to the recipe—the less fat a cookie has, the more the need for it. I prefer to spray my pans lightly with vegetable oil if the recipe calls for greased cookie sheets.

Parchment does not promote spreading, as a greased sheet will; it provides a nonstick surface. Spritz cookies are best baked on ungreased pans for little spread as it's important that they keep their pressed design and shape during baking. They also contain sufficient butter so they won't stick to their baking sheets. Chocolate chip cookies are best baked on ungreased sheets or parchment paper if the recipe is for puffy ones or on greased sheets if the recipe is written for the cookies to spread. If using parchment, to keep the paper from slipping dab some water on each corner of the pan, center the paper and press all four corners. Parchment paper can be reused several times, both front and back.

end up with a batch of cookies that are inconsistently baked, and have slightly different textures as a result. A measuring spoon or ice cream scoop will help you keep your cookies equal.

The type of sheet (page 8), and whether it is greased or not, also makes a big difference. And of course, the oven should be well preheated before you put the pan in.

Sarah Says: Make sure the baking pan has completely cooled before placing a new batch of dough on it. The fat in the recipe melts when placed on a warm sheet, causing it to spread more than it should before it's baked enough to hold the cookies' shape.

QUESTION: *How do I store drop cookies and dough?*

ANSWER: In a dry climate, crisp drop cookies can be kept for about five days, if stored in a cookie jar or container with a loose fitting lid. In a humid climate, store crisp cookies in a tightly covered container. Soft drop cookies should be kept in tightly covered containers for about five days or so with a piece of fresh-cut apple to add moisture. Place an apple half skin-side down on top of the cookies in the storage container. Remove and discard the fruit after a day or two. Baked drop cookies freeze beautifully for about three months.

Cookie dough can also be frozen for about four weeks, and will keep well in the refrigerator for three days. However, I've never had great luck freezing dough for snickerdoodles, peanut butter cookies, or heavy butter-based dough like spritz or shortbread. I've had good luck in freezing them already baked. Unbaked brownie batter does not store well because the leaveners will expend all of their leavening powers.

COOKIES: POINTERS, QUESTIONS, AND RECIPES

In all the years I've been taking baking questions, by far the most popular cookie is chocolate chip: it's the hands-down winner. The good news is that I've come up with a chocolate chip cookie recipe that is written to be somewhat chewy and puffy.

QUESTION: *My cookies bake just fine. But when I try to remove them from the cookie sheets, they fall apart. What should I do?*

ANSWER: Cookies usually break when removed from baking sheets while they're still too warm. Let the cookies cool on the sheets for a few minutes before transferring them to wire racks. Or if you have delicate cookies, bake them on a parchment paper–lined cookie sheet. When done, slide the entire sheet with the cookies to the wire cake rack to cool.

QUESTION: *Whenever I make chocolate chip cookies, they come out of the oven flat! It doesn't matter if I use butter, margarine, or Crisco. I have brand new cookie sheets (the shiny kind with the layer of air in them), which I didn't grease. The thickness of the cookies in the diners is what I'm looking for. Being a PTA mom I know they'd sell pretty fast at our bake sales.*

ANSWER: The thick and puffy chewy cookies we buy in malls and see in ads present a very different picture from those we bake at home, causing frustration of the kind you're experiencing.

The recipe for all chocolate chip cookies baked at home seems to be the one on the back of the Nestlé chocolate chips bag. It's the popular chocolate chip cookie that many of us grew up with and have been baking and eating since. It's been around since 1930, when it was invented by Ruth Wakefield of Massachusetts. This Nestlé recipe frequently produces a flatter and crispier cookie than most like; but it's only doing what it was written to do.

Making a chocolate chip cookie that is puffy and chewy is a challenge because these are two diametrically opposed attributes. When I simply added one or two tablespoons flour for more puff and chew, I got the puff but not the chew, and lost the buttery flavor. I also ended up with a dry cookie with little flavor that hardened into a rock when cooled. When I tried baking the Nestlé recipe for slightly less time, which resulted in more chew because the cookie's structure had set only a little, nine times out of ten, I ended up with a cookie that was gooey and fell apart. I then tried adding two tablespoons of butter, which gives flavor and prevents the cookie from hardening when cooled, but it spread more and became flat and crisp. For more chew, I used all brown sugar, instead of an equal combination of white and brown sugars, but this also made the dough spread too much, and gave the cookie a dark brown color as opposed to the light brown we associate with chocolate chip cookies. The cookie's taste also had a molasses undertone that was too strong for me. I tried using all baking powder instead of baking soda, which resulted in more puff, but I lost the browning and the flavor in the cookie. I tried using half baking soda and half baking powder which gave the best results: little spread and more puff, a nice brown color when baked, with more of a buttery, vanilla flavor.

SARAH'S THICK-WITH-A-CHEW CHOCOLATE CHIP COOKIES

MAKES ABOUT 4 DOZEN 2½ TO 3-INCH COOKIES

Here it is, the answer to your number one baking request: the thick and chewy chocolate chip cookie! You'll get a crunchy outside and a slightly chewy inside. Cookies made with this recipe will have the texture and taste that a chocolate chip cookie should. It wasn't easy—I went through 75 batches of cookies until I got it right. Since cookies are especially sensitive to the addition or subtraction of ingredients, testing was very intricate and took a long time, but I did succeed. Baking them at 400 degrees F helps them puff and then set quickly.

INGREDIENTS
2⅔ cups unbleached all-purpose flour; spoon into dry measuring cup and level
   to top
½ teaspoon baking powder
½ teaspoon baking soda
½ teaspoon salt
¾ cup sugar
¾ cup dark brown sugar, packed
1 cup (2 sticks) unsalted butter, room temperature
2 large eggs, room temperature
2 teaspoons vanilla extract
2 cups (one 11.5- or 12-ounce bag) semisweet chocolate chips
1 cup chopped walnuts, optional (page 26); chop, then measure

1. Adjust the rack in the center of the oven and preheat the oven to 400 degrees F.

2. In a medium bowl, combine the flour, baking powder, baking soda, and salt. In another medium bowl combine the sugars.

3. In a large bowl, beat the butter until softened with a handheld mixer on low speed. Add the sugars and cream on low until well combined (page 39). The mixture will look somewhat creamy and a little shaggy. With the mixer still on low, add the eggs and vanilla and mix until incorporated.

4. With a large rubber spatula, fold in the flour mixture (page 40). The dough will be stiff. With the handheld mixer, beat on low for 5 to 10 seconds to combine. Fold in the chocolate chips and walnuts.

5. Roll 1 tablespoon of the dough into a ball for each cookie, and place the balls about 1 inch apart on an ungreased baking sheet. The dough will spread very little when baked.

6. Bake for 7 to 9 minutes (about 5 minutes for smaller cookies) until just browned around the edges, and pale and slightly unset in the middle. Let the cookies cool on the sheet for 1 minute. Then remove the cookies from the sheet to wire racks to cool completely.

Storage: See page 96.

CLASSIC CRISPY SUGAR COOKIES

MAKES TWO TO THREE DOZEN 2½-INCH COOKIES

Most cookies use baking powder for leavening; I chose to use baking soda. It causes the cookie to spread rather than puff, perfect for a crispy cookie, and have a wonderful buttery flavor you can't get with baking powder. These cookies will get soft if they're exposed to high humidity levels or stored with soft cookies.

INGREDIENTS

1½ cups unbleached all-purpose flour; spoon into dry measuring cup and level to
    top
½ teaspoon baking soda
¼ teaspoon baking powder
¼ teaspoon salt
10 tablespoons (1¼ sticks) unsalted butter, room temperature
1 cup sugar
1 large egg, room temperature
1 teaspoon vanilla extract
½ teaspoon lemon extract, optional

1. Position a shelf in the middle of the oven and preheat the oven to 350 degrees F.

2. In a medium bowl, combine the flour, baking soda, baking powder, and salt. Set aside.

3. In a large bowl, beat the butter until softened with a handheld mixer on low speed. Add the sugar and cream on low speed until well combined (page 39). The mixture will look somewhat creamy and a little shaggy. With the mixer on low, add the egg and the vanilla and lemon extracts and beat until combined.

4. With a large rubber spatula, fold in the flour (page 40). The batter will be stiff. With the mixer, beat on low for 5 to 10 seconds to combine.

5. Form into balls 1 inch in diameter or drop by teaspoonfuls 2 inches apart on an ungreased cookie sheet. The batter will spread when baked. If the dough is too sticky to work with, refrigerate it briefly to firm up.

6. Bake for 15 to 20 minutes until just lightly browned. The cookies will puff in the oven and deflate when removed.

7. Leave the cookies on the baking sheet for 1 minute to harden slightly, and then move the cookies to a wire rack to cool completely.

Storage: See page 96.

QUESTION: *I would like to know if sugar cookies can be frozen after being frosted with royal icing. Also, can they be frozen after being decorated with different colors? If they can be frozen please give defrosting instructions.*

ANSWER: If you freeze cookies with icing you run the risk of the icing getting wet or cracking when it defrosts. Also, colors may run or turn "funky." It's best if you freeze the cookies unfrosted, then thaw and decorate. They're usually ready in just a few minutes. If you freeze them frosted, make sure the decorations are completely dried. Then, freeze the cookies on a cookie sheet, unwrapped, until hardened. Place them in a freezer container without touching, with waxed or parchment paper between layers. This way you won't mar the decorations. To defrost, let the cookies sit at room temperature in their wrappers.

QUESTION: *I cut out sugar cookies from the dough and they were lovely until I used a spatula to pick them up! They lost some of their shape and some of my cookies came out crooked. Do you have any tips so my cookies hold their shape?*

ANSWER: Dough gets soft when you work with it, causing the cookies to get out of shape. What I do is roll my cookies out on a cookie sheet and then cut them with a cutter. I quickly put the cookie sheet in the freezer just long enough to harden the dough. Then I can peel off the excess dough and safely move the cookies if I must. Bake right away; no need to thaw.

QUESTION: *My biscotti crumble when cutting and I can barely get a whole cookie.*

ANSWER: Biscotti are cut into individual cookies when the baked dough is still warm. Make sure the logs are baked a light golden brown and have cooled slightly. Cut the logs on the diagonal into $\frac{1}{2}$-inch thick slices. Cut them into individual cookies with an electric knife or with a sharp, serrated one. You'll have less crumbling if you do. Try out this method with my Orange Mocha Chip Biscotti (recipe follows).

ORANGE MOCHA CHIP BISCOTTI

MAKES 3 DOZEN COOKIES

This crunchy, flavorful Italian cookie is perfect for dipping into a steaming cappuccino or as an accompaniment to ice cream or a glass of wine. Sometimes biscotti turn hard if they're overhandled or too much flour is used. I like to add canola oil to keep them moist and a little soft.

INGREDIENTS
Vegetable oil cooking spray
1¾ cups unbleached flour; spoon into dry measuring cup and level to top
¼ cup Dutch-process cocoa powder; scoop into dry measuring cup and level to top
1 teaspoon instant espresso powder or instant coffee granules
1 teaspoon baking powder
¼ teaspoon baking soda
¼ teaspoon salt
1 cup sugar
2 large eggs, room temperature
3 tablespoons canola oil
1 teaspoon vanilla extract
1 tablespoon grated orange peel (from 1 orange) or ¼ teaspoon pure orange oil
½ cup chocolate chips; use mini if you can find them

1. Position a rack in the center of the oven and preheat the oven to 350 degrees F. Lightly spray a baking sheet with vegetable oil spray or line it with parchment paper.

2. In a medium bowl, whisk the flour, cocoa, espresso powder, baking powder, baking soda, and salt until well combined. Set aside.

3. In another medium bowl, using a handheld mixer set on high speed, beat the sugar, eggs, oil, vanilla, and orange peel until smooth, about 2 minutes. Make a well in the center of the dry ingredients and pour in the egg mixture. Then add the chocolate chips. Using a spoon, stir until just moistened. The dough will seem a little dry. Knead the dough briefly in the bowl until it just comes together. Shape the dough into two 7- by 2-inch logs on the prepared baking sheet, spacing them about 1 inch apart.

4. Bake for about 25 minutes, until the logs are light brown and covered with tiny

cracks. Remove the logs but do not turn off the oven. Transfer the logs to a wire cake rack and let them cool on the sheet for about 10 minutes.

5. On a work surface, using an electric or serrated knife, cut the logs on the diagonal into $\frac{1}{2}$-inch slices. Return the slices to the baking sheet.

6. Bake for 5 minutes. Turn the biscotti over and continue baking until the edges are crisp, about 5 minutes more. The edges will not be very brown and the centers will be soft, but the biscotti will crisp when cooled. Do not overbake. Transfer to a wire cake rack and cool completely.

Storage: These keep 2 weeks or so in an airtight container or for 3 months frozen.

QUESTION: *How do you get cookies to be soft?*

ANSWER: You must start with a soft cookie recipe, such as the Jumbo Oatmeal Raisin Cookies (page 104). Then, the keys are making larger cookies, and not overbaking them. Bake the cookies until just golden brown, since they will continue cooking after you have removed them from the oven. Don't leave them on the cookie sheet for more than a minute or two. This can be tricky because hot cookies can be fragile.

JUMBO OATMEAL RAISIN COOKIES

❖

MAKES ABOUT 4 DOZEN 3-INCH COOKIES

If you want a chewy cookie, this is it. The high oven temperature causes the cookies to puff and set on the outside before the inside sets, making a thicker cookie. Remember not to overbake for a good chew.

INGREDIENTS
2 cups unbleached all-purpose flour; spoon into measuring cup and level to top
1 teaspoon baking soda
½ teaspoon baking powder
½ teaspoon salt
1 cup (2 sticks) unsalted butter, room temperature
1 cup sugar
1 cup dark brown sugar, packed
2 large eggs, room temperature
1 teaspoon vanilla extract
2 cups quick-cooking oats (not instant)
1 cup raisins; if dry, soak in hot water for 5 minutes, then drain
½ cup chopped walnuts (page 26); chop, then measure

1. Position a rack in the center of the oven and preheat the oven to 400 degrees F.

2. In a medium bowl, combine flour, baking soda, baking powder, and salt. Set aside.

3. In another medium bowl, with a handheld mixer fitted with the beaters, beat the butter to soften. (You can use a stand mixer fitted with the paddle attachment.) Add the sugars and cream well (page 39). Add the eggs, one at a time, and the vanilla, blending well after each. Fold in the flour mixture with a rubber spatula. Blend 5 seconds with the mixer on low. The batter will be thick. With a heavy wooden spoon, fold in the oats, raisins, and nuts.

4. Drop by rounded tablespoonfuls onto ungreased or parchment-lined cookie sheets, 2 inches apart. For smaller cookies, drop by the teaspoonful. Put cookies in the oven, taking care to close the oven door immediately. Bake for 12 to 15 minutes until just lightly browned. The middle may not seem set, but if the edges are, remove the cookies from the oven.

5. Remove the cookie sheets to cool on a wire cake rack for 1 or 2 minutes. Gently remove the cookies from the sheets with a metal spatula or pancake turner, and put them on the rack to cool completely. The cookies will harden more when they cool.

Storage: See page 96.

BAR COOKIES: POINTERS, QUESTIONS, AND RECIPES

Bars are great to begin with, because with the right recipe you can produce delectable results that are just as you envisioned—without spending a lot of time in the kitchen. Bars include brownies—in this section you'll find recipes for both fudgy, gooey brownies and chocolaty, cakey ones—as well as citrusy bars and chocolate chip cookie bars!

There are essentially two types of brownies—fudgy and cakey. When looking for a fudge- or cake-like brownie, the recipe (ingredients, mixing, and baking methods) dictates which type of brownie you are going to get; you can't make a fudgy brownie from a cakey brownie recipe and vice versa. I can help you understand what to look for in your recipe and how it works, so you can choose the recipe that will give you the kind of brownie you want.

Fudge brownies are dense and intensely chocolaty, and have a moist interior. Similar to a flourless chocolate cake, the brownie recipe doesn't contain enough flour to hold its structure and, with a high proportion of fat from eggs, melted chocolate, butter, and sugar, it puffs in the oven and collapses in a pool of molten fudge when baked. Fudge brownies start with melted butter and chocolate and are best mixed by hand, for less fluffiness and more fudginess. The fat in the egg yolks, chocolate, and butter plays several critical roles in recipes, adding flavor and creamy, melt-in-the-mouth texture. Sugar also raises the temperature at which egg proteins set, permit-

QUESTION: *I want to get evenly sized bars. How do I do that?*

ANSWER: Let bar cookies cool in their pan on a wire cake rack before cutting. Although it's awfully tempting to cut into a pan of just-baked brownies or blondies, hold off. If you just can't wait, you can speed up the process by placing them in the freezer until they become more solid and easier to cut.

Before cutting, lightly score the cutting lines on the surface with a knife while the brownies are still warm. My tried-and-true method is to cut bars in their pan using a knife or, better still, a bench scraper (page 11). With a bench scraper you can cut straight down and lift straight out. You'll be amazed how neatly the squares come out.

Others recommend flipping the whole cooled "cookie" out of the pan and cutting from the bottom side, or flipping it right side up to cut. You'll have better luck with this method with cakier recipes, because they are more even in thickness, and solid with a flat top. For fudge brownies, cutting in the pan offers the needed support to prevent them from cracking and squishing.

ting the egg proteins to coagulate slowly and enmesh with the other ingredients, resulting in a less stiff recipe. Sugar also assists in moisture retention because of its hydrophilic characteristic, prolonging shelf life by keeping the brownies moist longer.

Cake brownies (page 110) are like a buttercake, only richer; with more flour in proportion to fat and eggs than fudge brownies, and leavening. They hold their structure—unlike fudge brownies—which makes them ideal for icing. A cake brownie recipe begins with the creaming step (page 39) reminiscent of cake making. They usually have baking powder unlike a true fudge brownie, and so will rise in the oven, which gives them their cakey lightness. Sometimes milk is added to make brownies tender and moist. A small percentage of recipes call for the ingredients to be mixed in one bowl, resulting in brownies with a cake-like texture, only denser.

Sarah Says: Some people like their fudge brownies thick, while others prefer them thin. You can control this by choosing a smaller or larger pan. But be careful: if you try to make your brownies too thick, they won't bake and you'll wind up with raw batter in the middle. On the flip side, if the pan is too big and the batter too shallow, the brownies will dry out quickly and have no flavor.

DOUBLE CHOCOLATE FUDGE BROWNIE BARS

MAKES ONE 8-INCH SQUARE PAN,
16 TO 24 BARS OF DENSE, FUDGY BROWNIES

The trick to fudge brownies is to mix until ingredients are just combined. If you merrily beat the ingredients at each and every stage, so much air will be beaten into the batter that it will rise only to collapse on itself during baking with a top surface separated from the main body of the brownies.

INGREDIENTS
Vegetable oil cooking spray
¼ cup Dutch-process cocoa powder; spoon into dry measuring cup and level to top (do not use natural cocoa powder)
1 cup unbleached, all-purpose flour; spoon into dry measuring cup and level to top
½ teaspoon baking powder
¼ teaspoon salt
3 ounces bittersweet or semisweet chocolate, chopped (three 1-ounce squares)
½ cup (1 stick) unsalted butter, room temperature
3 large eggs, room temperature
2 teaspoons vanilla extract
1½ cups sugar
½ cup chopped walnuts, optional (page 26)

1. Position a rack in the center of the oven and preheat the oven to 350 degrees F. Grease an 8 x 8-inch baking pan.

2. If the cocoa powder is lumpy, sift to a fine powder before combining. Push any lumps through a strainer; do not discard unless hardened (I use a small-gauge wire mesh strainer). In a medium bowl, blend the flour, cocoa powder, baking powder, and salt. Set aside.

3. Put the chopped chocolate in a small bowl. Warm the butter in a small saucepan until just melted, and remove from the heat. Pour the butter over the chocolate. Swirl the pan so the hot butter warms all the chocolate and covers it. Let the mixture sit 2 minutes. Stir to melt the chocolate. Let cool until slightly warm.

4. With a fork, beat the eggs and vanilla together in a medium bowl until just combined. Stir in the sugar with a rubber spatula. Pour in the cooled butter–chocolate mixture and mix until smooth. Do not whip. In 2 additions, fold in the flour mixture

(page 40) until almost combined, and then the walnuts until all are fully combined. Scrape the batter into the pan and smooth it. Tap the pan bottom lightly on the countertop a few times to remove excess air bubbles.

5. Bake for exactly 40 minutes. This recipe will puff slightly in the oven, then fall and crack; that's normal. The brownies will seem underdone in the middle but will harden as they cool. Do not overbake. Cool in the pan on a wire cake rack before cutting into squares.

Storage: Store well-covered at room temperature for 3 to 5 days. Freezes well for up to 3 months.

Sarah Says: Mix ingredients preferably by hand or with a handheld mixer on low, except the flour, which is folded in by hand with a rubber spatula at the end. This gentler mixing method prevents too much gluten from forming, and too much air from being beaten into the batter. Fudge brownies should be fudgy and dense, not light and airy.

Sarah Says: With the increased egg protein, fudge brownies become more sensitive to overbaking, a problem worsened by the fact that it is hard to tell when they are done. The batter around the outer edge of the pan bakes much faster and can appear dry after only 15 minutes. The center of the pan can remain moist even when the brownies are done. Overbaked, they dry out; underbaked, they are too runny. I find it best to follow the time in the recipe. As long as you are using the correct baking pan and the oven is functioning properly, the clock is your best guide.

QUESTION: *Hi, I've tried everything—recipes, different pans—yet my brownies get this thin crackly crust and sink in the middle. Are brownies supposed to be like that? Can you please tell me what's wrong?*

ANSWER: Nothing is wrong—you baked a classic fudge brownie. Whole eggs and butter both provide leavening by their water content turning to steam when baked (eggs are 65.5 percent water and butter is 18 percent water, plus 1 percent milk solids). Initially fudge brownies will rise in the oven from the steam and the leavening gas (CO_2) created by the baking powder. However, the brownies will then collapse because of a low gluten content, becoming characteristically dense and fudgy. The sugar crystallizes when the brownies cool, turning the top hard and crisp. It's normal. Perhaps you'd like to try my Chocolate Brownie-Cake Bars (page 110), which bake more like a cake.

CHOCOLATE BROWNIE-CAKE BARS

MAKES ONE 8-INCH SQUARE PAN, 12 BARS

This recipe makes a flavorful, dense brownie with a cake-like texture. Cake brownies are usually made with cocoa powder rather than the chocolate squares used in fudge brownies. Since cocoa powder contains starch like flour and has less fat per ounce than chocolate, the result is not nearly as gooey. Sometimes milk is added for moistness, and leaveners such as baking powder or baking soda to give the texture a lift.

INGREDIENTS
Vegetable oil cooking spray
1 cup unbleached all-purpose flour
¼ cup Dutch-process cocoa powder
¼ teaspoon baking powder
¼ teaspoon salt
⅓ cup (5 tablespoons plus 1 teaspoon) unsalted butter, room temperature
1 cup sugar
2 large eggs, room temperature
2 teaspoons vanilla extract

1. Position a rack in the center of the oven and preheat the oven to 350 degrees F. Grease an 8 x 8-inch square pan.

2. In a large bowl, combine the flour, cocoa powder, baking powder, and salt. If the cocoa powder is lumpy, sift the mixture. (I use a small-gauge wire mesh strainer.) Set aside.

3. Beat the butter until soft with a handheld mixer on low speed. Add sugar in a steady stream. Increase speed to medium and beat for a few minutes until shaggy. For more on creaming, see page 39. Add the eggs one at a time and beat for 20 seconds after each addition.

4. Fold in the dry ingredients with a rubber spatula. The batter is thick. Blend 1 minute with the beater on low. Spread batter in pan from the middle towards the edges, making sure it touches all sides of pan.

5. Bake for about 25 to 30 minutes until a toothpick inserted in the middle comes out with a few gooey crumbs attached. The top looks dull when baked, but becomes glossier as it cools. Cool in the pan on a wire cake rack before cutting into squares.

Storage: Store well-covered at room temperature for 3 to 5 days. Freezes well for up to 3 months.

QUESTION: *Why do my brownies have tough, hard edges? The crust on my brownies also blistered. What happened?*

ANSWER: It sounds like you're having a bad brownie day. Bar cookies tend to get crusty on their edges, especially when baked in a dark heatproof glass or nonstick pan. Remember to reduce the oven temperature by 25 degrees F if that's what you are using. This should help them turn out less crusty. If all else fails, trim the edges before serving.

A bar crust will blister when the egg content is too high and the sugar content too low. This phenomenon is observed primarily with cake-type brownies, which have a lower sugar-to-flour ratio than the fudge-type brownies.

Sarah Says: I've also developed a great chewy, gooey chocolate chip bar recipe, which my kids are wild about. It is contained in a pan, allowing me to make it thicker, with ingredient proportions similar to a fudge brownie.

CHEWY CHOCOLATE CHIP COOKIE BARS

MAKES ONE 9 x 13-INCH PAN,
ABOUT 30 SMALL 1½ x 2½-INCH BARS

I created these chewy, gooey chocolate chip cookies in a pan because my kids Tom, Liz, Alex, and Zach, kept asking for homemade chocolate chip cookies and I needed a fast way to make them! If you leave out the chocolate chips, you get a blondie—a brownie without chocolate—but they are a great addition. These cookies bars are moist with a thin, crispy crust, and are especially good when served warm. It is a great recipe for a beginning baker.

INGREDIENTS
Vegetable oil cooking spray
2⅓ cups unbleached all-purpose flour; spoon into dry measuring cup and level to
   top
2½ teaspoons baking powder
½ teaspoon salt
1¼ cups sugar
1 cup dark brown sugar, packed
1 cup (2 sticks) unsalted butter, room temperature
3 large eggs, room temperature
2 teaspoons vanilla extract
2 cups (one 11.5- or 12-ounce bag) chocolate chips
1 cup chopped walnuts (page 26); chop, then measure

1. Position a rack in the middle of the oven and preheat the oven to 350 degrees F. Spray a 9- by 13-inch pan with vegetable oil spray.

2. In a medium bowl, combine the flour, baking powder, and salt. Set aside. Combine the sugars in a medium bowl and set aside. Melt the butter on low heat in a medium saucepan. Remove from the heat and stir in the sugars until dissolved. Let cool for about 5 minutes until lukewarm.

3. Whisk the eggs and vanilla thoroughly in a medium bowl. Quickly whisk approximately ½ cup of the butter-sugar mixture into the eggs to warm (temper) them. Repeat until both mixtures are combined and are smooth and bubbly.

4. Make a well in the flour and pour in the egg mixture. Stir with large strokes

until almost combined (I like to use a folding action, page 40, with a large rubber spatula); the batter will slowly mix and then come together. Fold in the chocolate chips and nuts until fully combined. Do not overmix. The batter will be thick.

5. Spread the batter evenly in the baking pan. Bake for 30 to 40 minutes until lightly browned around the edges, and cookie sounds hollow when tapped in the middle. It will seem underdone in the middle but will harden when cool. Do not overbake. Cool in the pan on a wire cake rack before cutting into bars.

Storage: Store well-covered at room temperature for 3 to 5 days. Freezes well for up to 3 months.

Variation: Mint Chocolate Chip Cookie Bars: Mint chocolate chips are hard to find, so I devised this delicious recipe. If you do find them, just substitute mint chocolate chips for the regular chips. Otherwise, cut 2 peppermint patties (1.5 ounces each) into about 16 equal pieces each. Mix the batter as above. After spreading the batter in the pan, place the pieces evenly over the top. Push each one down into the batter until just covered. Do not push to the bottom. Bake as above.

FLORIDA LIME PIE BARS WITH A COCONUT-GRAHAM CRACKER CRUST

MAKES ONE 8-INCH SQUARE OR 8-INCH ROUND PAN,
12 BARS OR 8 PIE WEDGES

A key lime is a small, yellow-green, aromatic fruit. If you can't find key limes in the grocery store, use fresh limes of the Tahiti or Persian varieties.

INGREDIENTS
CRUST
Vegetable oil cooking spray
1¼ cups graham cracker crumbs, from 9 crackers (18 squares total)
¼ cup sugar
2 tablespoons sweetened flaked coconut, toasted (see Note, below); spoon into dry measuring cup, pack down lightly, and level to top
6 tablespoons (¾ stick) unsalted butter, melted; measure and then melt in microwave on HIGH for 1 minute
1 teaspoon vanilla extract

FILLING
3 tablespoons sugar
2 tablespoons cornstarch
One 14-ounce can sweetened condensed milk
1 large egg, room temperature, beaten
½ cup fresh lime juice (from 3 limes)
Grated peel of 1 lime
¼ teaspoon pure lime oil, optional

TO SERVE
Whipped cream, page 25

1. Position a rack in the center of the oven and preheat the oven to 325 degrees F. (Do not reduce the oven heat if using a glass or dark nonstick pan.) Lightly spray an 8-inch square or round nonstick baking pan with vegetable oil spray.

2. To make the crust: in the baking pan, combine the cracker crumbs, sugar, and coconut. Add the butter and vanilla extract and mix until well combined. Press the

mixture with a large spoon or the flat bottom of a measuring cup evenly and firmly into the bottom and up the sides of the pan. Place the crust in the refrigerator or freezer to firm.

3. To make the filling: In a medium bowl, combine the sugar and cornstarch. Gradually stir in the condensed milk, then the egg. Add the lime juice, peel, and lime oil, and stir just until combined. Take the crust from the refrigerator and immediately pour the filling over it.

4. Bake until the edges look firm, but the center is still slightly unset, about 25 minutes. Cool in the pan to room temperature on a wire cake rack. Cover with plastic wrap and refrigerate until chilled, at least 2 hours or overnight.

5. To serve, run a knife between the crust and sides of the pan to release it. Using a sharp knife, cut into 12 bars or 8 pie-shaped slices. Serve chilled with whipped cream.

Storage: To store, wrap well and keep refrigerated.

Note: To toast shredded coconut, spread evenly on a baking sheet. Bake for 5 to 7 minutes in a preheated 350 degree F oven. Stir often, until the coconut is dry and mostly toasted light brown with some white shreds.

7

❖

PASTRY

*Why did my cream puffs collapse
when taken from the oven? . . .
and other steps on the pathway to pastry wizardry.*

PIE CRUSTS . . . PHYLLO DOUGH . . . puff pastry . . . cream puffs. These are some of the mouthwatering and buttery pastries that can be made at home; however, the mere thought of making them from scratch can make any home baker shudder with trepidation. The same basic ingredients—flour, salt, fat, and water—are used to make all of them. When combined with other ingredients in different proportions, and mixed and baked by a variety of methods, these basic ingredients make versatile batters and doughs that can be shaped and filled.

Homemade pastry can be intimidating to both novice and experienced bakers—it was to me at first. I think many of us have a love/hate relationship with pastry. In spite of having so few ingredients, pastry can seem difficult to conquer. Whether or not you aspire to become a world-class pastry chef, there are some fundamental truths about pastry ingredients that you need to master.

PASTRY TYPES

Pastry dough is divided into multiple categories: flaky or crumbly, puff, choux (*pâte à choux*), phyllo or strudel dough, and sweet dough. Most types involve complex recipes and time-consuming preparation.

Pastry types can share characteristics. The chief difference is the method of introducing the fat, which results in different textures. In pie crusts, solid fat is cut into the dry ingredients for flakiness. In puff pastry, the fat is sandwiched between hundreds of layers of dough for puff and flakiness. In choux pastry, the fat is melted in hot water before being mixed with the flour and cooked with the eggs to make a dough that puffs into a shape when baked.

FLAKY OR CRUMBLY PASTRY

This includes pie and tart crusts. The key to success with this pastry is to keep all ingredients cold and evenly distribute the fat in the dough.

PUFF PASTRY

Also referred to as *laminate dough,* this is the richest of all the pastries, with even rising, and a crispy and flaky texture. It starts out with a sheet of dough and a slab of butter and becomes 500 to 1,500 paper-thin layers of dough and butter and air for a

pastry that is both light and rich. The layers are created through "turns": rolling, folding, resting and/or chilling and rotating the dough over and again. Puff pastry dough can be shaped into strudel, appetizers, and shells to hold sweet or savory fillings. Danish (sweet dough, page 118) and puff pastry are made by similar techniques, but Danish is made with yeast while the main rising agent in puff pastry is steam.

CHOUX

Pâte à choux, also known as choux paste or cream puff paste, is the dough used for éclairs, profiteroles, and cream puffs. It is prepared by beating eggs into a thick mixture of flour, fat, salt, and water. The steam from the water acts as a leavener, causing the pastry to swell and form a high shell around a cavity that can later be filled with whipped cream, pastry cream, cheese, or other fillings.

PHYLLO OR STRUDEL DOUGH

Phyllo, also called *fillo* or *filo,* is what you find in traditional Greek recipes. Phyllo dough is sometimes made of flour and water only, and is stretched to tissue paper thinness. Wheat flour is essential as it is the only type containing the gluten that allows this. Any use of phyllo involves special techniques—brushing butter between layers, and keeping phyllo moist—to produce reliable results. Phyllo layers puff, but not as much as puff pastry. Try my Pear Baklava (page 121), made with store-bought phyllo dough.

When the dough is hand made for strudel, it includes wheat flour, vegetable oil, eggs, warm water, and salt. The dough is kneaded until smooth and elastic, and rests for at least an hour so the gluten strands can stretch to their full length.

SWEET DOUGH

This type of dough produces cinnamon buns, raised doughnuts, sweet rolls, coffee cakes, Danish pastry, and more. Many recipes are finished with icing, glaze, fruit jelly, or nuts, which makes this yeasted dough more like pastry than bread. Sweet dough is made with a relatively high sugar content, and calls for all-purpose flour, although some potato flour can be added for lightness.

THE ALCHEMY OF PASTRY

The differences in texture of many pastries have to do with the nature of the flour, and the fats used, such as butter, margarine, solid vegetable shortening, lard, or vegetable oil. The method of incorporating the fat into the flour affects the final texture and taste. Whether the fat is cut in, rolled in, or melted, it should be evenly distributed throughout the mixture. In addition to adding flavor, fat tenderizes the dough. Cold fat and flakiness are connected.

SPOTLIGHT ON INGREDIENTS

Wheat flour is essential to pastry making because it is the only flour with gluten, allowing dough to stretch and expand in the oven. Too much flour results in a tough, dry, and flavorless product, and too little yields a flat, tough, and flavorless baked good.

Fats contribute to the flakiness and wonderful taste of your pastry. The choice of fat is often a trade-off between flavor and texture—butter gives the most flavor but shortening yields the flakiest pie crusts. Some bakers use both butter and shortening to capture the best qualities of each, but I prefer to use all butter because of its better taste. Margarine can also be used, but I prefer the flavor of unsalted butter.

Water and milk are the most commonly used liquids in pastry. Heavy cream or milk contribute to the flavor and texture of the pastry. The liquid starts the development of gluten in the wheat flour when manipulated. During baking, the liquid turns to steam, helping to leaven the pastry.

Leaveners. Steam acts as the rising agent in puff and flaky pastries, in combination with the air enclosed between the layers. In choux pastry the rising agents are eggs plus steam. Croissants and Danish depend on the thin layers of butter to help the yeast; water in the butter becomes steam which, along with the trapped CO_2 gas from the yeast, gives them their light and flaky texture.

Baking powder and baking soda may be included in pie pastry.

THINGS TO THINK OF WHEN YOU'RE THINKING OF PASTRY

A few basic guidelines for making pastry:

- Set your oven to preheat when you enter the kitchen to begin making dough. If your oven isn't hot enough, certain types of dough won't puff.
- Puff pastry puffs within the first few minutes of baking. If the oven is too cold, you won't get as much as a lift.
- When making and rolling a dough, use cold ingredients and a cold work surface. Work quickly as you don't want the butter to warm, causing you to lose those flaky layers.
- Roll out in one direction only, with firm strokes. Try to avoid forcing the pastry to stretch—that will make it shrink when baked.

A PHYLLO DOUGH RECIPE AND ANSWERS TO QUESTIONS

I've selected one of the most versatile—and most asked about—types of pastry to work with: phyllo dough. It comes ready-made, and with it you can make a near endless variety of sweet and savory pastries, especially your own innovations.

QUESTION: *When I make baklava, my ready-made phyllo always winds up cracking and crumbling, which makes it hard to work with. What am I doing wrong?*

ANSWER: Your problem is easily corrected: you didn't keep your phyllo dough moist. It only takes a few minutes of exposure to air for phyllo to dry out and crack. For the best results, thaw your phyllo dough, still wrapped, in the refrigerator, 24 hours ahead of time. When ready to bake, place the phyllo dough on a cool surface on top of a sheet of plastic wrap, and carefully unfold the layers you need, keeping them stacked; cover the top of phyllo dough with another sheet of plastic wrap, and place a cool and moist kitchen towel on top of that. The unused portion should be refrigerated or frozen right away.

PEAR BAKLAVA

Pears, honey, and pecans make a wonderful twist on the typical nut-filled baklava.
I am sure you will enjoy this lower-in-fat version.

INGREDIENTS

BAKLAVA

6 large Bosc or Bartlett pears, peeled, cored, and cut into ½-inch cubes
½ cup sugar
1 tablespoon lemon juice (from 1 lemon)
1 teaspoon ground cinnamon
Vegetable oil cooking spray
One 16-ounce box of 12 x 17-inch phyllo, thawed overnight in the refrigerator
3 tablespoons melted unsalted butter, or more as needed, or vegetable oil cooking
  spray
2 tablespoons pecans, finely chopped and toasted (page 26)

SYRUP

1 cup water
1 cup honey (I prefer wildflower)
½ cup sugar
1 tablespoon fresh lemon juice (from 1 lemon)
1 tablespoon grated lemon peel, optional (from 1 lemon)

1. In a large, nonstick skillet, bring the pears, sugar, and lemon juice to a simmer over medium heat, stirring often. Cook, stirring occasionally, until all the liquid has evaporated and the pears are tender, about 10 to 15 minutes. Remove the pan from the heat, stir in the cinnamon, and set aside to cool completely.

2. Position a rack in the center of the oven and preheat the oven to 350 degrees F. Spray a 9- by 13-inch ovenproof glass baking pan with vegetable oil spray.

3. Start with a stack of 6 phyllo sheets. Place flat on a work surface and set the pan on top. With a sharp knife, trace around the pan and cut through the phyllo stack.

4. Place one 9- by 13-inch phyllo sheet in the bottom of the pan and brush it very lightly with melted butter. Repeat with the remaining 5 sheets.

5. Spread ½ of the cooled pear filling evenly over the phyllo (it won't cover completely). Repeat Steps 3 and 4 with 6 more phyllo sheets, top with the remainder of

the filling. Cut the remaining phyllo sheets (approximately 16) to fit the pan and place them over the filling. Brush each one with butter before adding the next. Brush the top sheet with butter and sprinkle the pecans over it.

6. With a very sharp knife, score the baklava horizontally into 3 equal strips and then vertically into 4 strips to create 12 rectangles. Score each rectangle diagonally to make 24 triangles. Bake for 40 to 45 minutes in the preheated oven until golden brown. Transfer the pan to a wire cake rack.

7. When the baklava has been baking for about 30 minutes, combine the water, honey, and sugar in a medium saucepan. Bring the mixture to a boil over high heat, stirring often to dissolve the sugar. The honey prevents the sugar from crystallizing. Reduce the heat to low and simmer for 5 minutes. Stir in the lemon juice and peel and cook until the syrup is slightly thickened, about 5 minutes more.

8. Spoon the hot syrup over the baklava as soon as you remove it from the oven. Cool completely in the pan before serving.

Storage: Phyllo sheets can be kept refrigerated or frozen, and can be thawed and frozen again. The pear baklava can be stored well-covered at room temperature for a couple of days, but does not freeze well because of the pears.

QUESTION: *I'm having a dinner party and would like to assemble my phyllo pastries earlier in the day and refrigerate them until they need to go in the oven for dessert. Will the crust be okay?*

ANSWER: To avoid soggy pastry, the best way is to prebake phyllo pastries without a filling and store them at room temperature in an airtight container. Fill right before serving and bake immediately. Or if you prefill, place phyllo pieces on baking sheets sprayed with vegetable oil spray, cover with plastic wrap, and refrigerate until ready to bake. If using a cooked filling, let cool before using. If the filling isn't wet, the phyllo pastries will keep for several days.

QUESTION: *I'm making cream puffs and éclairs from a recipe that I've used for many years. For some reason they are not turning out today. Could it be my eggs? It is rainy and cold, could it be the low barometer?*

ANSWER: I think you answered the question yourself: the high humidity from the rain means the puffs aren't completely drying out inside. Poke a hole with a paring knife in the bottom of the puffs after removing them from the oven and put them back in a low oven to dry the inside, then cool and use immediately to keep their shape and crisp outside.

QUESTION: *Why did my cream puffs collapse when taken from the oven?*

ANSWER: The major step in making cream puffs is to make sure a stable emulsion forms during the addition of eggs to the flour mixture. First the fat and hot water are beaten with the flour, which distributes the fat throughout the mixture. During this step, the starch in the flour gelatinizes, contributing to the thickening of the batter. After the mixture cools, the eggs are added one at a time, and beaten in after each addition. The egg yolks contain lipoproteins, which emulsify and disperse the fat throughout the mixture.

If all of that was done properly, insufficient baking is probably the cause of your cream puff collapse. Even though the puffs are brown on the outside, it's still possible that the egg proteins coagulated insufficiently to maintain the structure. There also might not have been enough time for the baked dough to dry out and firm up after being removed from the oven. Steam within the puff can condense and cause it to soften and collapse. Bake choux pastry in a preheated 425 degree F oven until crisp and beginning to color, about 10 minutes. Lower the temperature to 350 degrees F and bake another 20 minutes until well colored and dry. A skewer inserted into the center should come out almost dry.

8

❖

P I E S

My pie crust isn't flaky. When I baked my crust,
it shrank horribly. How can I keep
my lemon meringue pie from weeping?
. . . and other pie puzzle solutions.

EVERYBODY LOVES PIE—at least to eat. But from what I hear from bakers, probably not to make from scratch. Making pies is demanding! That's because you're making two or three recipes—crust, filling, and maybe a topping—and trying to get them to work in concert. Many ask why the picture in the magazine is so perfect and "Mine doesn't compare"? I always explain that there are simply bad pie days. If you've had burnt pie crust edges, a crust like cardboard, edges that sink below the rim of the pie pan, or a beautiful crust with a soupy filling that didn't gel, you're in the right place.

Your pies don't have to be perfect—just served with love, pride, and (maybe) some last-minute beautifiers like whipped cream (page 25) (which, I like to say, always hides most baking sins). That's *really* good news, since most of us remember pie tragedies—I've dropped pies, had crusts shrink, and watched a meringue pie I slaved over "weep" in a way that made me want to weep myself!

Pies are what I call an American folk tradition with family recipes, some hundreds of years old, found from coast to coast. They used to be portable snacks for pioneers on the go. Some of us can still remember our grandmother or mother pulling a freshly baked pie out of the oven, setting it to cool on the windowsill, its warm scent beckoning like a dinner bell. There is no reason for you not to carry on the tradition. But, for many of us it's foreign territory relegated to that exclusive group of bakers who can bake anything and to which we don't belong. Not any more.

WHAT IS A PIE? WHAT IS A TART?

The typical pie is a composite of a pastry bottom crust; a filling of fruit, nuts, or a sweet or savory custard; and an optional topping of a dough crust (solid or woven into a lattice), meringue, or a loose, pebbly cookie-like mixture called a crumb crust.

A tart is a European-style open-faced version of a pie; it can be sweet or savory, with only a bottom crust, or a bottom plus lattice, meringue, or crumb topping. Many of the same crusts and fillings for pies may be used in tarts. However, more sugary cookie-like crusts and richer fillings are better suited to shallower tarts.

WE CATEGORIZE PIES BY THEIR FILLINGS

Fruit pies have fillings made from cooked or uncooked fresh or dried fruit. They are assembled in an unbaked or partially baked bottom crust, with or without a top crust. Crust, filling, and top usually bake together.

Cream pies have a custard or mousse filling spread in a prebaked pastry or crumb crust.

Icebox pies are a type of cream pie with a gelatin-like filling, rather than a mousse or custard, poured into a prebaked crust and refrigerated to set.

Custard pies contain uncooked custard filling poured into an unbaked bottom crust. Crust and custard bake together.

Nut pies have a sugar-based filling with eggs and butter, poured over nutmeats in an unbaked bottom crust, with no top. Both bake together.

Savory pies such as quiche, are main course or appetizer pies with savory rather than sweet fillings.

Stovetop pies have fillings that are cooked on a stovetop and poured into a pre-baked crust. They are cooled at room temperature and are ready to serve.

Deep-dish pies are fruit pies typically with a top crust only, made of either pastry or baking powder biscuit dough. This difference has to do with the baking method, as they are baked in a deeper pie pan or casserole dish.

Cobblers, crisps, buckles, grunts, brown Bettys, and slumps are the fruit pie's easier-to-make, less intimidating country cousins. All have fruit fillings and are baked with top crusts only. These old-fashioned, fruit-based desserts are our true American heritage. Fruit desserts go far back into the history of American cooking.

Galettes are free-form pies baked on a flat sheet instead of in a pie pan.

Basic pie crusts are usually made from just four ingredients—flour, solid fat, water, and salt—but may include sugar, eggs, leavening, or even vinegar. The dough is rolled and fitted into a pie pan. It can be prebaked, partially baked and then filled, or baked with the filling. There are different types:

American pie pastry, or *pâte brisée* (broken dough): The basic flaky pie crust for which chilled butter or shortening is cut into the flour. It may include baking powder or baking soda for an additional lift, color, and flavor. White wine, cider vinegar, or another acidic ingredient is sometimes added to tenderize the dough.

Sweet pie and tart crust, or *pâte sucrée* (sugared dough): A sweet, tender cookie-like crust, with added sugar, whole eggs or yolks, or cream cheese. Perfect for beginners, this dough can be handled less gingerly than a traditional crust; but it can be soft and should be kept well-chilled.

Cookie tart crust, or *pâte sablé* (sand dough) is a delicate dough made by beating the fat with sugar, then mixing in eggs followed by the flour (often cake flour). This dough is usually baked blind (page 139) and filled after it has cooled.

FLAKINESS IS A WELCOME ATTRIBUTE IN PIE CRUSTS!

It's American flaky dough that I get the most questions about. It should bake with a golden brown, flaky pastry crust without burned areas or overly crisp edges, and have a uniform, non-crumbly consistency. But it doesn't always turn out that way.

It is the layering effect of butter or shortening surrounded by flour that forms the flakes in baked dough. If the layers weren't separated from one another by air, the pastry wouldn't be flaky. The colder the dough's ingredients are, and the least water your fat contains, the more flaky the layers you'll produce. Let's start with the ingredients to understand what makes the difference between a flaky pie crust and a disappointing one.

Wheat flour is typically used, either unbleached all-purpose flour, or a mix of two-thirds all-purpose and one-third cake flour. This combination contains less gluten-forming proteins, giving the crust more lightness and tenderness. But it makes the dough softer and harder to handle when rolling.

With too much flour you'll have a hard crust; too little will produce a sticky one. I always recommend erring on the "too little" side rather than too much—for instance, don't use extra flour to roll out your dough, if you can avoid it. The gluten in flour is also responsible for shrinkage as your crust bakes.

Fat, butter, shortening, lard, vegetable oil, margarine, or cream cheese, is a necessity. The higher the percent of fat to water your choice contains, the flakier the dough. Shortening and lard are 100 percent fat. I prefer butter for its flavor, although it contains less fat (generally only about 81 percent). Some cooks compromise and use an equal combination of butter and shortening. Vegetable oil is 100 percent fat, but it is absorbed into flour rather than coating it. This produces a dough that is flat and crumbly, not flaky. Whatever fat you choose, be sure the solid form of fat is *cold* when you make the crust; that helps create the flakiness bakers strive for. Chill the fat while measuring the other ingredients: at least 15 to 20 minutes in the refrigerator or 5 to 7 minutes in the freezer.

Chemical leaveners have a definite role to play. Most pie crust recipes with chemical leaveners use baking powder, which adds puff to the crust. However, I prefer baking soda, as it helps with browning and crispiness, and brings out the buttery flavor. It also helps your crust retain its shape better and, I believe, counteracts shrinkage more.

Sugar can be any dry variety. You shouldn't use honey or other liquid sweeteners; they produce an unwanted stickiness.

Cold liquids such as ice water or buttermilk are used to bind the ingredients together lightly and puff the spaces left when the cold butter melts.

Eggs or egg yolks, sour cream, or cream cheese all add fat, giving the crust a tenderness, richness, and enhancing browning capabilities.

THINK! FOR FLAKY, TENDER PIE CRUSTS

Think of pie dough as a flour-coated stick of butter that softens easily when handled.

FOR FLAKY AND TENDER PIE CRUST, THINK COLD!

Elastic gluten strands develop when wheat flour and moisture are manipulated: mixed, rolled, handled. Chilling the dough for 1 to 2 hours—preferably 12 to 24—after mixing relaxes the strands and helps prevent shrinking when the dough is baked. I also chill mine between fitting it into the pan and baking; any time you work the dough, you need to let the dough relax in the refrigerator. However, don't

QUESTION: *Why do pie crusts shrink?*

ANSWER: Gluten, rubber band–like strands, develops when wheat flour and water or other liquid is mixed together and further manipulated, such as rolled, shaped, fitted into the pan, etc. The strands want to contract when stretched unless refrigerated (at least an hour or preferably 12 to 24 hours afterward). This precaution mostly concerns flaky dough and has less relevance to sweet dough because of its high sugar content, which tenderizes.

QUESTION: *What makes a crust flaky?*

ANSWER: Fat particles become trapped in the dough by gluten strands formed when wheat flour is moistened and mixed. When the dough is rolled out the fat becomes tiny flattened strata between layers of gluten and starch. The better distributed and larger the fat particles are without softening or melting, the greater the chance the dough will be flaky. When the crust is baked, the fat remains solid just long enough to enable the flour's starches to gelatinize (set), without the fat being absorbed. At the same time, steam from the liquid ingredients enlarges the air spaces. The fat in the recipe keeps the layers from joining so the pastry can remain flaky. But, because the gluten strands are in sheets with fat layered in between, the air has little room to expand. The flour's starches set around them, making the air spaces permanent.

When we eat a bite of pie, we experience the crust as flaky because we are biting into extra-thin sheets of dough with air pockets distributed throughout, giving a slight crunch. Next time you look at a flaky pie crust, take note of the strata (layering).

place it in the freezer to speed up the chilling; it isn't as effective as refrigerating to relax the gluten strands.

THINK HANDS OFF!

Handle the pastry as little as possible and always use your fingertips, the coolest part of your hands. Every time you touch the dough, you soften the fat and create gluten. In the oven, you want the fat to start out cold so its takes longer to melt before the flour's starches set around it; otherwise you'll get a mealy crust. Overmixing also results in a tough, not-so-flaky crust.

Scraps of dough should be stacked on top of one another to roll out a second time. Never knead them together because the dough will become rubbery and hard to work with.

THINK PEAS, NOT CRUMBS!

The larger the pieces of cold fat and the better distributed, the flakier the crust will be.

QUESTION: *Some instructions for making a pie crust say to make sure the fat is "crumb-sized" after it's cut into the dry ingredients, but you say "pea-sized." Which size suggestion should I follow? I'm confused.*

ANSWER: I like to cut the fat into the flour only until it becomes pea-sized so that the fat particles have a greater chance of staying solid in the oven long enough to produce many flaky layers. The finer the fat-and-flour bits are to start with, the less flaky and more mealy the baked dough will be.

THINK "LEAVE EXTRA FLOUR IN THE PANTRY"

Avoid using any flour to roll out the dough, if possible. If you must, use only the smallest amount of flour—mere pinches—when rolling the dough on the counter-top; the more flour you use, the tougher and less flaky the finished crust. I roll mine between two pieces of parchment paper.

FINALLY, THINK HOT!

Getting the shaped and chilled dough into an accurately preheated hot oven before the fat softens is important, as well. Too low an oven temperature will make the pastry pale, hard, and flat.

ALL-PURPOSE PIE DOUGH
(PÂTE BRISÉE)

❖

MAKES ONE 9 x 1¼-INCH PIE CRUST

A rolled dough should be pliable and handle like a thick fabric. I like to use baking soda in my crusts—it helps with browning and brings out the buttery flavor with a little lift. The amount of water is variable. When I make this recipe in the winter, I use about 2 tablespoons water; during the warm weather, I frequently use 5 or 6 tablespoons.

INGREDIENTS
8 tablespoons (1 stick) cold butter cut into tablespoon-size pieces,
   or ½ cup cold shortening
1½ cups unbleached all-purpose flour, chilled in the freezer (not refrigerator);
   spoon into dry measuring cup and level to top
1 tablespoon sugar
⅛ teaspoon baking soda
¼ teaspoon salt
½ cup ice water

1. Prepare the ingredients and cut in the fat. Cut the butter into tablespoon-size pieces and chill (page 127). In a pan or a large bowl, mix the flour, sugar, baking soda, and salt. With a fork, toss the chilled butter pieces in the flour mixture until covered. Use a bench scraper to push straight down on the butter to chop it. Toss flour with the scraper as you go. Stop when the butter is cut into pea-size pieces and evenly distributed throughout the flour. If using shortening, you will have moist clumps approximately the same size. Instead of a bench scraper, you can use two knives, one in each hand, cutting down the lifting to toss the flour and fat bits.

Quickly work the fat into the flour by pinching small pieces of the butter and flour between your fingers and thumb. Then let it drop back into the bowl and start again with another piece of fat and flour mixture. Continually pinch and squeeze all of the butter into the dry ingredients, so you get large flakes of fat covered in flour and the mixture looks shaggy. Reach into the bottom of the bowl with a fork from time to time and redistribute the ingredients. The fat needs to be incorporated into the flour as quickly as possible without overhandling so it doesn't soften or melt. If the fat starts to soften too much, refrigerate or freeze the dough until really cold, then resume. If you have "hot hands," occasionally run them under cold water, then dry them.

2. Mix the dough. Before you start mixing, evenly distribute the flour and fat in the large bowl or pan. Make sure the fat in the dough is still cold. Quickly pull out a small amount. Is it firm? If so, your butter is still cold enough and you can proceed with adding the water. If the butter feels soft and your fingers look greasy, put the mixture, bowl and all, in the refrigerator or freezer until the flakes are firm again.

Evenly sprinkle the water over the flour and dry ingredients one tablespoon at a time, gently tossing with the fork after each addition. Reach down into the bottom of the bowl with the fork to work in the liquid, before adding more water. Take care not to overwork the dough because the crust will turn from flaky to crumbly. When the mixture starts to look shredded and clumps together, while still on the dry side, stop adding water.

Test to see if you are finished mixing the dough: pinch two small clumps of dough together between your thumb and forefinger. I call this the "pinch test." When the dough clumps barely hold together when pinched, look dry on the outside and moist on the inside when broken open, the dough is mixed. You don't want wet, sticky dough, but it is better to have a slightly moister dough than a dry one. If you add more or less water than specified in the recipe, don't worry. The amount necessary to bring dough together can vary up to 50 percent depending upon the flour type and the humidity. Correct the dough with more water or flour, if necessary, adding 1 teaspoon at a time.

If in doubt, gather the mixture into a disk as best you can. Dough absorbs more water during resting and chilling, the next step, and afterward you may not have a problem.

3. Shape and refrigerate the dough: This step is not optional!

Shape the dough into a disk approximately 1 inch high by pressing, not kneading, the dough pieces together. This shape helps to chill it faster and more evenly, and makes rolling faster because it is already round and flat. (If you are making a double recipe for a two-crust pie, portion one disk with ⅔ of the dough and the other with ⅓. The larger portion will be the bottom crust and the smaller, the top.) Wrap the dough in plastic wrap, pressing any crumbly pieces back into the disk. Refrigerate for 1 to 2 hours, preferably 12 to 24 hours. Refrigeration makes the single biggest difference that I've ever seen in a pie crust: the gluten strands relax from the cold, so the dough will roll, stretch, and shape more easily.

4. Roll the dough: For rolling, a cool, flat surface is ideal. The goal is to roll the dough into as uniform a round as you can get, approximately 3 inches larger than the diameter of the pie or tart pan—in this recipe, roll the dough into a 12-inch circle. It should be approximately ⅛-inch thick. When baked, the entire crust should cut easily with a fork, and be flaky, tender, and not too crumbly.

After it chills for at least 1 hour, remove the single dough disk or the larger one for a two-crust pie from the refrigerator (leave the smaller one in). If frozen, allow it to defrost in the refrigerator for at least 3 hours, or overnight.

You can roll the dough on the countertop using pinches of flour to dust it, but I always roll my dough between two large sheets of parchment paper to lessen my chance of using too much flour, which can easily toughen and dry the pie crust. On one piece of parchment, place the pie pan upside down at dead center. Trace around the edge. Remove the pan. Take your ruler and mark $1\frac{1}{2}$ inches evenly outside the circle as if drawing a clock face: mark at 12, 3, 6 and 9 o'clock, and then halfway between each number. Draw a line connecting all points parallel to the circle. You now have a template. As you roll, you'll be able to see through the paper to make sure you're rolling evenly, and know to stop when you reach the outside marks.

Place the dough in the middle of the other piece of parchment and place the paper with the markings centered over it, so you'll have paper, dough, paper. Don't flip the top piece; you don't want the markings to touch the dough. Adjust dough to the center of the circle. Smack dough with the body of the rolling pin to flatten and warm it slightly. Repeat several times. Rotate a few degrees after each smack so you don't hit in the same place twice. If the dough is naturally soft or includes a lot of sugar, there is no need to soften it. Give the dough evenly round edges by gently and quickly pressing the sides together with the cupped palms of your hands. Rotate the dough doing this until it forms a round shape.

Make sure the dough is dead center in the circle. Starting in the center, push away from you with your rolling pin with firm, even pressure to the opposite side. Rotate the dough in its papers, so the next roll will be right next to the one you just left, and roll again. Roll the dough to the $1\frac{1}{2}$-inch markings all around the circle. Roll in one direction, not back and forth, so the gluten strands stretch in one direction only, giving strength to the crust. Don't roll over the same spot multiple times because you'll make the dough too thin.

5. Fit the dough into the pan: Slide the paper-dough-paper sandwich onto a cookie sheet and flip it over, so the marked paper is on the bottom. Carefully peel off the top paper, starting from one corner. If the dough sticks, slide it back onto the cookie sheet, quicky freeze, and try again when it has hardened.

Once the top paper has been removed, place the pie pan upside down on the center of the dough. Slide the dough, still on the paper, onto the cookie sheet and flip it over. Remove the cookie sheet. Gently position the dough so the lines drawn on the parchment paper line up with the pie pan's edge.

Carefully peel off the parchment. Quickly freeze the dough, if the paper resists. Carefully ease the dough down into the pan so that it is flat and air pockets have not formed between the pan and the dough. Gently press the dough down into the bottom with the side or the heel of your hand; don't press too hard, or the dough will later shrink from the gluten strands snapping back.

If you rolled the dough right on the countertop, use your bench scraper or a spatula, to gently lift up the edges and fold it in half onto itself. Slide both hands underneath to support it. Lift the dough and position the fold of dough over the center of the pie pan. Let it rest on one side, draping over the edge. Carefully unfold it to cover the other side, and let it drape over the side. If the dough is too warm and tears, place the pan and dough on the cookie sheet, patch, and chill. Take out of the fridge and let it soften a bit, and try again.

Some bakers roll the dough loosely onto a rolling pin, unless the dough is soft and sticky. Place a floured rolling pin on the dough, centered on the edge nearest you. Roll away from you and at the same time pick up the edge (use a bench scraper or spatula if the dough sticks to the countertop) and support the dough as you wrap it around the pin, being careful not to press it. Keep rolling until all of the dough is rolled onto the pin. Drape the loose end over the far edge of the pan and gently unroll toward you, lowering it into the pan. Do the same for the top of a two-crust pie after the bottom has been filled.

6. Decorate the edges: After fitting the dough into the pie pan, you can flute the border. It serves as a decoration, prevents the filling from overflowing, provides a double layer of dough at the rim for strength and, for a two-crust pie, seals in the filling. For a pie, trim the excess dough around the edge of the pan with kitchen shears to an even overhang of $\frac{3}{4}$ to 1 inch. This is for both one- and two-crust pies after the top crust has been placed. A tart pan is trimmed when the excess is hung outside the edge and a rolling pin is rolled over the edges of the pan. The excess dough will get cut off.

To prepare a one-crust pie crust edge for fluting, fold the dough overhang underneath itself in a ridge. Push the ridge outward and down so it rests entirely on the rim or edge of the pan. Do not press down. For a two-crust pie, first adhere the crusts together: brush the bottom rim with water, place the top crust, and press the edges together. Trim and fold the dough overhang underneath itself in a ridge. Push the ridge so it rests entirely on the pan's rim.

One of the easiest decorative borders to make is a pressed edge around the edge. First pinch the edge of the crust. Then seal it with the tines of a fork pressed into the rim of the dough in a plain or crisscross pattern. Do not press all the way through the dough. If the fork sticks to the dough, dip the tines in flour and shake off excess. To make a crisscross pattern first press with the times pointing to the left. Rotate the pan slightly. Then press with the tines pointing to the right, overlapping the first pattern. Repeat the pattern all the way around the edge of the pan. For a quick decoration press the edge of the crust with the tines of the fork pointing toward the center. A scalloped edge is popular for one- and two-crust pies. To make, take your index and next finger, and bend them in a knuckle. Hold them slightly apart in a "v." Align the top of your knuckles on your left hand with the top of the rolled dough, and the other finger's knuckle on the right hand, centered towards the "v." Rest your knuckles on the pie crust rim and press against the outside of the wall of dough toward the center while at the same time pressing your knuckle against the inside of the wall between the "v" on the other side of the dough. For the next one, place the left side of the "v" in the right indentation of the previous "v" and press against the left index finger on the inside. Repeat all the way around to make a scalloped edge. Don't press too hard; you only want to shape the dough, not stretch it.

Right before baking, lightly brush the top of the dough with an egg wash of one egg beaten with 1 to 2 teaspoons of water, or lightly brush with milk and sprinkle with sugar. Cut steam vents in the top crust. There are several choices: Cut a $\frac{3}{4}$-inch circle in the top of the crust with a sharp paring knife or make five or six 2-inch-long slashes starting about 1 inch from the center of the pie and radiating toward the edge. During baking a pie filling releases steam through the vents so it won't boil over or cause a gap to form between the filling and the top crust.

Protect the edges of the crust, which burn easily during baking. Take three long pieces of foil and place them on top of one another, like a star without points. Place the filled pie into the center. Gather and fold the foil up and over the sides of the pan, covering the edges.

If desired, make decorations. Stack pie crust scraps on top of one another on a parchment-lined cookie sheet and roll, chill until cold, and cut out decorative designs either free-form with a sharp knife or with a small cookie cutter. Chill again for 1 to 2 hours.

First brush the tops with egg wash (see above), cream, or half-and-half (milk will work, too, but the others are better), and sprinkle with sugar. Bake immediately on a parchment paper–lined baking sheet at 425 degrees F for 6 to 12 minutes, or until golden brown. Remove to a rack to cool. For a one-crust pie, place baked and cooled designs on top of the baked or cooked filling.

To decorate the top or rim of an unbaked pie, brush the spot where the decoration made from dough will be placed lightly with water. Gently press the shape into place. Before baking brush with egg wash, cream, or half-and-half, and sprinkle with sugar.

Note: Double the recipe for a two-crust pie.

Variation: Whole Wheat Crust: Substitute $\frac{1}{2}$ cup of whole wheat flour for $\frac{1}{2}$ cup of all-purpose.

Storage: See page 139.

Sarah Says: Instead of a bowl, I like to mix my ingredients in an 8-inch square pan (for a double recipe for a two-crust pie, use a 7- by 11-inch pan). I can cut in the butter with a bench scraper, and I have more surface area when I sprinkle the water—meaning I can hydrate the flour more evenly and quickly.

Sarah Says: Here are some other ways to mix dough:

STAND MIXER

You can mix together the fat and the flour, and other dry ingredients, in a stand mixer fitted with the paddle attachment. Mix on low speed and be careful not to over-process. Scrape down and continue to mix until the fat resembles small peas, with no larger pieces of fat visible. Stop the mixer, remove the bowl, and pinch and press the fat into the flour (page 130). Clamp the bowl back on the mixer. Change to the dough hook, mix on low speed and slowly add ice water. Continue mixing until the dough pulls away from the side of the bowl. The dough doesn't need to be completely homogenized. Stop the mixer and do the pinch test (page 131) to see if you've added enough liquid. If you have, move to the next step.

FOOD PROCESSOR

Add flour and the other dry ingredients to the bowl fitted with the steel blade and pulse once or twice until mixed. Add the pieces of chilled fat and pulse until you have pea-size fat pieces. Stop the food processor, remove the bowl, and pinch and press the fat into the flour (page 130). Clamp the bowl back on the food processor. Fit with the dough blade. After cutting in the fat, pour the water through the food tube over the flour mixture and pulse it 5 to 6 times at one-second intervals. Don't allow the dough to start clumping together. However, I don't recommend using a processor for this stage, as it's easy to overwork the dough. Finish mixing the dough by hand so it comes together.

Sarah Says: You can further layer together the fat and flour and increase flakiness by a technique known in French as *fraisage*. This smears flat pieces of fat in the flour, which is optimal when making a very flaky crust.

To do: break off a walnut-sized lump of dough, put it under the heel of your hand on the counter, and push on the dough as you slide it forward about 4 inches. Scrape up and set aside that piece of dough and repeat with the remaining dough. Stack the pieces of dough and press together; do not knead the dough.

QUESTION: *When I rolled my dough, it just cracked and fell apart. Should I just add more water?*

ANSWER: Press the cracks together and if the dough seems somewhat dry, roll it between two pieces of plastic wrap.

If the dough is really dry, you need to correct it: break up the dough into walnut-size pieces of dough and place on the countertop. Sprinkle one or two drops of water on each piece and *fraisage* the dough (page 135).

Sarah Says: The dough must be rolled quickly after being removed from the refrigerator, before the fat in it becomes too soft and unworkable. However, if the dough is too cold, it will crack and break up during rolling, so let it sit a few minutes at room temperature to warm. Press the cracks together to fix, otherwise they'll get bigger and bigger as you roll.

If the dough becomes too soft, cover and refrigerate it for 15 minutes or until chilled without gathering or kneading it. The freezer can speed up the process, but watch the dough carefully so it doesn't get too cold. If it does, let it warm a few minutes at room temperature before proceeding.

If the dough is naturally soft and sticky from egg yolks, sugar, sour cream, cream cheese, etc., roll the dough between pieces of parchment or waxed paper on the countertop with extra flour.

Patch pie dough where necessary so the filling doesn't leak through. Remember, when the crust is filled, no one will see any patching.

If the dough's edge looks ragged after rolling, don't worry, it will be trimmed.

QUESTION: *I mixed my dough all right, but it keeps sticking to my rolling pin and tearing. It is impossible to roll. Please help!*

ANSWER: Roll the dough between two pieces of parchment paper. A dough with inadequately distributed fat is problematic—it will be difficult to roll out; the butter will stick to the rolling pin, the butter chunks will melt and the dough may tear. If the dough is too wet and sticky you can use a light sprinkling of flour on the countertop, but I try to avoid this and roll between two pieces of parchment paper (not plastic wrap because it makes the dough stickier). Chilling the dough also helps.

QUESTION: *How do I roll dough for a square or rectangular tart pan and fit it into the pan?*

ANSWER: After mixing the dough, gather the dough into a rectangular or square "disk." After refrigerating, roll it into the desired shape, rolling from the center out. Make the shape about 2 to 3 inches larger than the tart pan on all sides, and about $\frac{1}{8}$-inch thick. To fit the dough, it is the same as fitting a round pan. Fold the dough in half lengthwise. Position the dough over the center of the pan and unfold. Gently guide the dough into the pan. Don't trim it so it fits better in the corners—you need the dough to be a solid piece so the filling won't leak through. Patch it if necessary. Before trimming, make sure the top of the crust is secure by pressing gently with your index finger and thumb. Trim off the excess by running a rolling pin over the pan's edge. Chill in the refrigerator, as usual.

Sarah Says: Here's my method for an easy lattice-topped pie. The more intricate the strips are, the more problems occur. Working with larger pieces will make your life easier. Roll the dough between sheets of parchment paper to a 9- by 18-inch rectangle about ⅛ inch thick. Cut the dough the short way into six strips 2½ to 3 inches wide by 9 inches long. Weave the strips three across and three down on a parchment paper–lined baking sheet. Refrigerate. When ready to bake, brush the pie crust edge with water. Invert the lattice onto the pie, press both crusts together, and peel off the parchment. Trim the overhang to ½ inch. Then roll the excess pie crust edge toward the center of the pie and stop when there's an even edge all the way around sitting on the pan rim. Flute the rim (page 133).

QUESTION: *Why do pie crusts shrink when baked?*

ANSWER: A pie crust will shrink because the gluten strands contract. Think of your crust as having rubber band–like strands inside, stretched from rolling. They develop when wheat flour and moisture are manipulated (mixed, rolled, fitted into the pan, etc.). They slowly return to their original shape if not relaxed sufficiently through chilling.

QUESTION: *How long can I store pie dough?*

ANSWER: Raw dough, unrolled or rolled, can be kept in the refrigerator for 2 to 3 days. The dough can be frozen for longer storage of 6 to 8 weeks. If frozen and not yet rolled, thaw it in the refrigerator for at least 3 hours or overnight before using. You can also roll it out first, shape it into a pan, and then freeze it. Wrap the unbaked pie crust in plastic wrap and then place it in an airtight plastic bag before storing. You need not thaw before using.

An empty baked pie shell can be kept at room temperature for a couple of days and in the freezer for about 6 to 8 weeks.

You can freeze a fruit pie raw or baked, although a baked pie will lose some of its most desirable qualities when thawed. Don't defrost an unbaked frozen pie first. Position a rack in the lower third of the oven. Preheat the oven to 450 degrees F. After about 15 minutes cut steam vents (page 134) in the top of the pie. Reduce the oven heat to 350 degrees F and bake for about 45 minutes or until the crust is brown and the filling is bubbling. Remove to a wire cake rack to cool. To reheat a baked frozen pie, allow it to thaw at room temperature for an hour, then bake it at 350 degrees F for 30 to 40 minutes, until heated through. I don't recommend freezing custard or cream pies.

HOW TO PRE-BAKE (BLIND BAKE) A CRUST

Blind baking refers to baking an unfilled pie or tart shell to produce a partially or fully baked crust. It is done when making cream pies or tarts, if fillings are particularly moist, or when precooked fillings are part of the recipe.

Empty pie shells need to be pricked (docked) with the tines of a fork or a tool called a "docker" and weighed down during baking. The crust must release steam and air through the holes you create; without vents the crust can fill with air pockets, puff up, then shrink dramatically, resulting in an uneven shell. Bubbles also occur on the bottom of the crust, causing it to puff up. Prick all over the bottom and sides of a pie crust; prick all over the bottom of tart crusts only at ½-inch intervals.

You can weigh your crust down in a variety of ways for the first part of baking. Line the pastry shell with foil, leaving an excess of foil on all sides so you can fold it over the pie edges to protect them from getting too brown when baked. Some bakers use parchment paper or waxed paper to line their pie shells, but I like foil because you can press it right against the side of the crust. In addition, foil promotes better heat conduction for more even browning, which parchment and waxed paper don't.

Fill the shell almost to the top with pie weights—clean pennies, rice, or dried beans—to hold its shape during baking. I also like to place my weights on a flat coffee filter for easy removal. The large, flat ones are used in coffee urns and are a perfect size for an 8- or 9-inch pie pan. Plus, a filter won't stick to the crust when removing, which sometimes happens when you use foil. Metal pie weights or pennies outperform rice and beans because they are heavier and better able to keep the shell from puffing. Also, being metal they are better conductors of heat.

When the first stage of blind baking is done, carefully remove the weights. Cool and store them. Rice and beans can be used two or three times as weights. After that, discard them; don't cook with them.

Once the weights are lifted off for the final browning of the crust, you should check the pie shell every few minutes and re-prick the crust if air bubbles form under the dough. When baking is done, remove the crust from the oven and place it on a wire cake rack to cool completely before filling. If any parts of it have bubbled up, press them down gently or gently prick with the tines of a fork while the crust is still warm. The baked shell can be stored or frozen if not being used right away (page 139).

Optionally, moisture-proof a partially or fully baked pie or tart crust immediately after baking to prevent a soggy bottom crust. Apply the moisture-proofing with a pastry brush on the bottom of the crust and about an inch up the sides right after the crust is removed from the oven to the wire cake rack. After applying, the pie shell is thoroughly cooled on a wire cake rack.

Options for an 8- or 9-inch pie or tart: $\frac{1}{2}$ beaten large egg white; 2 to 3 tablespoons seedless red currant or any flavor jelly or 2 squares (2 ounces) semisweet or sweetened chocolate or chocolate chips. Do not use butter as it contains water.

For a partially or fully baked crust: Apply the egg white with a pastry brush after the crust has cooled 3 to 4 minutes. The heat from the crust will bake on the egg white. If not, return it to the warm oven for 1 to 3 minutes to set or look opaque and dry. This can also be done before filling an unbaked crust. Just apply, let the egg white dry, and fill.

When using preserves or jelly: Briefly heat in a heavy-bottomed pan under medium-low heat or in a microwave on HIGH until boiling. Then strain mixture through a fine-mesh strainer to remove any lumps or seeds. If it gets too cold and solid, briefly reheat. Brush carefully over the bottom of the crust with a pastry brush. Let set about 15 minutes or less.

For a fully baked crust: Brush with melted chocolate or chocolate chips and let harden before filling. Grate chocolate over the warm crust bottom and then spread it. As it melts, it makes a perfect moisture barrier because it contains a lot of fat.

BLIND BAKING PIE CRUSTS PARTIALLY

Many times a bottom crust will become soggy when filled with fruit or other moist fillings. The solution is to partially bake it first, then fill it and bake again. The procedure is the same for both pie crusts and tart shells.

1. Position a rack in the lower third of the oven. Place a baking sheet on the rack. Preheat the oven to 425 degrees F for at least 20 minutes.
2. Take the well-chilled crust from the refrigerator or freezer. If the dough isn't very cold, return it until it is.
3. Line the shell with foil and fill it with weights. Put the pie pan on the baking sheet and bake for 8 to 10 minutes. Pull out the rack or remove the pie pan from the oven. Carefully remove the foil and the weights.
4. Put the pie shell back in the oven, this time without weights. Bake for another 4 to 5 minutes, until the crust starts to turn golden brown. Remove the baking sheet with the pie pan from the oven.
5. Optionally, moisture-proof the crust (page 140). Cool the crust completely in its pan on a wire cake rack. Fill the crust and proceed to bake it according to the recipe. Don't subtract the pre-baking time from the recipe's total.

BLIND BAKING PIE CRUSTS COMPLETELY

This is done when the filling is already fully cooked and it will not be baked again.

1. Position a rack in the lower third of the oven. Place a baking sheet on the rack. Preheat the oven to 425 degrees F for at least 20 minutes.
2. Take the well-chilled crust from the refrigerator or freezer. If the dough isn't very cold, return it until it is.
3. Line the crust with foil and fill it with weights. Put the pie pan on the baking sheet and bake for 12 minutes. Pull out the rack or remove the pie pan from the oven. Carefully remove the foil and the weights.
4. Reduce the heat to 350 degrees F. Put the pie shell back in the oven, this time without weights. Bake for another 12 to 15 minutes. Watch the crust carefully until it turns golden brown all over. The crust is done when it is golden brown. If using a heatproof glass pan, look through its bottom and make sure the bottom crust is golden brown, too. If the top or edges are becoming too dark, loosely cover with aluminum foil to shield it from the heat. Remove the baking sheet with the pie pan from the oven. If moisture-proofing (page 140), do it now.
5. Cool the crust completely in its pan on a wire cake rack before filling or storing.

Do the same as for pie crusts, but bake at 425 degrees F for 10 minutes. Remove the foil and weights; bake until the pastry is golden, another 5 to 10 minutes. Optionally, moisture-proof (page 140). Cool on a rack.

QUESTION: *I want to assemble my pie ahead of time and bake it later. Do you have any tips for me?*

ANSWER: If you're not baking the pie right away, keep the filling and crust separate and assemble right before baking. When a filled pie sits, the filling can make the bottom crust soggy, or the filling can separate and need an extra stirring. The same goes for freezing a pie. You can freeze it whole, depending on the pie, but if you can freeze the crust separate from the filling it's so much better—fillings can make the crust soggy when they thaw.

QUESTION: *The bottom of my crust never seems to bake right. It is always undone and mushy. How can I prevent it?*

ANSWER: A fully baked bottom crust is crucial; a mushy, gummy crust means a messy wedge of pie. Here are four different solutions:

1. Use a heatproof glass pan so you can see the crust browning, or use a perforated pie pan. Chicago Metallic Bakeware company sent me one so I could develop a pie recipe for them, and I fell in love with it.
2. Bake the pie in the oven on a preheated surface such as a baking sheet, baking stone, or quarry tiles. They do a good job with baking and browning the bottom crust thoroughly before the top crust browns because they retain the heat so well (the pizza stone and quarry tiles do it best). Adjust the oven shelf to the lowest rung and place the baking surface on it, covered with foil to catch any drips. If using a pizza stone or tiles, allow longer for them to heat, 30 to 40 minutes instead of the usual 20 for preheating.
3. For certain juicy fruit pies (peach, nectarine, raspberry), some cooks bake their pie directly on the floor of the oven for a truly crispy bottom crust. I have found that the bottom burns too quickly this way, though. If you do try it, put a piece of foil down first to catch any drips.

4. Moisture-proof the bottom crust before filling and baking; do not prebake (page 140).

QUESTION: *The edge on my pie crust turns a really dark brown and tastes burnt, while the rest of the pie is fine. What can I do to prevent this from happening again?*

ANSWER: Before filling the pie, protect the edges from over-browning: center the pan in a long crisscross of foil and fill. Right before baking, gather the foil around the pie pan, bringing it up and over the edge. It is easier to do this before baking rather than take the pie out of the oven halfway through and try to cover the crust without burning yourself. There are also pie crust shields you can use, but they can stick to the crust if the filling leaks. I don't use them.

PIES: POINTERS, QUESTIONS, AND RECIPES

Perhaps more than any other kind of baking, achieving the perfect pie is filled with long-treasured recipes, handed-down folklore about what works best, and prejudices against specific methods. Rather than seek to go against generations of tradition, in this section I'm just going to tell you what works for me—and share some new recipes I've developed that achieve good results.

One very important point to remember: always cool a cooked pie filling to room temperature or cooler before putting it into a raw dough shell. If the filling is too hot, you will melt the butter in the crust.

Sarah Says: I often make extra fruit pie filling so that I have it on hand if the urge for pie strikes. If you want to do this, freeze a batch in an aluminum foil pie pan. Then, when you need a pie, just thaw the filling slightly and slide it from the foil pan into a dough-lined pie pan. Cover with a top crust or streusel and bake.

FRUIT PIES AND TARTS

Fruit pies are best eaten the day they are made. With leftovers don't expect the crust to hold up; it will begin to soak up the juices from the filling and there isn't too much you can do about it!

QUESTION: *I am confused about the different types of thickeners for fruit pies. Which one is best?*

ANSWER: Thickeners are used in fruit pies to gel the liquid that comes from the juicy fruit when it's baked. Without them you would have baked fruit in a puddle of juice and a soggy bottom crust. If the recipe is properly thickened, the cut edges of the pie will ooze only slightly, the pieces of fruit will look distinct, and the color will be bright. A fruit pie filling needs to boil in order to thicken. Be sure it's boiling for several minutes before removing the pie from the oven.

Typical thickeners for fruit pies include the obvious (flour, cornstarch, tapioca) and the not-so-obvious (ClearJel). All are available in the supermarket. The amount needed varies with the kind of fruit and the quantity of sugar in the recipe. Certain thickeners are best used with certain types of fruit. However, I must warn you that everyone has their favorite thickener and will swear by it as the very best!

THICKENING EQUIVALENTS

Each of these has the same thickening power:

- 3 tablespoons Instant ClearJel
- 3 tablespoons cornstarch
- ⅓ cup unbleached all-purpose flour
- ¼ cup tapioca

INSTANT CLEARJEL POWDER (CLEARJEL STARCH)

This modified cornstarch is my favorite thickener for all fruit pies. You can use it one for one in place of cornstarch. It is what many commercial bakers use in their fruit pie fillings. ClearJel makes a fruit filling that's clear and bright; it has absolutely no floury or starchy taste; and it is freezer stable: you can freeze an unbaked pie and then bake it later without a chance of the thickener losing its strength. All you have to do is whisk together the ClearJel and the sugar in a bowl, and sprinkle this mixture over the prepared fruit. Stir or toss well.

Unbleached All-purpose Flour

Flour is a favorite thickener for apple pies. The rule of thumb is about ⅓ cup of flour to each quart of fruit, but each recipe will vary. I like to toss my cut fruit with flour before filling my pie; this distributes it more evenly. The starchy flavor flour imparts can be a drawback.

Cornstarch

This is also a good thickener to use with fruit. It has twice the thickening power of flour, but like flour, it imparts a slightly starchy flavor, especially in juicy fruit pies. That's why I recommend cooking part of the fruit and cornstarch first. Cornstarch doesn't work if your filling is high in acidity, such as from cherries, or if you plan to freeze the filling at any time. It loses its thickening power over time if stored. On the plus side, it does not thin when a slice of pie is reheated.

Tapioca (Pearl or Quick-cooking)

In general, fruit fillings thickened with tapioca allow the flavor of the fruit to come through cleanly. Tapioca can hold more fruit juice than other thickeners without becoming rigid. But it isn't recommended for a lattice top or other open fruit pie, as it becomes hard when the tapioca grains on the surface are exposed to the hot air of the oven. A finer grind, instant tapioca, can be used instead. If you find only pearl tapioca, just place it in a spice grinder or food processor and pulse to make "instant" tapioca.

Tapioca has no flavor of its own and it cooks quickly. If you use tapioca, to prevent uneven thickening and lumps let the filling mixture stand for at least 15 minutes before you spoon it into the crust to bake.

QUESTION: *Why, after baking, do apple pies always have a space between the filling and the crust?*

ANSWER: As the apples soften during cooking, steam is released. Steam collects beneath the top crust, where it then expands and rises in a hot oven, causing pressure from beneath that supports the crust as it sets in the oven. Meanwhile, the apples inside have collapsed.

Precooking and cooling the apples partially solves this problem. They will shrink, but much less. Slice the apples into wedges. Thick slices promote air space and create a gap between the fruit and the crust, which you don't want. To prevent fillings that are too juicy, toss apples with sugar right before using. Sugar draws water from the apples, and the longer they sit, the more watery the filling becomes. Finally, build up the filling to look like a mound. Pour any juices in the center of the pie; they will distribute themselves evenly.

MIXED-UP APPLE PIE

MAKES ONE 9 X 1¼-INCH DOUBLE CRUST PIE

In this recipe, no space forms between the top crust and the filling. The reason? I use apples that hold their shape during baking. Also, I choose types that cook at the same rate; I don't want one variety overbaking and turning to mush before the others are done. Granny Smith, Golden Delicious, Jonathan, and Cortland are all good choices because these tart apples hold their shape best. More acidic apples like the Red Delicious and McIntosh, break down a little faster when baked and have a tendency to cook up mealy or into mushy applesauce, not good for pie baking. If you can only choose one apple, choose Granny Smith.

For this recipe, the apples should be peeled, cored, and cut into ½-inch wedges. Five pounds of apples is about 10 large apples, and will yield 5 cups of prepared apple wedges.

INGREDIENTS

CRUST

2 recipes All-Purpose Pie Dough (page 130), divided into ⅔ and ⅓ portions

FILLING

5 pounds mixed Granny Smith, Golden Delicious, Jonathan, and Cortland apples
⅔ cup sugar or ⅓ cup sugar and ⅓ cup dark brown sugar, packed
2 tablespoons lemon juice (from about 1 lemon)
¼ cup (½ stick) unsalted butter
3 tablespoons unbleached all-purpose flour
1 teaspoon ground cinnamon

TO FINISH

1 tablespoon heavy cream or milk
½ teaspoon sugar

1. Roll out ⅔ of the All-Purpose Pie Dough between sheets of parchment paper to a 12-inch round approximately ⅛-inch thick (page 132). Fit into a heatproof glass pie pan. Do not trim. Cover and place in the refrigerator. Roll out the remaining dough, place flat on a cookie sheet, cover with plastic wrap, and chill in the refrigerator.

2. Set a rack in the lower third of the oven. Place a foil-lined baking sheet on it and preheat the oven to 400 degrees F.

3. To make the filling: In a large bowl, toss the apple wedges with the sugar and lemon juice. Melt the butter in an 11-inch skillet over medium heat. Add the apples. Cook about 5 minutes, stirring occasionally, until the apples are barely tender. Transfer to a 7- by 11-inch or larger pan to cool. In a small bowl, combine the flour and cinnamon; sprinkle evenly over the apples and toss.

4. Remove the top crust from the refrigerator and let it sit to warm so it will be pliable. Fill the bottom crust with the cooled apple mixture (dump it in the middle so the juices will distribute evenly). Before placing the top crust, brush the rim of the bottom crust lightly with water. This will serve as the glue to hold the two together.

5. Fit the top crust over the apple mixture. Pinch around the entire edge to stick the two crusts together. Trim the dough with scissors leaving a 1-inch overhang from the pie pan and pinch together again. Finish the pie's edge by fluting it (page 133). Cut several slashes in the top crust for steam vents. Brush the top of the pie lightly with the cream and sprinkle with the sugar.

6. Immediately place the pie on the hot baking sheet in the oven and reduce the heat to 375 degrees F. Bake for about $1\frac{1}{4}$ hours, until the pie crust is golden brown and the filling is bubbling through the vents. Look through the glass pie pan to see if the crust is evenly browned. If the top or edge is browning too fast, cover loosely with foil.

7. Remove the baking sheet and pie from the oven. Place the pie still in its pan on a wire cake rack to cool, about 1 hour. Serve warm.

BLUEBERRY CRUMBLE PIE

❖

MAKES ONE 9 X 1¼-INCH PIE

A staple of our early ancestors, blueberries are as much a part of our heritage as apple pie or lemon meringue pie. I simply cannot get enough of them! For optimal storage, refrigerate unwashed fresh berries, where they'll keep for 10 days to 2 weeks; they'll keep even longer in the freezer. Both frozen and fresh berries should be rinsed and drained just before using. If thawed berries are not used immediately, cover and refrigerate and use within three days. To guarantee that the filling sets, I precook it, leaving nothing to chance.

INGREDIENTS
CRUST
1 recipe All-Purpose Pie Dough (page 130)

FILLING
3 tablespoons cornstarch
3 tablespoons water
3 pints (6 cups) blueberries (fresh or frozen)
⅔ cup sugar
3 tablespoons unsalted butter
1 tablespoon lemon juice (from 1 lemon)
1 teaspoon grated lemon peel (from 1 lemon)
1 teaspoon salt

TOPPING
1 cup all-purpose flour
½ cup sugar
½ cup quick-cooking oats (not instant)
½ teaspoon cinnamon
¼ teaspoon salt
½ cup (1 stick) unsalted butter, cold

1. Set a rack in the lower third of the oven. Place a foil-lined baking sheet on it and preheat the oven to 400 degrees F.

2. Roll out the All-Purpose Pie Dough between sheets of parchment paper to a

12-inch round approximately $\frac{1}{8}$-inch thick (page 132). Fit it into a heatproof glass pie pan and flute it (page 133). Cover and place it in the refrigerator.

3. To make the filling: Combine the cornstarch and water in a medium bowl. Combine 1 cup of the blueberries and $\frac{1}{3}$ cup of the sugar in a large saucepan. Bring to simmer over low heat, and cook until the sugar liquefies, 5 to 7 minutes. Add to the cornstarch mixture and mix well. Return both to the saucepan and add the remaining 5 cups of blueberries. Cook the blueberry mixture over low heat stirring constantly, until it thickens like syrup and becomes clear, 7 to 8 minutes. Pour it back into the same medium bowl and stir in the remaining $\frac{1}{3}$ cup of sugar, butter, lemon juice and peel, and salt. Press a piece of plastic wrap on the surface and cool to room temperature.

4. To make the topping: Mix the flour, sugar, oats, cinnamon, and salt in a medium bowl. Cut the butter into tablespoon-size pieces and toss with the flour mixture. With your fingertips, pinch the mixture together until it forms large crumbs. Set aside; refrigerate if the room is warm.

5. To assemble the pie: Pour the cooled filling into the pie shell. Sprinkle the topping evenly over all. Immediately place the pie on the baking sheet in the oven and reduce the heat to 375 degrees F. If the rim of the crust or the topping begins to brown too quickly, place a piece of foil over the top of the pie.

6. Bake for about 1 hour, until the fruit is bubbling. Look through the glass pie pan to see if the bottom crust is evenly browned. When the pie is done, remove the pie from the oven. Cool the pie still in its pan on a wire cake rack until the filling solidifies more, about an hour, and serve. It is delicious with vanilla ice cream. For longer storage, cool thoroughly.

QUESTION: *I have always wanted to make a crust with cornmeal. But it always falls apart.*

ANSWER: The trick is to replace $\frac{1}{4}$ to $\frac{1}{2}$ cup of the flour in the recipe with the cornmeal. You need to mix it with unbleached all-purpose flour because cornmeal doesn't contain gluten and your crust will crumble, as you sadly discovered.

QUESTION: *I made a peach cobbler and it was a little runny. What should I have done?*

ANSWER: It probably means your peaches were a little extra-ripe. You can always mix a little flour into the filling before baking.

RASPBERRY TART WITH A CORNMEAL CRUST

MAKES ONE 9-INCH OR 9½-INCH TART

The golden, sweet cornmeal crust is a perfect base for the tangy, red raspberry filling. This is also good with boysenberries.

INGREDIENTS

CRUST
2 tablespoons unsalted butter, chilled
1 cup unbleached all-purpose flour; spoon into measuring cup and level to top
½ cup yellow cornmeal, fine grind (regular)
½ cup sugar
½ teaspoon baking powder
¼ teaspoon salt
1 large egg yolk
3 tablespoons ice water

FILLING
1 cup water; measure in liquid measuring cup
2 tablespoons sugar
2 tablespoons cornstarch
2 cups fresh or frozen raspberries
Vegetable oil cooking spray

1. On the large holes of a box grater, shred the chilled butter onto a plate. Freeze for 10 minutes until frozen.

2. In a medium bowl, whisk the flour, cornmeal, sugar, baking powder, and salt until well combined. Toss in the frozen butter and quickly press it into the mixture between your thumb and forefingers until it resembles small bread crumbs (pea-size pieces are not necessary with this crust). In a small bowl, mix the egg yolk and ice water. Gradually add the egg mixture to the flour mixture while tossing with a fork until thoroughly moistened but not wet. The clump of dough should hold together when pressed between your thumb and forefinger, but look dry on the outside. You may not need all of the egg mixture. Gather the dough in the bowl to bring it together (the dough will remain somewhat crumbly) and make a thick disk. Wrap in

waxed paper; plastic wrap makes the outside sticky. Refrigerate until well-chilled, about an hour.

3. In a medium saucepan, whisk the water with the sugar and cornstarch until the cornstarch dissolves. Cook over medium heat about 3 minutes, stirring occasionally, until thickened. Stir in the raspberries and immediately remove from heat. Cool completely with a piece of plastic wrap pressed on its surface.

4. Position a rack in the center of the oven and place a foil-lined baking sheet on it. Preheat the oven to 350 degrees F. Generously spray a 9-inch or 9½-inch tart pan with removable bottom with vegetable oil spray.

5. To make the crust, place the dough between two sheets of waxed paper. Make a circle about 12 inches in diameter and about ⅛-inch thick (page 132). If the dough crumbles, just press it together. To harden, place it on the baking sheet and freeze until it is very cold and the top sheet of waxed paper pulls away easily, 10 to 15 minutes.

6. Fit the crust into the tart pan: Set the tart pan bottom on the center of the dough. Position the tart pan side over the bottom. Flip the cornmeal crust and tart pan over at the same time so the crust is in the pan. Peel away the paper. Gently press the dough to fit the corners of the pan. Patch any cracks with leftover dough. Before trimming make sure the top of the crust is secure by pressing gently with your index finger and thumb. Trim the tart dough by running a rolling pin over the top of the pan. Pour the cooled raspberry filling into the crust.

7. Place the tart pan on the baking sheet and bake until the crust is lightly browned and the filling is lightly bubbling, about 45 minutes. Remove the tart still in its pan to a wire cake rack to cool. Lightly spray a piece of plastic wrap with vegetable oil spray and place the sprayed side directly on the surface of the filling so it won't harden. Poke a few holes in the wrap with the tip of a knife to allow the steam to escape. Cool completely in the pan at room temperature. Remove the plastic wrap, side, and bottom of the pan (see below) and serve at room temperature.

8. **Storage:** Cover tightly with plastic wrap and store at room temperature. Keeps for 2 to 3 days.

QUESTION: *How do I remove a tart from its pan side?*

ANSWER: Set the tart pan on a stable base at least 3 inches high, such as a coffee can. Holding the bottom, let the side slip down and fall to the countertop. To remove the bottom, set the tart on a flat surface and carefully slide a long, thin metal spatula (an offset one works best) between the tart and the pan bottom. Slide the tart to a flat serving plate placed at equal height.

> QUESTION: *Can you freeze fruit pies after baking? Will this ruin them?*
>
> ANSWER: It is much better to freeze a fruit pie before baking than after; the texture suffers substantially if frozen after baking. If you freeze the pie before baking, don't defrost it when the time comes to bake. Bake it unwrapped at 425 degrees F for 15 to 20 minutes, then lower the temperature to 350 degrees F for the remainder of the cooking time. The total baking time will be about 20 minutes longer than for an unfrozen pie.

STOVETOP AND ICEBOX PIES

At least weather-wise, summertime is the most perfect time for a stovetop pie or an icebox pie. Not only are these pies refreshing treats, but it's great to have a do-ahead dessert waiting patiently in your fridge while you grill your dinner outside, or to enjoy after a night out of pizza with the kids.

Some recipes can be easily assembled with a store-bought crust and easy-to-make pudding from a box (shh! . . . don't tell). Many times a graham cracker crust (page 82) or a one-crust pie crust (page 130) is used.

> **Sarah Says:** When making an icebox pie with frozen fruit, always thaw and drain the fruit before using. If it thaws in the pie, it will leech water and ruin your recipe.

LEMON MERINGUE PIE

Stovetop pies covered with meringue, such as the Luscious Lemon Meringue Pie recipe that follows on page 155, often have special problems. When you cut the pie, you should see a bright lemon-colored filling that keeps its shape, stacked between a lightly browned crust and white meringue. But have you ever made a lemon meringue pie and had the meringue slide off the filling? Have you had to pour off water from the bottom of the pie after taking it from the refrigerator, which means you'll have a mushy bottom crust? How about a filling that oozes out of the sides of a cut piece of pie, flattening it?

Meringue doesn't hold up for long periods of time, particularly in humid weather, which is when most of us choose to make these summery-seeming pies. I think lemon meringue pie is intended to be eaten right away; when the pie sits, especially in the refrigerator, water can collect in the bottom of it. This weeping may also make your meringue slide off the filling.

QUESTION: *When I take my lemon meringue pie out of the oven, I see what looks like a sugary juice starting to come out of the pie. When the pie has cooled, I place it in the refrigerator. By the time I take it out a few hours later or the next day the crust bottom seems to be swimming in a watery liquid. What can I do?*

ANSWER: The water is called weeping and is caused by the egg whites in the meringue denaturing or breaking down over time. It has to do with refrigeration, heat, timing, and the eggs themselves and how you handle them.

Lemon meringue pies are meant to be eaten in one day. Some weeping comes from moisture condensing on a pie after it is been refrigerated. Pies can be stored at room temperature for a day and don't have to be refrigerated, as long as there is sufficient sugar in the meringue. Don't cover the pie at any point after preparing, as that too, speeds up weeping. If there is anything left over, refrigerate it.

The temperature of the filling also influences the tendency of meringue to weep. The meringue and filling must seal together to prevent weeping. This happens when the meringue is spread on a hot filling. I don't fill my crust with the hot filling and then make the meringue, as many recipes suggest. Instead, I keep the filling in the pot I made it in, and briefly reheat it after the meringue is made. I heat the filling on low heat, stirring constantly, until hot. It only takes about a minute. I pour in the filling and immediately top it with the meringue, sealing the meringue to the filling and crust.

Be sure you are using fresh eggs. The older the egg white, the less stable it will be after whipping.

Eliminate the cream of tartar from the meringue. Although it may help initially in whipping the egg whites, over time it destabilizes them and causes them to weep. It is really only worth using cream of tartar if you don't have an electric mixer and have to whip the egg whites more slowly by hand.

The right amount of sugar helps prevent weeping. Optimally, you should have about two tablespoons per egg white for a meringue-topped pie. Egg whites really have to be beaten well once the sugar is added. Insufficient beating can cause weeping; the peaks on the meringue need to be quite stiff. However, overbeating the egg whites before the sugar is added can also contribute to the problem. Add the sugar when the egg whites reach the soft peak stage.

A small amount of heated cornstarch and water added to the meringue helps prevent weeping. I take a tablespoon of the cornstarch mixture from the filling after it becomes opaque. Add that to the egg whites when they reach the soft peak stage.

LUSCIOUS LEMON MERINGUE PIE

❖

To all of us pie connoisseurs, a lemon meringue pie should be a delicious, mouth-puckering dessert with a marvelous contrast of textures. It is a classic American dessert with the ultimate flaky pastry (or graham cracker crust) and a tart, fresh lemony custard-like filling under a dazzling mound of fluffy meringue that's either swirled into a spiral or puffed into peaks and baked to a golden brown. However, there are many potholes in the lemon-scented road to this sensation, of which weeping water is the main one. Another problem is fillings that don't set. The trick I use is to thicken my cornstarch mixture first to ensure the filling will set, and then combine it with the rest of the ingredients.

INGREDIENTS

CRUST

1 recipe All-Purpose Pie Dough (page 130), blind-baked and cooled (page 139),
   or an unbaked graham cracker crust (page 82)

FILLING

4 large egg yolks (save the whites for the meringue)
1½ cups sugar
⅓ cup plus 1 tablespoon cornstarch (6 tablespoons plus 1 teaspoon)
1½ cups water
2 tablespoons unsalted butter, softened
½ cup lemon juice (from about 3 small lemons)
1 teaspoon grated lemon peel (from 1 lemon)
¼ teaspoon lemon extract
¼ teaspoon vanilla extract

MERINGUE

4 large egg whites
⅛ teaspoon salt
½ cup sugar or superfine sugar
1 tablespoon cornstarch mixture (reserved from the filling recipe)

1. Position a rack in the center of the oven and preheat the oven to 400 degrees F.

2. Thoroughly beat the egg yolks in a medium bowl. Mix the sugar and cornstarch in 2-quart heavy-bottomed saucepan; gradually stir in the water to dissolve the

sugar. Cook over medium heat, stirring constantly, until the mixture thickens and boils for about 1 minute. (I like to stir with a flat whisk. It works better than a wooden spoon because you can get it into the corner of the pan.) The mixture will be shiny and opaque when done. Remove from the heat. Set aside 1 tablespoon of the mixture in a microwave-safe cup to be used later for the meringue.

3. Immediately whisk a large spoonful of the hot cornstarch mixture into the egg yolks. Repeat a couple of times until 1/3 of the cornstarch mixture is added. Pour the eggs back into the rest of the thickened cornstarch. Cook on medium-low heat stirring constantly for 1 minute until steam breaks through the cornstarch mixture from the bottom; remove from the heat. Stir in the butter until incorporated. Add the lemon juice, lemon peel, and extracts (the vanilla tempers the lemon's acidity). Leave in the saucepan. Set aside with a piece of plastic wrap pressed on top. Don't let the filling cool.

4. Microwave the reserved cornstarch mixture at 50% power for two 5-second intervals to soften; do not boil. Cover and set aside. In a dry, clean mixer bowl, with the mixer on medium speed, beat the egg whites until foamy. Add the salt. Continue whipping until the foam is white and opaque and soft peaks form. Increase the mixer speed to high and add the sugar at the side of the bowl. Add the reserved cooked cornstarch in 3 equal portions. Beat until the egg whites are glossy and form stiff peaks. Set aside.

5. If the filling isn't hot, return the saucepan to low heat, stirring constantly. Heat until just hot. Pour into the crust. Spread the meringue over the filling immediately, carefully sealing to the edge of the crust to prevent shrinking or weeping.

6. Bake for 8 to 12 minutes, until the meringue is lightly browned on the high points. Cool completely on a wire cake rack. Serve immediately.

Note: For a higher meringue, use 6 egg whites and increase the sugar to 3/4 cup. For safe meringue use egg white powder.

QUESTION: *I usually make my lemon meringue pies—usually quite a hit—with no problem. But when I made it yesterday, it was properly chilled but the lemon layer didn't "gel." What did I do wrong?*

ANSWER: It's best to add the lemon juice and lemon peel after the cornstarch mixture has thickened. The acids in these ingredients break down the starch's thickening properties, if you add them earlier.

Another cause of a cornstarch-thickened filling not gelling is when the cornstarch is under- or over-cooked. You have to make sure you heat it to boiling for one minute while stirring constantly. Then it must be removed from the heat and used immediately.

BLACK AND WHITE CHOCOLATE MOUSSE TART

MAKES ONE 9-INCH TART

A showstopper. This good example of an icebox pie is like a cream pie, but is made with a gelatin-enhanced filling poured into a prebaked crust and refrigerated to set the filling. Top with shaved chocolate. This pie is rich so I advise serving smaller pieces—it will yield 16 slices instead of the usual eight.

INGREDIENTS

CRUST

Vegetable oil cooking spray

1¼ cups Oreo cookie crumbs or chocolate graham cracker crumbs, from 9 full-size crackers (18 squares total)

¼ cup sugar

½ teaspoon instant espresso powder or instant coffee granules

⅓ cup (5 tablespoons plus 1 teaspoon) unsalted butter, melted

MOUSSE

2 tablespoons water

½ envelope powdered gelatin (1¼ teaspoons, ⅛ ounce by weight)

2 cups (one 12-ounce bag) white chocolate chips

½ cup milk

2 teaspoons vanilla extract

¾ cup heavy cream

¼ cup sugar

1 teaspoon vanilla extract

GARNISH

1 ounce semisweet or bittersweet chocolate (1 square)

1. Position a rack in the center of the oven and preheat the oven to 375 degrees F. Generously spray a 9-inch tart pan with removable bottom with vegetable oil spray. Place the tart pan on a baking sheet lined with foil.

2. To make the crust in the tart pan, lightly toss the cookie crumbs, sugar, and espresso powder until well combined. Drizzle with the melted butter and mix together. Press the mixture into the bottom and up the side of the pan with your fin-

gertips. Use a metal measuring cup to tamp down the crust next to the side. Make sure the crust is evenly distributed, and the side is compacted. Bake for 6 to 8 minutes until it smells done and the crust is just becoming firm. Do not overbake. Looks are deceiving. Slide the tart shell from the baking sheet to a wire cake rack; do not pick up the pan by its bottom, or you'll crack the crust.

3. Put the water into a small heatproof cup. Sprinkle the gelatin over the water and let soften for 5 minutes. Microwave uncovered at 50% power at 10-second intervals for 30 to 45 seconds until clear. Don't let it boil.

4. Place the chocolate chips in a medium bowl. Heat the milk in a small saucepan over low heat until just boiling. Pour the hot milk over the chips. Push down any chips not covered in milk with a fork. Let stand 1 minute. Stir until the chocolate is melted and smooth. Let it sit a few seconds again if not completely melted and stir again. Stir in the hot gelatin mixture and the vanilla. Place the bowl in an ice water bath in a larger bowl stirring every couple of minutes for 10 to 15 minutes until the mixture is cool. Don't refrigerate or freeze to cool it; the gelatin will make the mixture stiffen. Strain through a fine-mesh strainer if there are any small pieces of unmelted chips. Set aside.

5. Using an electric mixer at medium-high speed, beat the heavy cream, sugar, and vanilla in a large bowl until medium-soft mounds form. Do not overwhip or the mousse will be grainy. You can do this step in advance and refrigerate the cream. Whisk (don't beat) again right before using.

6. Fold (page 40) one-half of the whipped cream into the chocolate mixture to lighten it. Then fold in the remaining whipped cream. Spread the mousse in the cooled pie shell so the top is smooth, and refrigerate under an inverted bowl for at least 8 hours, preferably overnight, until the mousse is firm.

7. Set the tart pan on a stable base at least 3 inches high, such as a coffee can. The outer ring will slip away from the crust and fall to the countertop. To remove the bottom, set the tart on a flat surface and carefully slide a long, thin metal spatula (an offset one works best) between the shell and the pan bottom. Slide the tart to a flat serving plate placed at equal height.

8. Right before serving, garnish with dark chocolate shavings: Warm a 1-ounce square of semisweet or bittersweet chocolate in the microwave for 45 seconds on 50% power. (Just warm the chocolate slightly; don't let it melt.) Using a vegetable peeler, shave the chocolate by pressing down lightly on the smoothest side or top of the piece. The harder you press, the thicker the pieces will be. Let them fall onto a sheet of waxed paper, then refrigerate for about 5 minutes to harden. Sprinkle evenly over the tart right before serving.

Storage: Store the tart in the refrigerator, covered, for 2 to 3 days.

Note: I use ice baths often to cool down mixtures quickly. To prepare an ice bath, pour ice cubes into a 4-quart bowl. Generously sprinkle salt over the ice and add water to cover. Place in the ice bath the bowl containing the mixture to be cooled carefully.

9

CHOCOLATE

*I was melting chocolate and it turned into
a lumpy, grainy mess; what did I do wrong?
Can I substitute one kind of cocoa powder for another?
. . . and many other chocolate dilemmas.*

CHOCOLATE IS BOTH an ingredient in recipes, and the main ingredient in the process of chocolate making. Bakers have more questions about chocolate than almost any other single ingredient. Chocolate can be especially tricky to melt, and cocoa powder is a mystery to most of us.

There is specialty chocolate sold in thick chunks, measured by the pound or fractions of a pound. It is generally found in gourmet and baking specialty shops. Melted to liquid form, poured into molds or sculpted, chocolate becomes confections. There are convenient baking chocolate squares found in the grocery store in one-ounce portions, perfect for recipes. Chocolate can be pressed into cocoa powder and used for baking and making ice cream and sorbets. Chocolate chips or chunks can be added to a batter before baking, creating a recipe studded with chocolate throughout.

HOW IS CHOCOLATE MADE?

All chocolate comes from the same source: the cacao bean, the seed of the *Theobroma cacao,* a tropical evergreen tree found in Central and South America and Africa. But its ultimate manifestations can be quite different. The important thing is to buy "real" chocolate which contains cocoa butter. If it doesn't, it's not the real stuff.

The chocolate maker starts by roasting the beans to bring out the most flavor and enhance the richness of color. The beans are cracked and winnowed to expose the cocoa nib, the meat of the cacao bean. The chocolate nibs are crushed and ground by

QUESTION: *How would you describe a perfect chocolate flavor in a recipe?*

ANSWER: It is all a balancing act to find that point at which you have enough chocolate or cocoa powder added to a recipe. Frequently I like to combine part cocoa powder and part chocolate squares for a more complex taste similar to a fine European chocolate, or for greater impact such as in the Double Chocolate Fudge Brownie Bar recipe (page 108). I've also found that a pinch of salt helps enhance the chocolate flavor in a recipe.

The higher priced Dutch-process cocoas have had the bitterness removed and as a result they don't deliver the same flavor as natural cocoa (Hershey's, for example) or bittersweet chocolate squares. Rich chocolate flavor can be achieved in a cake, because cake recipes have a lot of sugar and fat, which are synergistic with the chocolate flavor profile. On the other hand, muffins have less fat and sugar and so would not be as chocolaty. As a result so many chocolate "muffins" are really cupcakes parading as muffins. I ran into this issue when Chicago Metallic Bakeware Company asked me to formulate a Chocolate Muffin Top recipe (page 220) for the celebration of the tenth anniversary of their bakeware invention, the muffin top pan. One can't make a true muffin sweet enough to carry the chocolate flavor, so my rich and chocolaty "muffin" recipe more resembles a cake formula.

large stone mills while hot from roasting, into a thick rich-looking "liquor" or "mass" called cocoa or chocolate liquor. Despite its name, it is nonalcoholic, and is what makes chocolate chocolate. Chocolate liquor is pure unsweetened chocolate made up of 50 to 58 percent cocoa solids, that give it its marvelous and distinct chocolaty flavor and dark color, and 42 to 50 percent cocoa butter, the fat that gives it its smooth, creamy richness. The more cocoa butter chocolate contains, the higher quality and more expensive the chocolate becomes.

The cocoa butter is removed and the liquor becomes a powder that is blended back with a specific amount of cocoa butter and other ingredients such as sugar, flavors (like vanilla), and often milk powder. The chocolate maker adds these ingredients according to his or her secret recipe, resulting in different kinds of dark chocolate that we find in the store, called unsweetened, bittersweet, semisweet, sweet, or milk chocolate. (White chocolate is technically not a chocolate.) In general, the darker the chocolate, the more chocolate liquor it contains—from 100 percent in unsweetened chocolate to 10 percent for milk chocolate. The darkest chocolate will provide the most chocolaty, almost bitter flavor.

After the ingredients are mixed, the product is further refined and conched to smooth it and tempered (page 170) to create chocolate suitable for solid bars and pieces. Premium chocolates are conched longer than others.

WHAT ARE THE DIFFERENT VARIETIES OF CHOCOLATE?

Unsweetened chocolate sometimes called "bitter chocolate," is pure chocolate liquor. It does not contain any sugar; don't confuse it with sweetened chocolate, which does.

Bittersweet chocolate has a rich, deep, chocolaty taste, but still retains some bite. Like pure, unsweetened chocolate, bittersweet chocolate contains more antioxidants than most other varieties.

Semisweet chocolate is the classic dark chocolate. It has a mellow, almost sweet flavor, smooth texture, and contains more sugar than you'll find in bittersweet.

Sweet chocolate is sweet dark chocolate, also called sweet baking chocolate. It contains more sugar than semisweet.

German chocolate isn't really German; it was developed by Baker's Chocolate Company by a man named German. It is sweetened chocolate, ideal for icings and cakes; you can substitute dark sweet chocolate for German chocolate.

Milk chocolate is a popular choice. It contains chocolate liquor, cocoa butter, sugar, flavorings, and of course, milk solids. It is creamy and somewhat less chocolaty and milder for baking. Due to its dairy content, milk chocolate burns easily.

Chopped milk chocolate doesn't do very well in place of chocolate chips in cookies, it tends to seize and become very hard after baking. Save the milk chocolate to melt and spread on the top of already baked cookies.

Couverture (French for covering) is used by professionals to coat candies, for molding, and for dipping. It has a higher percentage of cocoa butter than ordinary chocolate which makes it "melt in your mouth" and gives it a richer flavor and glossier finish. The high fat percentage enables it to form a much thinner shell than regular tempered chocolate. It is rather expensive, and you may need to go to a specialty store to find it. Available in bittersweet, semisweet, white, and milk chocolate, it

Sarah Says: If you want to add cocoa powder to your recipe, start by substituting one-fourth cup of cocoa powder for the same amount of wheat flour. Remember a little cocoa powder goes a long way and can dry a recipe more than flour does. Depending on whether you use Dutch-processed or natural, an adjustment of the leaveners may be desirable, but not necessary. You can use cocoa powder in place of baking chocolate: one ounce of baking chocolate equals three level tablespoons cocoa plus one level tablespoon of melted butter, shortening, or vegetable oil (canola is my recommendation). You may want to adjust the sugar in the recipe but not by more or less than one-fourth cup. I never bother to, because different types of chocolate yield different and interesting results.

comes in small discs and solid blocks which you'll need to chop into little chunks for melting. It sets with a deep color and a definite shine.

Cocoa powder comes in two types: natural and Dutch-process (also called alkalized). Dutch-process cocoa has been treated with a mild alkali, such as baking soda, to neutralize its acidity. It has a milder, more well-rounded taste than natural cocoa. It also has a deeper, redder color. Natural cocoa powder is more flavorful, with a hint of fruitiness. Unless you find it unavoidable, you shouldn't substitute one variety for another; you'll produce quite different results in taste and texture. Baking chocolate contains cocoa butter (15 grams fat per ounce of unsweetened chocolate) which gives creaminess and richness to a recipe, while cocoa powder has three grams of fat.

CHOCOLATE BLENDS

Chocolate chips, also known as morsels, are miniature drops of chocolate. Chocolate chips are easy to work with and are always foolproof. They are made from chocolate

QUESTION: *My devil's food cake recipe calls for unsweetened chocolate, but I only have semisweet. If I use the semisweet chocolate, what will happen?*

ANSWER: If you're substituting a couple of squares, the cake will be a little sweeter—that's all! If you have a recipe that relies heavily on chocolate for its texture, then the sugar and other ingredients may have to be adjusted on a case-by-case basis.

liquor, sugar, cocoa butter or vegetable oil, milk fat, vanilla, and soy lecithin (an emulsifier) to combine the water-loving ingredients in chocolate with the oil-loving. By providing a way for these opposites to get together, this chocolate requires less cocoa butter, making it less expensive.

Chocolate chips have about 29 percent cocoa butter—less than chocolate bars—so they retain their shape better when they're baked in the oven. Avoid chips that contain vegetable oil instead of cocoa butter; they have a waxy flavor. There are several flavors of chips: bittersweet, semisweet, milk, and white. One cup of chips weighs six ounces.

Although you may be tempted to melt chocolate chips to flavor frostings, fudges, other confections, and baked items, they cannot be substituted for regular chocolate in a recipe; they don't behave the same way. Solid chocolate will melt to a smoother, creamier consistency. There are specific recipes written that use melted chocolate chips for making chocolate dipped candy, fruit, or pretzels.

You can try to make your own chocolate chips by chopping regular chocolate into small size pieces, but they won't exactly work the same way that the chips do.

Chocolate bark is both a candy and an ingredient. It is a blend of chocolates that have been melted with vegetable oil and mixed with nuts, fruit, or other add-ins. You can make your own from compound coating or chocolate chips plus add-ins. As a candy, it is dried in thin sheets and broken into large pieces with a texture resembling tree bark.

NON-CHOCOLATE VARIETIES

White chocolate isn't really chocolate at all; it contains no cocoa solids. It is a mixture of cocoa butter, sugar, milk, and vanilla (imitation white chocolate doesn't even have cocoa butter—it is made with vegetable oil and doesn't taste the same). To me, it gives recipes a buttery, milky-sweet, vanilla flavor. White chocolate melts easily and at a low temperature due to its dairy content; you must watch it carefully.

Compound, Confectionery, or Summer Coating are all names for a sort of chocolate-flavored candy created to melt easily and harden quickly. It contains palm kernel oil instead of cocoa butter, making it less expensive. It needn't be tempered and can withstand higher heat than true chocolate. If you want quick and easy, use confectionery coating; if you want the real thing, use real chocolate and patience.

QUESTION: *When a recipe calls for "cocoa powder" which type do I use?*

ANSWER: "Cocoa" means natural. If "Dutch-process" or "alkalized" is specified, use that.

QUESTION: *How can I tell which cocoa powder is Dutch-process and which one is natural? I saw a label that said "alkalized." What is that?*

ANSWER: Cocoa powder must be labeled as "processed with alkali" or "alkalized" if it has been Dutch-processed. If these terms don't appear on the label, it is natural cocoa. Most recipes will either specify Dutch-process or simply say "cocoa." In the latter case, use natural cocoa (such as Hershey's).

QUESTION: *Please help! My brownie recipe says to use Dutch-process cocoa powder and I only have natural. Can I use it?*

ANSWER: It is best to use the type of cocoa powder specified in the recipe since the leavening agent is matched with it. Cocoa goes through a fermentation and drying process that affects its pH or acidity level; depending on the type, it may affect the leavening system in your baking. Most recipes pair baking soda with natural cocoa powder and baking powder with Dutch-process.

If you absolutely need to substitute, go ahead and experiment, but it is not a simple exchange—expect some disappointments before you get the desired color, flavor, and texture. I find that by adding a pinch ($\frac{1}{8}$ teaspoon) of baking soda to natural cocoa, I can achieve an affect similar to that of alkalized cocoa, but only if the recipe doesn't already contain any soda. Natural cocoa has more flavor and the addition of baking soda gives it a darker color, but some people notice a slight bitterness in their recipes. It is entirely possible to make a cake-like brownie with natural cocoa by adding baking soda and baking powder, or a denser, fudgier one with just baking soda (provided there is enough fat in the recipe).

QUESTION: *I noticed that sometimes a chocolate cake recipe calls for "dissolving" the cocoa powder in hot water before adding to the recipe. What is the purpose?*

ANSWER: When you dissolve the cocoa powder it disperses better in batter than if it were added with the flour, and it dissolves more quickly in hot water than in cold. Cold water molecules tend to be attracted to each other and as a result the powder many clump together. In the hot water, the water molecules are moving faster and bouncing off the walls of the cup, causing the cocoa powder to break up and dissolve.

QUESTION: *When I add cocoa powder directly to the batter it is hard to combine. Why?*

ANSWER: Cocoa powder clumps easily because of its starch content and develops considerable viscosity in water. Because of this, it is best to combine the cocoa powder with the flour and dry ingredients and then sift them together. If the recipe calls for "1 cup sifted flour," sift the flour, measure, and resift with the cocoa powder. If there are cocoa powder clumps left in the sifter, don't throw them out; simply press them through the sifter. If the flour-cocoa mixture has clumps after sifting, sift again and again until silky smooth before using.

QUESTION: *My recipe calls for low-fat cocoa powder. I thought cocoa powder didn't have any fat in it. Please explain.*

ANSWER: Cocoa powder still retains some cocoa butter after pressing. Low-fat cocoa, the kind most commonly used, has 10 to 12 percent fat; medium-fat, 14 to 16 percent; and high-fat cocoa, sometimes called drinking cocoa, has 22 to 24 percent. Nestlé's Quick, a high-fat cocoa, should not be used as a baking ingredient.

CHOCOLATE: POINTERS, QUESTIONS, AND RECIPES

In a fluid state obtained by melting, chocolate can be used in a wide variety of recipes.

MELTING CHOCOLATE

The optimal way to melt chocolate—take it from a solid state to a fluid one—requires low temperatures, indirect heat, plenty of time, and constant stirring and attention. The process starts a little below 90 degrees F as the cocoa butter begins to melt. Chocolate melts best when it reaches about 105 degrees F, only as warm as warm water. Melting temperatures must never exceed 115 degrees F for more sensitive milk and white chocolates, and 120 degrees for dark; otherwise the chocolate will burn and be ruined. Chocolate chips (which aren't real chocolate) melt at a higher temperature, making them less susceptible to burning and more foolproof. Measure all temperatures with a mercury-gauge chocolate thermometer, page 7. Don't melt over actively boiling water or direct heat. Do not cover chocolate with a lid or condensation may form and drop on the chocolate causing seizing.

DOUBLE BOILER METHOD (BAIN MARIE; PAGE 76)

When melting chocolate, I like to fashion my own double boiler with a wide bowl for the top; more of the chocolate will be exposed to the heat from the water below, and it will melt evenly. A wide bowl also enables you to stir the chocolate more easily and vigorously.

1. Chop the chocolate into $\frac{1}{4}$- to $\frac{1}{2}$-inch or smaller evenly sized pieces. Put it in the bowl or top pot and set aside.
2. Fill the bottom of the double boiler about half full with water, making sure it won't touch the bowl above. Heat the water to boiling, and remove the pan from the stove. Some recommend using simmering water, but boiling the water first and removing the pan is safer for the beginner.
3. Carefully wipe any condensation from the rim of the pan. Never place the double boiler top over the bottom pan while the water is actually boiling, because a tiny splash of water or steam will cause your chocolate to seize.
4. Fit the top over the bottom part. The chocolate will begin to melt. Stir with a heatproof spatula. Don't use a wooden spoon, because wood may contain moisture and odors.
5. When the chocolate is almost melted, remove the top from the double boiler, wipe the condensation from its bottom with a towel, and place it on a heatproof surface. Stir the chocolate vigorously until it is fully melted. This is where patience comes in! If it is taking a long time, don't give in to the temptation to place it over the double boiler, back on the stove. Keep stirring. The heat from the melted chocolate will continue to melt the rest. Be careful, the bowl will have become quite hot. (If the chocolate is really stubborn, boil the water again, remove it from the heat, and return the chocolate back over it, stirring.)

MICROWAVE METHOD

For melting only a couple of chocolate squares, you may wish to use a microwave oven. Place the chocolate in a microwave-safe bowl and microwave on a medium setting (50% power) checking every 10 to 15 seconds. Let the chocolate stand for 30 seconds outside the microwave, then stir. Appearances can be deceiving, especially when microwaving chocolate: chocolate holds its form and looks shiny even when melted. When the chocolate is almost melted, remove it and stir until completely melted. Milk and white chocolate burn very easily, so check them every 5 to 8 seconds.

OVEN METHOD

This technique was inspired by my mom and Julia Child. Put a few squares in a heatproof bowl or on a piece of foil with the edges turned up, and place on the middle shelf at 350 degrees F. It will take 5 to 10 minutes for a couple of squares to melt, but watch them carefully, especially milk and white chocolate. Remove when almost melted (the squares will still retain their shape and look shiny) and stir until thoroughly melted. For melting large quantities, put the chopped chocolate in a heatproof bowl or large pan and place it on the middle shelf in an oven set at the lowest temperature with the door ajar. It takes awhile, sometimes an hour or more, but keep an eye on it.

Sarah Says: If you have a pound or more of melted chocolate you want to cool quickly, blend it with an immersion blender. Stirring cools liquids, but you don't want to use a mixer, because it will beat too much air into the chocolate.

QUESTION: *One moment I was stirring chocolate pieces that were just beginning to melt and the next thing I knew, I had a lumpy, grainy, mess that looked like thick paste. What caused this? Can I fix it?*

ANSWER: Called *seizing,* this problem is caused by the tiniest amount of liquid, even a single drop of water—the moisture clinging to a just-washed strawberry, or the steam from a double boiler. Make sure all utensils are clean and dry every time before using. Oddly, while small amounts of liquid can spoil melted chocolate, large amounts are okay so long as the liquid is warmed to match the temperature of the melted chocolate. If you add cold cream or milk, for example, the chocolate will begin to solidify and you'll end up with a mess. Instead warm liquids properly before adding them to the chocolate.

Chocolate is also heat-sensitive and may clump and seize if it has burned.

When melting chocolate, keep the heat low and indirect, especially for milk and white chocolate which are most vulnerable. Keep stirring and watching the melting chocolate at all times. Never let chocolate go above 115 degrees F for milk and white chocolate or 120 degrees F for dark chocolate. Use a chocolate thermometer to be sure.

Whether or not you can fix seized chocolate is a hit-or-miss proposition. If it is burned, throw it out. If it is being used as an ingredient in a recipe, my recommendation would be to melt it with a few drops of vegetable oil or clarified butter (melted butter with its milk solids removed). This will sometimes soften the seized chocolate enough so it will mix with other ingredients; however, it is no longer considered pure chocolate and cannot be used for tempering (page 170).

QUESTION: *I melted 2 squares of chocolate in the top of a double boiler. When I added it to the batter, it formed small streaks that looked like unmelted or rehardened chocolate. Did I ruin my recipe?*

ANSWER: Unfortunately, you can't save the batter once chocolate has seized or formed streaks. In the future, before adding it to a recipe let the chocolate cool until close to the batter's temperature but still molten. Temper it—not to be confused with chocolate tempering (page 170)—by adding a spoonful of warm chocolate to the batter and quickly mixing to raise the temperature of the batter gradually. Mix in a couple of spoonfuls of chocolate before adding the rest to the main bowl of batter. Mix both until thoroughly combined. You shouldn't have any more problems.

You'll also temper the same way when your recipe calls for you to combine warm melted chocolate with colder eggs. Add a tablespoon or two of the chocolate to the beaten eggs and stir to combine. Repeat a couple of times until at least half of the chocolate is added. Slowly add the chocolate mixture to the main egg mixture in a steady stream while stirring. This prevents the eggs in the main bowl from scrambling and the chocolate from seizing.

QUESTION: *What if the recipe calls for melting the chocolate together with fat or some other liquid?*

ANSWER: If fat such as butter or vegetable shortening, or a liquid such as milk or cream, is to be melted or heated with chocolate, make sure you have at least 1 tablespoon for every 2 ounces of chocolate. A lower ratio can cause seizing.

TEMPERING CHOCOLATE

Tempering is done for chocolate work such as candy making, sculpting, and molding. It's a precise method, allowing chocolate to harden with specific desirable attributes. When you bite into a chocolate confection that has been properly tempered, it will have a nice crispy crunch or, if it is a thicker covering, it will snap. It will be creamy, not chalky, and won't melt easily when touched. Molded candies will release out of the molds more easily and still retain a glossy finish.

There is much confusion as to when to temper chocolate and when not. The way I remember: temper unadulterated (nothing added) chocolate when it will be a stand-alone structural component and you need it to harden properly. This is true for molded chocolates, dipped or coated centers such as truffles, and for sculpted decorations, intricate ribbons, or chocolate curls. For making simple candy bars in which chopped nuts, dried fruit, or candy are added the chocolate also needs to be tem-

QUESTION: *What kind of chocolate should I use for tempering? Why can't I temper baking chocolate squares?*

ANSWER: Chocolate for tempering comes in the form of solid blocks, bars (not candy bars), or tablets. It is available in dark (sweet, semisweet, and bittersweet), milk, and white. Couverture chocolate can also be tempered.

Baking chocolate squares don't contain the amount of cocoa butter and sugar of a chocolate you'd want to use for coating. You could temper baking chocolate, but it is usually too bitter and brittle to enjoy as a proper chocolate coating.

pered. When chocolate is an ingredient in recipes, such as Chocolate Frosted Fudge Layer Cake (page 177) or Chocolate Ganache Fudge Sauce (page 175) it need not be tempered. In those recipes, melted chocolate is blended with other ingredients. Its role is to add flavor and texture, not structure. Small confectionery work doesn't require tempering either. You can use untempered melted chocolate for dipping if you're going to eat your dessert right away and don't need it to harden.

Always temper more chocolate than you need, and certainly no less than $1\frac{1}{2}$ pounds at a time. Use a large bowl. A large quantity will hold its temper longer and is less apt to burn than a smaller quantity. You can also temper leftover melted or previously tempered and hardened chocolate, as long as it is unadulterated by other ingredients, hasn't been used for dipping fruit, such as strawberries, and hasn't previously seized or burned. But if chocolate hardens after tempering, you need to re-temper it every time you melt it for recipes that require tempering.

TEMPERING IN THREE STEPS

To assure that the temperatures are accurate, always use a mercury-gauge chocolate thermometer (page 7) and pay attention! To be perfectly safe, it's better to target for a temperature between about 2 degrees above the lower limit and 2 degrees below the upper limit. Consult the manufacturer's label for the best temperature for the chocolate you are using or follow the temperature zones (page 173) as a guideline. The temperature must be *exact*.

PREPARE THE CHOCOLATE

Chop the chocolate with a serrated knife into evenly sized ¼-inch pieces so they will melt at the same rate. You can also purchase pure chocolate discs, which can be used as is. Place two-thirds of the chocolate in the top of the double boiler; reserve one-third.

PREPARE THE DOUBLE BOILER

Half fill the bottom of a double boiler with water, making sure the top part won't touch the water below. Bring the water to a boil. Remove the bottom from the heat. Fit the top part holding two-thirds of the chocolate on the top.

STEP 1

Melt two-thirds of the chocolate to 115 degrees F (milk or white chocolate) or 120 degrees F (dark).

Sarah Says: A simple method to test temper is to apply a small quantity of chocolate to a piece of paper or the point of a knife. If the chocolate has been tempered correctly, it will harden evenly and show a good gloss within five minutes. If it is dull and cloudy, you have to start over again. Another way to test is to spread a thin layer on a scrap of parchment, wait five minutes, and then try to peel the chocolate from the paper. If you can, and it's not blotchy, you're in business. If you can't, start the tempering process again from Step 1.

Remove the top part of double boiler and dry its bottom immediately. Rapidly stir in the one-third of reserved chocolate, a few tablespoons at a time; this is called *seeding*. The added chocolate pieces are at room temperature and will cool the mixture. The molten cocoa butter does a kind of follow-the-leader, arranging itself after the fashion of the seeds, which are still tempered by the manufacturer. When the chocolate has cooled to 84 or 85 degrees F (for all types of chocolate), stop. Don't add too much at a time as it may not melt completely and the mixture will become lumpy. If it does, mix with an immersion blender, not an electric mixer.

While cooling the chocolate, heat—but do not boil—the water in the bottom of the double boiler and remove from the heat to prepare for Step 3. Make sure the bottom pan has at least an inch of water.

STEP 3

Place the top part of the double boiler back on the bottom. Warm dark chocolate to 88 to 91 degrees F (89 degrees F being its ideal working temperature), and milk or white chocolate to 86 to 87 degrees F. It happens quickly.

It is necessary to keep chocolate in temper while using. The chocolate must stay in the ideal temperature range in Step 3. If the chocolate cools to lower than 84 or 85 degrees F and is still melted, you can reheat it multiple times back to "temperate zone" of 88 to 91 degrees F (dark) or 86 or 87 degrees F (milk and white).

Never let the chocolate's temperature exceed 92 degrees F for dark chocolate or 88 degrees F for milk and white, or the stable cocoa butter crystals will start to melt and the temper will be lost.

If you've added cream, butter, or any other ingredient to the melted, pure chocolate, it can't be tempered again because it is no longer considered "pure." Instead, you can use it in recipes or for small chocolate confections.

Sarah Says: My mentor Nick Malgieri—baker, teacher, and cookbook author—taught me a simple and nearly foolproof way to keep chocolate in temper without constantly reheating it: set the bowl on a foil covered heating pad (the type used for backaches) on a low setting. Fit the heating pad into a larger bowl to cradle the smaller bowl of tempered chocolate. As you work, stir the chocolate frequently and check its temperature. You must be diligent in this; it is very easy for the tempered chocolate to overheat and go out of temper, even when warmed gently.

Most molded, enrobed, and dipped chocolates set best in a cool, dark place at approximately 59 to 64 degrees F. Afterward, if they're tempered properly, they should be fine at 68 degrees or even a few degrees above. For quick cooling, place molten chocolate in the refrigerator to set, but don't store it there, because it will bloom; that is, the cocoa butter will start to separate out from the chocolate and form a thin whitish layer on the surface.

As the tempered chocolate cools, it should become hard and shiny. If it doesn't harden properly, be more patient when tempering the next batch. (If nothing has been added to the chocolate, you can temper it over again.) The flavor will be the same even if you did not get the temper right, unless you burned it, and with practice, you will soon achieve the right chocolate "feel." Here are some temper-gone-wrong symptoms:

QUESTION: *My chocolate won't harden. I tempered it; what did I do wrong?*

ANSWER: If the chocolate remains sticky and takes over an hour to harden, the tempering process did not work. Most likely, the chocolate was over- or underheated during the 3-step tempering process, and you'll have to start again.

QUESTION: *What is ganache?*

ANSWER: You may not know this but that creamy, delicately flavored chocolate stuff found in the center of a rich truffle is called *ganache*. You may also recognize it as a shiny glaze on a cake, as a whipped filling or icing, or as a piped decoration. I use it as a base for my thick Chocolate Ganache Fudge Sauce (recipe follows). All ganache is a rich mixture of chopped chocolate and boiled heavy cream. The hot cream is poured over the chocolate, which melts after sitting for a few minutes. A smooth emulsion is formed as they are whisked together; the result should look shiny and thick. It can be poured, or cooled and whipped to thicken and become fluffy. Ganache can be also be flavored or have extra ingredients added, such as butter or corn syrup.

CHOCOLATE GANACHE
FUDGE SAUCE

❖

MAKES 1½ CUPS

This is an excellent example of how to melt delicate chocolate with boiled cream. I had been trying to create a thick chocolate sauce for some time, and a lot of times it became gritty from undissolved or crystalized sugar. One day a light bulb went on and I thought, "Why not use ganache as the base?" This rich sauce, thickened with confectioners' sugar, which dissolves faster than granulated, is delicious with ice cream. Spoon it over your favorite scoop and watch the warmed sauce slowly slide its way over the mound of ice cream, covering it perfectly in a layer of dark chocolate. Don't use bittersweet chocolate, it has less sugar and cocoa butter, causing it to be less fluid than semisweet.

INGREDIENTS

6 ounces (six 1-ounce squares) semisweet chocolate
½ cup heavy cream
2 tablespoons unsalted butter, softened; leave at room temperature until spreadable
1 tablespoon light corn syrup
2 teaspoons vanilla extract or 1 tablespoon liqueur, any flavor
1 cup confectioners' sugar, sifted; measure and then sift

1. Chop the chocolate into ¼- to ½-inch pieces and place in a medium heatproof bowl or cut 1-ounce squares in half.

2. Bring the cream to a boil in a small saucepan, or microwave in a heatproof glass measuring cup for about 1½ minutes on HIGH. Check every 15 seconds. Remove from the heat.

3. Immediately pour the cream over the chocolate. Swirl the bowl a few times so the chocolate is covered. Push down any uncovered pieces with a whisk or heatproof rubber spatula so that the chocolate is completely submerged. Let stand for 2 to 3 minutes; whisk or mix on low speed with a handheld mixer until smooth.

4. Add the butter, corn syrup, and vanilla extract and mix the ganache on low until it is incorporated. (The mixture will be hot.) Add the confectioners' sugar ¼ cup at a time and beat on medium speed until the sauce pours like corn syrup. To use

right away, cool quickly: place the bowl of ganache in a larger bowl of ice water until cooled (page 174). Don't let it get too cold.

Storage: Chocolate Ganache Fudge Sauce can be stored at room temperature in an airtight container. Before you store it, press a piece of plastic wrap on the surface so a film does not form. If you refrigerate it, bring it back to room temperature before using by setting it in a warm place in the kitchen; it takes about an hour to soften. You can also warm it by stirring it in a heatproof bowl over a pan of simmering water—don't subject it to direct heat.

CHOCOLATE FROSTED FUDGE LAYER CAKE

MAKES TWO 8 x 2-INCH ROUND LAYERS OR
ONE 7 x 11-INCH CAKE

My mother's Chocolate Frosted Fudge Layer Cake is a tried-and-true family favorite. Growing up, she baked this for us for every special occasion, and so made every occasion special. For me, this isn't just a delicious cake—it is also one which evokes countless special memories. In fact, I learned how to bake cakes from this very recipe. I think you'll find it becomes a family favorite for you, too.

INGREDIENTS

CAKE

2 cups cake flour, not self-rising; don't use all-purpose flour; spoon into dry
    measuring cup and level to top

½ teaspoon salt

1 cup (2 sticks) unsalted butter, room temperature

2 cups sugar or superfine sugar

3 ounces (three 1-ounce squares) bittersweet or semisweet chocolate, melted

½ cup buttermilk, well shaken; measure in liquid measuring cup

2 large eggs, room temperature

1 teaspoon baking soda

1 cup strong hot coffee (see Note)

ICING

4 ounces (four 1-ounce squares) bittersweet or semisweet chocolate, melted

4 cups (1 pound) confectioners' sugar

4 or more tablespoons milk

1 tablespoon vanilla extract

1. Position a rack in the center of the oven and preheat the oven to 350 degrees F. Generously grease two 8-inch pans. Or lightly grease the pans, line them with parchment paper, and then grease the paper lightly.

2. In a medium bowl, combine the flour and salt, and set aside.

3. In the bowl of a stand mixer, beat the butter with the paddle attachment on low speed until soft. Add the sugar in a steady stream. Increase the speed to medium and beat for 5 minutes until the mixture is light yellow and fluffy (page 39).

4. With the mixer on low, add the melted chocolate and the buttermilk in a steady stream at the side of the bowl. Add the eggs. Beat until smooth.

5. Turn off the mixer and remove the bowl. Add the baking soda to the cup of coffee, holding it over the center of the mixing bowl as the mixture tends to bubble up and spill over the side. Even if it doesn't react so dramatically, as long as you see a few bubbles, the soda is doing its job. Add the dissolved baking soda to the batter. Reattach the bowl to the mixer and resume mixing on low until the batter is smooth. It will be very thin. Using a soup ladle, divide the batter evenly between the two pans.

6. Bake for approximately 30 minutes or until the top feels firm and gives slightly when touched with a cupped palm. If you insert a toothpick in the middle and remove, it should have a few moist crumbs attached, but not batter. The cake will shrink a little from the side of the pan; it will also smell done. You will still hear a few air bubbles popping.

7. Remove the pans to a wire cake rack, let cool for 10 minutes, and unmold. Turn the layers upright to cool completely. While the cake cools, make the icing.

8. Prepare the icing: Beat all the icing ingredients together with an electric mixer set on medium speed or by hand with a wooden spoon. Start with the smallest quantity of milk. If the icing seems too dry to spread properly, add more milk a teaspoon at a time, and mix to incorporate before deciding whether to add more. If it seems too runny, add confectioners' sugar a tablespoon at a time, mixing to incorporate before you decide whether to add more. This icing can be made in advance and sit, covered with plastic wrap, at room temperature. The sugar in it acts as a preservative.

Assemble: page 50

Storage: page 48

Note: Use brewed coffee or 2 teaspoons instant espresso powder or instant coffee granules dissolved in 1 cup hot water. The coffee has to be hot enough to dissolve the baking soda.

QUESTION: *How can I make my cake more chocolaty?*

ANSWER: I like to use melted chocolate squares instead of cocoa powder, which has a drying effect. The rule of thumb I use is: if a chocolate cake has cocoa powder, substitute about 2 or 3 chocolate squares per recipe. You'll need to substitute a few ingredients, plus do some testing: 3 level tablespoons Dutch-process or natural cocoa LESS 1 tablespoon oil or melted shortening or butter equals 1 square of unsweetened baking chocolate.

10

YEAST BREADS

Why won't my bread rise? . . .
and other secrets of the (almost)
lost art of bread making.

WHEN I WAS A LITTLE GIRL, my mother didn't believe that commercially prepared bread was adequate; she thought it was long on chemicals and short on nutrition. So we made our own every week. For me, then, it is not just the final bread product that I relish; it is also the process of making a fragrant bread loaf from a bowlful of basic ingredients. If you want this process to become fulfilling for you, it will help to understand the basic way yeast bread is made.

If you haven't experienced the wonderful aroma of bread baking in the oven, and eating some slathered in melting butter as soon as it's cool enough to handle, you're missing something. Fragrant homemade bread is a triumphant accomplishment for bakers of all ages. I know it frightens many home bakers to think of making their own yeast bread. I will try to minimize your fears and show you both the science and art of bread making so you too can turn out beautiful and flavorful loaves.

Yeast breads that are kneaded include two major types: pan or homemade yeast breads, and sourdough or sponge starter breads. There are also old dough and salt-rising methods, and yeast batter breads. The big difference between pan and starter breads is the source of the yeast and how it's fermented.

TYPES OF YEAST BREAD

PAN BREADS

I call these homemade yeast breads. They are smooth looking loaves typically with a fine, even grain (air holes) on the inside. If you look closely at a piece of sandwich bread, you can see a honeycomb texture in it where hundreds of tiny air bubbles formed and then burst. This type includes a wide variety of breads: white, whole-wheat, dinner rolls, yeasted coffee cakes, and many of the sweet holiday breads. The category also includes pizza crusts, bagels, pretzels, and some pancakes and waffles.

Pan bread recipes are mixed using the "Straight Dough Method." It is a single-step mixing process in which all of the ingredients are placed into the same mixing bowl. Bread machine breads also fall into this category. Homemade yeast bread dough takes three to four hours (less with instant yeast) for mixing, kneading, two risings, and one shaping. Some breads are now made by the "Quick Mix Method" in which a newer strain of instant yeast is blended with the flour, then mixed and kneaded with one resting period and one rise instead of two.

SOURDOUGH OR SPONGE STARTER BREADS

Sponge Method (page 205) includes breads with large, irregularly shaped air holes and crusty crusts. They are also called European-style, ethnic, rustic, or artisan breads. This type includes sourdough bread, French baguettes, ciabatta, Italian bread, Pugliese, and lots, lots more. Other recipes that use yeast from a starter include sourdough pancakes, biscuits, waffles, and some cakes.

Sourdough starter breads are leavened by a *pre-ferment,* a culture of wild yeast and bacteria that feed in a batter made of flour and water which you make in your kitchen. Sponge starters also contain packaged yeast, which is fermented before being added to the bread's ingredients. This is called the "Indirect Method." The dough then goes through bread making steps tailored to the specific type being made.

In past times, a sourdough starter was the primary way yeast was cultivated and preserved from one baking day to the next. Only a piece of it is necessary to leaven bread. California gold rush miners in the San Francisco area discovered that they could keep sourdough starters alive for years to bake and cook with while traveling from gold strike to gold strike. I personally know someone who has had her prized starter for 150 years, passed down to her from her grandmother.

NO-KNEAD YEAST BATTER BREADS

This type includes Amish friendship bread and Sally Lunn, which are among the easiest breads to make. Amish friendship bread is made from a sponge that is kept alive and often handed down from generation to generation—I have heard of one that's over 150 years old. They require no kneading and have the shortest fermentation time of all the yeasted breads. You can generally have one on the table in under two hours. They are not discussed here.

THE ALCHEMY OF YEAST BREAD

The ingredients and fermentation set the tone for the entire bread making experience.

INGREDIENTS

The magic of bread is that the ingredients interact in such a complex way; there are lots of different choices you can make that affect the final outcome. To make a loaf of bread, essentially all you need is flour, liquid, and yeast—and don't forget the salt! But you can add other ingredients as well, to make all sorts of unique and fragrant breads and to improve the taste and texture of the finished product.

WHEAT FLOUR

Wheat flour is the predominant ingredient in bread, by weight. Bread, whole-wheat, and all-purpose flour are ideal types because their ample gluten-forming proteins when developed withstand the strong leavening power of yeast, and can stretch yet hold its shape. In a bread machine, bread and whole-wheat flour can withstand the rigors of mechanical processing. You can generally substitute unbleached all-purpose flour for bread flour, one for one, but you'll get different qualities.

The flour's protein percentage less than its starch content affects the texture of the bread. Increased protein increases the potential loaf volume but too much protein that is developed into gluten causes low volume. Using all bread flour makes a chewier loaf because of its high gluten content. All whole-wheat flour can make for very dense, heavy, and dry bread. I recommend using one-half the whole-wheat flour and one-half all-purpose flour for lighter and more flavorful results. Whole grain bread can be dry and flavorless.

LIQUID

Liquid may be tap water, milk, buttermilk, potato water, and the water content in butter and eggs.

> QUESTION: *When dissolving the yeast in milk, it always clumps. What should I do?*
>
> ANSWER: Dehydrated yeast typically clumps when dissolved in milk. To solve this, first dissolve the yeast in $\frac{1}{4}$ cup of 110 to 115 degree F water. Then add the milk, warmed to the same temperature, less the amount of water used to dissolve the yeast.

YEAST

Yeast is the heart of bread making. There are basically two types of yeast: packaged yeast—also known as baker's yeast—and sourdough. Before packaged yeast was available, bakers developed a leavener called a sourdough from a fermented mixture of water and flour; later, they added packaged yeast for a sponge (page 205).

You can't mention yeast without discussing fermentation. One of the secrets to making great bread lies in fermentation, which all yeast goes through. Most of us are familiar with yeast as a leavening agent for bread; developing flavor and texture are another of its functions.

SALT

Salt is a critical bread ingredient. You can't do without it, so don't be tempted to leave it out or reduce it. Salt in a yeast bread recipe moderates (slows) the action of yeast and allows it to produce carbon dioxide (CO_2) at a reasonable rate, resulting in a better texture. It also enhances flavor. However, if salt comes into direct contact with the dissolved yeast, it will kill it, so be careful to mix the salt in with the second or third cup of dry ingredients.

SWEETENERS

Sugar plays a role in fermentation, as well as adding flavor and rich brown color to bread's crust. Table sugar is commonly used, but brown sugar, honey, molasses, jams, and dried or fresh fruits may also be used. Fruit juices also add significant amounts of sugar. Don't use sugar-free sweeteners, unless the recipe is written specifically to include them. Sugar-free sweeteners contain chemicals that can damage or kill the yeast.

OTHER INGREDIENTS

To change the character of your bread, you can add other ingredients to the dough. Whole eggs and egg yolks make a richer dough and add color; whites make a drier dough. Milk makes softer and cakier dough with a more tender crumb. Fats like extra virgin olive oil and butter result in a tender and moist texture. Fats increase the keeping qualities of a bread loaf, preventing it from drying out too quickly. However, don't use light or tub margarines; if their first ingredient is water they will not work. Don't substitute oil for butter or shortening unless the recipe permits it.

FRUITS AND NUTS

Seeds, nuts, dried fruits, herbs, spices, cheese, and bran are just a few of the many ingredients you can use to create unique and flavorful breads. Remember they slow down fermentation so follow the recipe for how much to add. Breads laden with extras don't usually double in size during rising. It is best to add them right after the dough is deflated from its first rise and before shaping the dough. Knead them in a few times until evenly distributed. If using dried fruit in a yeast bread recipe, it is best to soak it in hot water and then drain it. Otherwise, it absorbs a lot of water from the bread's ingredients, resulting in a dry loaf.

DOUGH ENHANCERS

Dough enhancers can improve the texture, taste, and crust of the bread, but they aren't necessary. There are several:

- **Vital wheat gluten** is gluten added to a recipe to give extra rise and consistency; it contains a high amount of gluten-forming proteins (40 to 80 percent per cup). I use it in heavier breads that rise slowly, such as oat, whole grain, and ones loaded with sugar, dried fruit, and nuts. Your loaves should rise higher and have better volume. Always follow package instructions;
- **Ascorbic acid** creates an acidic environment and also acts as a preservative to deter mold and bacterial growth. You can use Fruit Fresh (found in the canning aisle of the supermarket) or a crushed or powdered vitamin C tablet, but measure accordingly. Use $\frac{1}{8}$ teaspoon per recipe;
- **Dough relaxer** is a combination of all-natural gluten relaxing ingredients;
- **Lecithin** helps keep bread fresh longer and makes lighter bread. It also helps make the bread moister and acts as a mild preservative;
- **Non-diastatic malt** is a super food source for the yeast which gives the bread better structure and makes the bread softer and more tender.

FERMENTATION

The secret to making great bread lies in the fermentation of the yeast, one of the most critical steps. What is it and how does it work? Yeast as the leavener in bread recipes is supplemented with steam and expanding air from oven heat. Before any dough can yield a light, aerated loaf of bread, it must be fermented for a certain amount of time depending on the type of yeast used. A prerequisite to fermentation is a well mixed and fully hydrated dough.

All yeast goes through the same process, whether packaged or cultivated in a starter. Yeast's magic starts to happen the minute you rehydrate baker's yeast (*Saccharomyces cerevisiae*) and mix it with flour and/or glucose and to a lesser extent fructose, such as honey, or when wild yeast and bacteria take hold in a starter. Yeast is a living organism that needs food, moisture, warmth, and air to survive, ferment, and grow.

During fermentation, yeast breaks down flour's hydrated starches into simple sugars, glucose and fructose, so it can feed and stay alive. There is a small amount of simple sugar present in flour due mainly to damage during the milling process. Yeast uses some of the sugar; the rest contributes to the flavor and color of the bread. As the yeast feeds, it gives off carbon dioxide (CO_2) bubbles and alcohol and, in the case of sourdough starter breads, another gas-producing microorganism, wild *Lactobacillus*. The gas is trapped eventually in the elastic gluten structure of the dough, causing the bread to rise.

All fermentation stops when the yeast is subjected to a temperature of 140 degrees F and it begins to die. Keep in mind that fermentation is subject to many other influences such as the character of the flour, yeast level, temperature, and the balance of the recipe's ingredients.

The intensity of flavor and texture depend on the type of yeast and how long it is cultivated and fermented, and the other ingredients. Homemade yeast breads are made with ingredients that have not been previously fermented. As a result, they tend to have soft crusts with fluffy insides and evenly spaced air pockets.

Starter breads are leavened with a pre-ferment (page 205) that takes minutes, hours, weeks, or months to cultivate and ferment before being added to the bread's other ingredients. Because of the added boost from packaged yeast, a sponge starter ferments much faster and more reliably than a sourdough. The resulting bread has a mild-tasting tangy or wheaty flavor, a finer air-pocket (cell) structure, and a less crusty crust than a sourdough. Sourdough's fermentation is the longest, measured in days, weeks,

Sarah Says: A prerequisite to fermentation is a well mixed and fully hydrated dough.

Sarah Says: Precise temperatures are essential when working with yeast. Always measure with an instant read thermometer. Temperatures for yeast can vary by manufacturer, so always read label instructions first.

Essential temperatures are:

- Dissolving active dry and cake yeast: Liquids used to dissolve yeast should be in the range of 100 to 110 degrees F. If the temperature is below 90 degrees F, the yeast will be inhibited and the loaf won't rise to its fullest, if at all: if too high (above 115 degrees F), the yeast begins to die, also affecting the rise in your loaf.
- Dissolving cake or fresh yeast: It can be crumbled in the dry ingredients or softened in 80 to 90 degree F water.
- Hydrating instant yeast, combined with flour and other dry ingredients: liquid used to combine with dry ingredients should be in the range of 120 to 130 degrees F.
- Rising place (fermentation): about 75 to 85 degrees F.
- Bread is done baking: 190 to 210 degrees F.

and beyond. This results in bread with more taste and "sourness" or "wheatiness," a crustier crust, and a unique crumb with irregular air holes.

Yeast is sensitive to temperature. Below 50 degrees F it goes into a state of suspension, allowing dough to be left overnight in a cool area, such as a refrigerator; fermentation slows. This is called a cool rise. It results in less carbon dioxide gas, and more alcohol, and acids, and a sourer flavor. A cool rise works best for a sourdough starter and high-sugar doughs. If you are interrupted during the bread making process and need a place to park the dough, the refrigerator is fine. If you freeze dough, the yeast goes into a state of suspension, which allows the dough to be kept there for long periods of time without fermentation. Freezing a starter is a hit or miss proposition, especially a sourdough.

Fermentation can be quickened by warm temperatures; usually 75 to 85 degrees F is best. Although needing warmth, yeast can be killed at temperatures around 115 to 120 degrees F.

YEAST BREAD: STEP-BY-STEP WITH RECIPES AND LOTS OF TIPS

Baking bread, pizza, rolls, and anything else with yeasted dough at home is a wonderful experience, which I recommend you try at least once.

The goals in mixing are to uniformly incorporate the ingredients, hydrate the flour, develop the gluten, and start the fermentation process, later ended during baking. Homemade pan breads rely more on their ingredients than on fermentation for their flavor and texture, as do starter breads.

You can take any recipe and make it foolproof. Just dissolve the yeast first and add the flour after.

STEP 1: PREPARE THE YEAST

The first step is to rehydrate the yeast. Dissolving the yeast properly is essential to a successful yeast bread recipe. The liquid must be at exact temperatures. If not specified, follow these instructions below.

ACTIVE DRY AND FRESH CAKE YEASTS

These yeasts are dissolved and activated in a liquid, usually water, but can be done in milk, although yeast tends to clump. (Cake yeast can also be crumbled into the dry ingredients, instead.)

1. Warm the mixing bowl by filling it with warm (not hot) tap water, then pouring it out. Fill the bowl with the water called for in the recipe, at 100 to 110 degrees F unless otherwise indicated by the manufacturer. If you don't have a thermometer, drop water on the inside of your wrist; it should feel "blood warm." This is clearly not as accurate.
2. Sprinkle active dry or crumble cake yeast over the surface of the water. After 2 or 3 minutes, the yeast will have absorbed enough liquid. Whisk until dissolved. If the yeast clumps, let it sit another minute or so, then whisk again. Cake yeast will soften and break apart. The mixture will look cloudy, you should start to smell a yeasty odor and see some bubbles in a few minutes.

How to Dissolve Yeast in Milk

Yeast really clumps when added to warm milk. If the recipe calls for milk only, not in combination with water, for an easier time first place the yeast in $\frac{1}{4}$ cup of water at 100 to 110 degrees F and let it sit a few minutes until it dissolves. Then add the milk, minus $\frac{1}{4}$ cup, warmed to the same temperature.

How to Add Melted Butter, Scalded Milk, and Other Liquids to the Yeast

Some recipes call for adding a mixture of milk and melted butter directly to the re-hydrated yeast. Make sure you first cool the liquid to tepid (100 to 105 degrees F) or close to body temperature before adding it to the recipe. (If the mixture has cooled, the melted butter may clump; it is ok, just leave as is.)

Instant Active Dry Yeast or Bread Machine Yeast

Sprinkle instant active dry yeast evenly over the flour and other dry ingredients (including salt) and blend. Add water, milk, melted butter, and other liquid ingredients, heated to very warm (120 to 130 degrees F or whatever the manufacturer suggests). Stir into dry ingredients. You then simply mix the dough, let it rest for 10 minutes—instead of the first rise—shape it into loaves and let it rise before baking. But keep in mind that according to some bakers, with a fast rise the flavor of the bread cannot develop and the texture may suffer (I agree).

STEP 2: MY FOOLPROOF DOUGH-MIXING METHOD

I add the flour to the dissolved yeast, rather than the other way around, until the dough is tacky. This way I have more control over the process and can stop adding flour when the dough is just right. You must learn to work with a slacker (tacky) dough. It is the moisture content in the dough that turns to steam to give it the oven rise, creating an open, light, and airy texture and crumb. The gluten strands in the dough will also stretch and shape more easily, creating a well-formed loaf.

First combine the dissolved yeast, milk, eggs, melted butter, other liquid ingredients, and sugar. Make sure liquid ingredients are between 100 and 105 degrees F so as not to inhibit or kill the yeast. Never add cold water or milk to the dissolved yeast, otherwise you'll retard its activity. Too hot, and you kill it. Add the flour and salt as indicated in the recipe. Mix until the dough is tacky but no longer sticking to your hands and work surface. Dough should be smooth and cohesive. When properly mixed, you can hear a slight sticky sound in the bowl of a stand mixer when mixing. If you have straggling dough pieces on the sides or in the bottom of the bowl, it usu-

QUESTION: *I'm having trouble with my bread recipe. It says to use 5 cups of flour and 1 cup water. Sometimes I need more or less flour or water in the recipe. I double checked my measurements. What am I doing wrong?*

ANSWER: You're not doing anything wrong. The amount of flour or liquid used in a bread recipe is always variable with baking recipes that call for wheat flour. It has to do with how much the flour will absorb on a given day.

Higher-protein flour absorbs more water, faster, than lower protein flour. For example, a dough made with 2 cups of high-protein flour will absorb 1 cup of water to form a soft, sticky dough. It takes $2\frac{1}{2}$ cups low-protein flour to get the same consistency. Protein levels change depending upon the brand of flour and where and when the wheat was grown. Bakers have blamed the difference in absorption on humidity which only makes a minute difference. This means that flour's protein level directly affects the ratio of wet ingredients to dry, which is mainly noticed in bread recipes where flour is the greatest percentage by weight.

ally means your dough is a tad dry and needs to be corrected. Properly tacky dough will clean the bowl by picking up every last scrap in the bowl during mixing. It shouldn't have small lumps of flour on its surface and shouldn't be shaggy, but rather smooth (whole wheat will be smooth with flecks of bran). The stickier the dough, the wider the bread's crumb (the inside of the bread), the drier and denser the dough, the more dry and compact the crumb will be.

After the dough has been mixed, if it's too dry or wet keep it in the mixing bowl, and correct it with a teaspoon of water or pinches of flour at a time. You'll be surprised at how far a little of each goes. Mix thoroughly before deciding to add more. Don't go back and forth between too wet and too dry because you'll overmix and create excess gluten.

Once the dough is out of the mixer, you can correct the dough the same way when kneading. If your dough is on the dry side of tacky, leave it alone; don't try to make it perfect. During kneading the ingredients are incorporated better and the gluten becomes more hydrated, sometimes correcting the problem.

Sarah Says: Mixing can be done in a very large bowl with a wooden spoon and a strong arm, with an electric stand mixer (a handheld mixer does not have enough power), a food processor, or a bread machine.

STEP 3: KNEADING

Kneading is the process of working the dough with a pushing, folding, and turning technique. It serves many important purposes in developing texture, flavor, and rise. Kneading

- creates air bubbles that expand from the yeast's fermentation and heat;
- develops gluten that is elastic and can stretch fully from the yeast's fermentation;
- activates the yeast by making more food available by redistributing it;
- equalizes the temperature throughout the dough so it can rise evenly;
- gets rid of excess carbon dioxide gas so it won't retard the yeast;
- introduces oxygen, which has a stimulating effect on the yeast.

Underkneading creates dough that won't hold its shape, is dense, and cracks when baked. Overkneading creates too much gluten, causing dry and tough bread that doesn't rise as high as it should.

Sarah Says: Before I decide whether to correct the dough, I knead it for a few turns. Often it corrects itself. If not, I do.

A nonstick Silpat baking mat, a granite or marble slab, a wooden cutting board, or even a formica countertop makes a great kneading surface. Flour is typically called for to prepare the work surface, so the dough won't stick. If the dough is mixed properly and tacky, you really don't need to add any flour during the kneading process. However, if your dough is excessively sticky or wet, prepare the kneading surface by lightly flouring it with pinches of flour instead of handfuls.

To Knead by Hand, "Push, Fold, and Turn"

Kneading should take about 8 to 10 minutes to complete. I'm a big fan of hand kneading. It dawned on me one day to use a kitchen timer to help me keep track of the time; afterwards, I realized that I hadn't been doing it long enough in my previous recipes. Ever since, my loaves rise even higher and have a creamier texture! The right amount of kneading is important, but once you start overdoing it, it is easy to overwork the dough.

1. Knead on a clean, smooth surface, at a comfortable height. Avoid sprinkling flour on the kneading surface. Start with the dough in a rough ball shape.
2. Use the heels of your hands to push the dough away. Don't tear or pull on the dough. You want to stretch the gluten strands gently rather than forcing

them to lengthen. If you do, they'll eventually snap right back into place and your bread won't rise as high or will shrink when baked.

3. Pick up the edge furthest away from you and fold it toward you.

4. Give the dough a quarter-turn.

5. Vigorously repeat the "push, fold, and turn" steps.

6. Knead the dough for 5 to 7 minutes, then review whether you have kneaded the dough long enough to make it silky and smooth. The Windowpane Kneading Test (see below) will help you decide. If you need more time, 8 to 10 minutes total is best.

7. After kneading, the dough should be smooth (whole wheat will be smooth with flecks of bran) and "feel like a baby's bottom"—silky, smooth, and soft—without small lumps of flour on its surface or surface tearing that indicates it's too dry. If it is, flatten the dough with your fingertips into a thick, rough disk. Sprinkle 1 teaspoon of water all over the surface. Fold the dough like a book and then fold again into a rough square shape. Knead the dough until you get the right consistency or determine that you need to add more.

To Knead in an Electric Mixer

Knead the dough on low speed with the dough hook for 5 minutes or until the dough is smooth and elastic as well as tacky. You should not have any dough sticking to the bowl, especially at the bottom center of the bowl. Knead a bit more on a countertop without flour to make it smooth.

To Knead in a Food Processor

Pulse for 45 seconds after the dough forms a ball around the steel blade; longer processing will cause too much gluten to form. Remove the dough, feel the moisture in it, and knead a bit more on a countertop without flour to make it smooth. Or use the food processor to make the dough come together, but finish it with a good hand kneading, which is my recommendation.

To Knead in a Bread Machine

Many people use their bread machine to mix and knead the dough. Follow the manufacturer's instructions.

When to Stop: Windowpane Kneading Test

When you have been kneading for 5 to 7 minutes by hand or for the full time with a stand mixer or with a food processor and your dough is smooth, perform this test to see if you should continue for the full 8 to 10 minutes or for just a few more seconds or minutes.

1. Pinch off a piece of dough.
2. Using both hands, grasp opposite sides of the dough with your fingertips.
3. Slowly pull your hands an inch or two apart and stretch the dough in between.
4. The dough should look like a window, also known as a gluten window, with a thin membrane in the center. Evaluate the results:

   - If the dough window stretches without breaking, STOP KNEADING.
   - If the dough window stretches and then tears, KNEAD FOR 1 MINUTE MORE.
   - If the dough window falls apart before it makes a windowpane, KNEAD FOR 2 MINUTES MORE.
   - If the dough won't stretch easily and tears right away, KEEP KNEADING.

Whole-wheat or fruit-and-nut studded breads are hard to test because the dough window tears away from the pieces. In that case, knead the dough for the full 8 to 10 minutes.

STEP 4: FIRST RISING (FERMENTATION)

If you've used instant active dry yeast, simply let the dough rest for 10 minutes after kneading. It isn't required to go through a formal first rising.

During rising, you'll witness a magical transformation. On the outside, you'll see the dough rising, expanding like a balloon. But on the inside, where it is invisible to the eye, lots of things are happening, too.

Recipes typically instruct you to "place dough in a warm place until doubled in size." Because these instructions are vague, bakers have problems with this step. Dough rests, rises, and ferments best with warmth (about 75 to 85 degrees F), and humidity. The ball of dough must be smooth and rounded. It must be covered and sit in a warm, draft-free place to rise. Rising time is also influenced by the amount of kneading (if too little or too much, the dough won't rise well).

It normally takes 1 to $1\frac{1}{2}$ hours for the yeast to accumulate a volume of carbon dioxide gas strong enough to stretch the gluten strands that hold it in and to make the dough rise. It should typically double in volume (size), but heavy breads with lots of sugar, whole-wheat flour, and add-ins won't grow so dramatically. That doesn't mean you've done anything wrong; it is just the ingredients working together in the right way. You can hold the dough in fermentation for only so long; there are a number of chemicals naturally present in dough that will eventually break down the gluten.

When the dough is formed, turn the ball around in a large, well greased bowl (vegetable oil works best) until it is greased on all sides. Place the rounded dough seam-side down with the smooth top up. I prefer a deep bowl, rather than a wide one. You can more easily see if the dough has risen to double its volume. My KitchenAid 4.5-quart mixing bowl is perfect. Cover the bowl tightly with plastic wrap; don't use aluminum foil. The plastic wrap stretches when the dough rises and retains moisture better. If the dough isn't correctly covered during rising, it will develop a dry sur-

tion of the time needed to raise dough for a loaf of bread (provided you don't open the door too often).

3. Check on the rise and the warmth in the microwave after 35 minutes by opening the door a crack. If the atmosphere isn't noticeably warm or there is no longer steam rising from the water, remove the dough and temporarily put it in a warm place while you microwave the water again. Replenish the water before you do. Return the dough to the microwave and close the door.

face that slows or stops the rising, and will give the bread a hard crust that will not brown correctly and may even separate from the rest of the bread when baked.

The microwave proofer (page 193) is my rising place of choice because it works well every time. Another good option is the lower shelf of an unlit oven. Place a large, shallow pan inside and pour in boiling water. Position the covered bowl of dough on the shelf above, centered over the pan; close the oven door. Remember not

QUESTION: *My bread loaves wouldn't rise. Why?*

ANSWER: Won't rise? Probably a problem with the yeast:

- Yeast is expired. To test, page 20;
- Water or liquid was too hot when proofing the yeast and it killed the yeast. Tips, pages 187.

QUESTION: *My dough is rising slowly. Can you tell me why?*

ANSWER: There are a number of possible causes:

- Rising place is too cold. Try my microwave proofer, page 193;
- Dough has been overworked and forced during shaping. How to shape dough, page 196;
- Used too much flour, or all whole-wheat flour. All about flour, page 181;
- Too many add-ins such as dried fruit, whole grains, sugar, eggs, etc. Tips, page 184;
- Under- or overkneaded. Solutions, page 190;
- Problems with sourdough or sponge starter. All about, page 205.

QUESTION: *How can I tell when my dough has risen enough?*

ANSWER: To determine if your dough has doubled in size or has sufficiently risen, press the tips of two fingers lightly and quickly about $\frac{1}{2}$ inch into the dough. If the impression you made stays, the dough is ready. If the indent disappears—which sometimes takes as long as 5 minutes—the yeast still has some energy left and needs a little more time; cover and let it rise longer.

QUESTION: *I checked on my rising dough and it looks fallen, with a flat, wrinkled top. What do I do now?*

ANSWER: It sounds like your dough has over-risen. This can cause a dense and sour tasting loaf with a flat top, the opposite of what you intended. To fix over-risen dough: go through a complete kneading of 8 to 10 minutes and let it rise again. Whether you can fix the dough depends on how over-risen it was; only the dough knows for sure. If the dough collapses during baking, there is nothing that can be done to save the loaf because the gluten strands have been overstretched or broken.

to turn on the oven until the risen dough is taken out. You can also keep the covered dough in the laundry room while doing the wash, or any other place where there is a constant supply of warmth and moisture.

STEP 5: PUNCHING DOWN (DEGASSING) DOUGH

Punching down the dough after it has doubled in size gives it a fresh start. It is deflated to expel some of the carbon dioxide—too much chokes the yeast—to redistribute the yeast cells more evenly throughout the dough for a new source of food, and to equalize the temperature throughout so that when shaped, the dough can rise evenly. It allows the gluten to relax, making the dough easier to shape in the next step. Punching down also divides the air pockets in the dough, making them smaller and more numerous, which ultimately contributes to the fine texture of the bread.

1. When the dough has doubled in size, gently take off the plastic wrap. Try not to pull on the dough if it gets stuck to the underside of the wrap; gently separate the two.

2. Deflate the dough with a couple of pushes with your fist straight down through the dough. Don't beat the dough. You will hear a "fisss" as the carbon dioxide is released and the dough deflates. Don't tear or pull on the dough while doing so, or you will tear the gluten strands and release too much of the air, carbon dioxide, and alcohol needed for oven rise and flavor.
3. After deflating the dough, tip the bowl sideways so it falls out onto the clean countertop. The dough will have enough oil on it so it won't stick. Sometimes you have to use your fingertips to ease the dough out, as it may be sticky.

STEP 6: SHAPING, PANNING, AND FINISHING TOUCHES

Shaping is about more than appearance. It forms the dough for optimal rise and containment. Make sure you use the pan size specified in the recipe; if too small the bread will rise over the sides; if too large the bread won't seem to have risen very much.

SHAPING A BREAD LOAF

The goal is to shape the dough without popping the air bubbles, losing carbon dioxide, or tearing the gluten strands in it. Gently stretch the dough with your fingertips away from you in an opposing motion only enough to shape the dough into a rough rectangle about five to six inches wide and six to eight inches long. Starting on one of the short sides, tightly roll the length of the dough. With each rotation, pinch the crease by pressing down with both thumbs or the heel of your hand along the seam to seal. The roll will eventually spread to eight or nine inches, perfect for a standard-size bread pan.

PANNING A LOAF

After shaping, place the dough seam-side down in a well-greased pan. For an even rise, the short edges should touch the ends of the pan, but not necessarily the sides. The dough should be centered between the long sides of the pan. If the pan is the proper size, the dough should fill it one-half to three-quarters full and rise accordingly.

Sarah Says: Pan bread loaves are typically baked in pans—hence their name—usually in a bread loaf pan, but includes pans of all sorts of shape and size. There are two standard loaf pan sizes: 9- by 5- by 3-inches and 8- by 4- by 2-inches. I prefer to use heavy, shiny pans for a lighter crust. Artisan breads are usually more free-form and baked in special pans, on a baking sheet, or directly on a baking stone.

> QUESTION: *My rolls are always unequal in size. Do you have any tips so they look more uniform?*
>
> ANSWER: If dough has to be divided in two or more equal pieces, get out your scale. Weigh the dough and get the total. Divide the dough by the number of servings to get what each piece should weigh. Portion the dough by cutting straight down with a sharp knife or bench scraper. Don't use a sawing motion and don't pull it apart; you want to avoid tearing the gluten strands. Weigh each portion to double-check. Avoid having to cut or add pieces to come to the right weight of each piece because you create a weak spot in the dough everytime you do.

SHAPING ROLLS

Divide the dough in half, then proceed.

- **Round:** With each piece of dough, while lightly pressing down, form a sphere by rotating the palm of your hand over the top. Pinch the creases on the underside to close.
- **Crescents:** Roll each half into a 14-inch circle. Cut each into 12 pie wedges. Roll up the wedges tightly from the wide end, pinch them closed, and curve the ends slightly to form crescents. Place with the points down on a baking sheet.
- **Knots:** Divide each half into 12 equal pieces; roll each into 5- to 6-inch snakes. Tie once.

STEP 7: SECOND RISE OR PROOFING

The second rise is an extension of fermentation and is the final step before baking. It is shorter than the first rising, usually only about 45 minutes for a bread loaf, because the yeast cells are now highly active. Among professional chefs, fermentation is referred to as *primary fermentation,* while the second one is called *proofing.* You'll also hear proofing used to refer to the process of testing the yeast to see if it is still active, which is different (page 20). I use my microwave proofer (page 193), but any place where the temperature is between 75 and 85 degrees F and there's humidity is ideal.

Some loaves need to double in size after shaping, or the recipe may indicate that rising is done when the middle of the dough reaches the rim of the pan. As with the first rising, you can check if the dough has risen enough by pressing the tip of your moistened index finger lightly and quickly about ¼ inch into the side of the dough.

QUESTION: *I want to make my cinnamon rolls and bread dough tonight and then bake them in the morning. Is it possible?*

ANSWER: If you need to interrupt the bread making process at almost any stage, you can park your homemade yeast breads in the refrigerator for a few hours or overnight, or freeze them. Freezing puts the yeast in a state of suspension, and refrigeration slows down its fermentation. Dough will last approximately three days in the refrigerator, although it is best to use it within forty-eight hours. It can be frozen for about one month.

When you store dough in the refrigerator, place it in the baking pan and cover it with an inverted pan or bowl. If you have a wire cake rack that stands three inches tall, place it over the dough as a frame; wrap plastic film around the pan and frame. Place the covered pan in the coldest part of your fridge. Note that instant yeast ("rapid rise") does not work well in a cool rise; it ferments too quickly. So that it won't "overproof" and spill over its container or collapse you need to punch the dough down every twelve to twenty-four hours once it has been placed in the refrigerator.

When you need it, take the dough out and let it sit at room temperature, still covered, until it completes its rise. It may take longer because the dough is still cold.

My favorite times to freeze dough are after kneading or after shaping. You can also freeze just-mixed dough. Move the dough directly from the freezer to room temperature; covered and left in a warm place, it will thaw and rise at the same time.

Freeze shaped loaves without wrapping them until they are hard; then wrap them. This way you won't mar the shape. Individual shapes such as rolls will stick together if they are frozen in one bag. Instead, place them on a cookie sheet and freeze them for one hour or until hardened. Once hardened they can be placed in one airtight bag without sticking and returned to the freezer.

If the impression stays, the dough is doubled and ready to bake. Don't let the loaf over-rise; it is better to err on the side of caution. The indent will fill during baking. A final rise called "oven spring" will take place in the hot oven, so don't allow shaped loaves to over-rise before baking or they will fail to rise as they should in the oven and may even collapse.

Sarah Says: When proofing rolls, I can't fit a sheet pan in my microwave proofer, so I place the dough on a piece of parchment paper which I can slide in and out of the pan. (You can bake the rolls right on the parchment supported by a baking sheet.)

STEP 8: BAKING

Before preheating, position one oven shelf on the rung below the middle one and another on the very bottom rung. Remove the other higher shelves so the bread has room to rise, sometimes 3 inches above the pan sides. I place a cookie sheet on the shelf on the bottom rung, near the heat source, to deflect the heat from the bottom of the loaf. This prevents the sides and bottom of the bread from becoming dark and hardened.

Turn on the oven to preheat; the dough is left to rise before the shaped dough has doubled in size and passed the rising test (page 197). Unless the recipe tells you otherwise, always preheat your oven for 30 to 40 minutes to the recommended temperature before placing the loaves in for baking—the longer the better. If baking a starter bread such as sourdough on a baking stone, preheat your oven and the stone for at least 45 minutes.

If you have more than 2 loaves in the oven, place them on the same shelf with at least 1 inch between them, and between them and the oven walls.

Most breads are baked at 375 to 400 degrees F. Recipes generally give a range for baking time (such as 45 to 55 minutes). The type and size of the oven, its accuracy, the material of the baking pan, and many other factors can affect how long it takes for bread to be done. Check your loaves about 10 minutes before the recipe says they should be done.

If your bread is browning unevenly, rotate the pan once the bread's structure is set, otherwise keep the oven door shut. If the loaf is browning excessively, make an aluminum foil "tent" and rest it over the top of the bread. Don't remove the loaf to do so.

Loaf appearance can be deceiving; the bread may look nicely browned on the outside and sound hollow when tapped—two traditional tests for doneness—but still not be done on the inside. To be sure, use the ever reliable instant read thermometer. Remove the loaf from the oven and unmold it. Insert the thermometer through the bottom of the loaf to its middle to measure the bread's internal temperature; if it's between 190 and 210 degrees F, it is done. If not, place the loaf back in the pan and return it to the oven. Check it again in 5 to 7 minutes.

STEP 9: COOLING

Take the finished bread out of the oven and let it sit in the pan for 10 minutes on a wire cake rack. If necessary, release the bread from the sides of the pan by running a thin knife between it and the sides of the pan.

Unmold by turning the loaf pan on its side; the bread should fall out. Cool freshly baked loaves on their sides on wire racks, so air can circulate—the bottom of the loaf is the hottest part. Make sure there is plenty of room between the loaves; I use one wire cake rack per loaf of bread. My wire cake racks are elevated 3 inches from the countertop to prevent condensation from forming between the countertop and the bread, lest the side get soggy. To elevate yours, place an upside-down glass under each corner of the rack.

The bread is actually still baking, so resist the temptation to cut into the loaf immediately. If you do, the bread will fall apart or mush together. Also, you won't experience its full flavor until the bread has cooled an hour or two or even more. I find my loaves always taste best the next day if there's anything left. How do I know? Let's just say I got impatient waiting for the loaf to cool for a taste!

STEP 10: STORING

Wait until the bread cools completely before wrapping the loaf in plastic wrap or foil and storing it in an airtight plastic bag or in a bread box. Bread is best stored at room temperature in a cool, dry place for 2 to 3 days (some starter breads last less, some longer).

Don't store it in the refrigerator because that dries out the bread and hastens staling; homemade bread stales quickly. However, after 1 or 2 days, store the bread in the freezer, where it keeps fresh for 2 to 3 months. Pre-slice it, if you want to, so you can take out one or two slices at a time. Use a sharp serrated knife or an electric knife.

CLASSIC WHITE SANDWICH BREAD

MAKES ONE 9 X 5 X 3-INCH LOAF, OR
TWO 8 X 4 X 2-INCHES LOAVES, OR 24 ROLLS

This is my favorite loaf to make as an everyday loaf, especially for the kids' school sandwiches. The bread slices beautifully because of the eggs, milk, and butter, and it is great for toast.

INGREDIENTS
Vegetable oil cooking spray
¾ *cup warm water, 100 to 110 degrees F; measured with an instant read thermometer*
4½ *teaspoons active dry yeast*
1 cup milk, 100 to 110 degrees F
½ *cup (1 stick) unsalted butter, melted and cooled*
½ *cup sugar*
6 cups unbleached all-purpose flour; spoon into dry measuring cup and level to top; variation: use ½ *all-purpose and* ½ *whole-wheat flours and blend together*
2 large eggs, lightly beaten
1½ *teaspoons salt*
Optional toppings: 1 egg, beaten; poppy or caraway seeds; milk or cream

1. Spray the bread pan with vegetable oil spray (even if it's nonstick). Preferably use one that is heavy, dull metal. Set aside.

2. **To mix with a stand mixer:** Fit the mixer with the paddle attachment. Place the water in the mixing bowl. Sprinkle the yeast over the surface. After 2 to 3 minutes, whisk the yeast until it has fully absorbed the water. Turn the mixer on low speed. Add the milk, butter, and sugar; combine. Add 2 cups of the flour in ½-cup portions. Increase the speed to medium and beat for 2 minutes. Reduce the speed to low, add the eggs and ½ cup flour mixed with the salt. Beat at high speed for 2 minutes.

Reduce the mixer speed to low and continue to add the remaining flour, in ½-cup portions, thoroughly blending after each. Switch to the dough hook when the mixture is like a very thick paste, after adding about 2 to 3 cups.

Continue adding the flour, ½ cup at a time. When the dough starts to come together in a solid shape, add flour only 1 or 2 tablespoons at a time. Take your time and don't rush the process; it is critical that you get the consistency of the dough right. Stop adding flour when the dough pulls away from the side of the bowl and all ingredients are incorporated. The dough should be tacky, not sticky, wet, or dry. You may end up needing more or less flour than called for in the recipe.

To mix by hand: Dissolve the yeast in the water in a large bowl (page 187) and add the milk, butter, and sugar; slowly add 2 cups of flour, ½ cup at a time. Add eggs, combine, and then add ½ cup flour mixed with the salt. Add the rest of the flour ½ cup at a time while you stir with a wooden spoon, adding only enough to form a rough, shaggy dough. The rest of the flour will be kneaded in. Let the dough rest for 5 to 15 minutes.

To use a food processor: Dissolve the yeast (page 187) in the food processor bowl. Secure the bowl onto the machine and insert the metal chopping blade (not the plastic dough blade). Add the milk, butter, and sugar. Process on low speed while slowly adding 2 cups flour and the salt, and then the eggs, through the feed tube. Continue to add flour until a slack, slightly tacky ball of dough forms. Add more water or flour if necessary and process for 45 seconds; rest for 1 minute; then process for another 45 seconds or until the dough is elastic.

At this point, with any method, set the dough aside to rest, covered, in its bowl for 15 minutes. It is now ready to be kneaded.

3. **Knead** (page 190) in the mixer bowl at low speed with the dough hook for 5 minutes—8 to 10 minutes by hand; 45 seconds in the food processor—until smooth and elastic. I prefer to knead by hand (page 190). Shape the dough into a ball. Transfer the dough to an oiled bowl and turn the dough to coat all over.

4. **First rising and punch down dough:** Cover in plastic wrap making sure to seal the bowl tightly. Place in the microwave proofer (page 193) or in a 75- to 85-degree F spot for 1 to 1½ hours until just about doubled in size. Punch down the dough to deflate.

5. Shape into a loaf, loaves, or rolls (page 196).

6. **Second rising:** Cover the pan tightly with plastic wrap and place it in the microwave proofer or in a 75- to 85-degree F spot until the top of the middle of the loaf reaches the rim of the pan, about 1 hour. Individual rolls should be placed 2 inches apart on a greased cookie sheet and left to rise until they double in bulk, 20 to 40 minutes.

While the dough is rising, prepare the oven. Position one rack on the rung below the middle one and another on the very bottom rung. (Remove the higher racks, if any.) Place a sheet pan on the lowest rack. Preheat the oven to 350 degrees F.

When the dough has risen, for a shiny finish brush the bread or each roll just before baking with beaten egg and optionally sprinkle with toppings, such as poppy or caraway seeds. You can also brush with milk or cream for a dull finish. Immediately place the loaves or rolls in the preheated oven.

7. **Bake** at 350 degrees F for 45 minutes to 1 hour (15 to 25 minutes for the rolls) until the bread (or each roll) reaches an internal temperature of 190 to 210 degrees F,

measured with an instant read thermometer. Remove the loaves or rolls from the oven and let them sit for 10 to 20 minutes before unmolding. Let the loaf cool on its side (rolls on their bottom) on a wire cake rack for at least one hour before slicing. Slice the bread with a serrated or electric knife.

Storage: If storing, cool for 2 hours or more before wrapping.

Notes: Two packages of Fleischmann's yeast equal 4½ teaspoons; different brands may have different measurements. The butter can be reduced to 4 tablespoons (½ stick), but that will change the taste and texture.

> **Sarah Says:** Always stop the mixer and scrape the side and bottom of the bowl with a rubber spatula between changes in speed.

SOURDOUGH AND SPONGE STARTER BREADS

French baguette, ciabatta, sourdough, Pugliese, focaccia: these are just a few of the delicious European-style loaves that are the true bread lover's bread—crusty, flavorful, and full of hearty character. This category of bread goes by many names: starter breads, sourdough, ethnic, hearth, natural, rustic, or my personal favorite, artisan bread. To me, the name aptly carries the idea of the Old World craft of bread making using a starter, both a medium and a method of growing a fermented batch of packaged or wild yeast and sometimes bacteria you cultivate in your kitchen, purchase, or obtain from an existing starter.

Artisan breads are generally formed by hand, in traditional shapes. Depending on the type, artisan breads can be baked directly on a "masonry hearth" (pizza pan, baking stone, or unglazed quarry tiles) with steam introduced during the first 5 to 10 minutes of baking to get a browner, crustier loaf. In a home environment, this can also be done with a pan of hot water placed right below the loaf, heated in the oven.

A starter is cultivated and fermented in a warm place in your kitchen or the refrigerator and is known as a pre-ferment. A starter comes in two types, sourdough and sponge. A sourdough is an old-fashioned natural leaven populated with wild yeast and bacteria in a batter of flour—for example, all-purpose, bread, whole-wheat, and sometimes rye—and water. In time, hopefully it becomes a bubbling, yeasty-smelling symbiotic culture of wild yeast (fungus, often *Saccharomyces exiguus,* and strains of the bacteria *lactobacilli*), and other strains native to where you are making the starter. A sponge, considered a more modern yeasted leaven, includes packaged yeast, a portion of an existing sourdough, or another sponge called "spiking the dough"), and as a result ferments faster and with more predictable results than a sourdough.

The success of the starter, degree of flavor (sourness), and texture in the final bread loaf depends on many factors including the temperature, length of fermentation, type of grain (flour), amount of water, the balance between gas production and retention, baking techniques, and for a sourdough the particular strains of yeast and lactobacilli that live in the starter.

Fermentation also causes what the French call "long kneading" in which you do nothing and the dough forms an elastic strand network known as gluten. When wheat flour is moistened and manipulated—mixed, kneaded, and shaped, for example—two proteins found in wheat flour, glutenin and gliadin, grab water and connect. Kneading further develops and strengthens this network. However, a weaker gluten network can also develop slowly and partially during fermentation with not as much kneading required, especially in breads made with a sourdough starter. The age of the starter and how long and much you knead the dough determine the texture of the bread. You can see the stringy gluten strands when you put the starter in the recipe. The warmth of the rising place or the oven will expand the air bubbles in

Sarah Says: The yeast's enzymes convert complex starches and sugars from carbohydrates in the hydrated flour to simple sugars that the yeast and, in a sourdough starter, bacteria, feed on, and ferment. This interaction releases carbon dioxide, which is trapped within tiny bubbles in the culture, part or all of which is added to a bread recipe, resulting in the dough expanding to produce the leavening of the bread. A sourdough becomes an ongoing culture that is fed flour and water and then stirred at regular intervals. This synergistic interaction also creates lactic acid and acetic acid (vinegar) from lactobacillus and ethanol (alcohol) from the yeast. They evaporate during baking and give the bread its unique flavor. Acetic acid is a natural preservative, preventing invading microorganisms from attacking the starter. You can detect their presence if the starter is a bubbly, frothy, yeasty, wheaty, and/or sour smelling culture. The most apparent physical change you see is a steady increase in the volume of the dough mass containing lots of tiny air bubbles called rising.

the dough (and some in the starter), raising the bread, as if it contained a million tiny balloons.

Using a starter in baking—particularly sourdough—is more unpredictable than using packaged yeast. The vibrant flavor and unique texture—the tangy taste and chewy crust of a homemade sourdough bread, the airy texture and crackling crust of French sourdough baguettes, or my flavorful Whole Grain Wheat Bread (page 208) made with a sponge starter—just can't be achieved any other way. There are recipes for sourdough cakes, waffles, pancakes, biscuits. This kind of bread, in many sizes, shapes, and flavors, has been baked and enjoyed for centuries in Europe and else-

QUESTION: *How does bread differ depending on which starter you use?*

ANSWER: A bread loaf made with a sponge will produce a milder tasting and more delicate bread with a finer cell structure than a sourdough, but not as much as homemade yeast bread (page 202). Because of the added yeast a sponge starter ferments faster—in hours or a fraction thereof, rather than the days and months for a sourdough; it can be used in a recipe right away. A bread loaf made with a sourdough starter has more sour and tangy or sometimes wheaty flavor and irregular air holes than a sponge starter.

where. Recipes and instructions for sourdough and sponge starters vary greatly. By controlling temperature, time, and other variables, the fermentation of bacteria and yeasts are facilitated.

Sarah Says: It is interesting to note a starter will attract only the yeast and bacteria unique to where it is made. That's why San Francisco sourdough bread can be made only in San Francisco, even if you bought a starter there and took it home to anywhere else.

QUESTION: *I had a recipe for chewy, delicious bread that started with a sponge made with whole-wheat flour and a little sugar. This bread was almost as good as the artisan breads I've eaten in good restaurants. Unfortunately, I lost the recipe. Do you have one?*

ANSWER: Try my Whole Grain Wheat Bread (page 208).

WHOLE GRAIN WHEAT BREAD
FROM A STARTER

MAKES ONE 9 x 5 x 3-INCH LOAF

This is my favorite bread with complex flavor—it is has a delicate wheat flavor with some sour notes, and is chewy, rich, and moist thanks to pre-fermenting part of the yeast in a sponge starter. It is a good recipe to try before you graduate to a sourdough starter. The bread also keeps longer than a pan bread loaf (Classic White Sandwich Bread, page 202), about 4 days well-wrapped at room temperature.

Instead of using whole-wheat flour, for a better texture and more fiber I make my own blend: unbleached all-purpose flour with raw bran. It is my signature blend. The resulting bread has a lot of fiber—1 cup of bran contains 24 grams of fiber versus 12 grams in 1 cup of whole-wheat flour—and is lighter because of the lower protein content of unbleached all-purpose flour. You'll need a part of one 1/4-ounce active dry yeast package.

If baked in a dark pan, nonstick or not, the crust will be crusty, which is what I prefer.

INGREDIENTS

SPONGE
1/4 *cup water, 100 to 110 degrees F*
1/2 *teaspoon active dry yeast; don't use instant yeast*
1/2 *cup unbleached, all-purpose flour; spoon into measuring cup and level to top*

BREAD
Vegetable oil cooking spray
1 cup water, 100 to 110 degrees F; use an instant read thermometer
1 teaspoon active dry yeast; don't use instant yeast
1/4 *cup honey, any flavor*
2 1/2 *cups unbleached all-purpose flour; spoon into measuring cup and level to top*
1 1/2 *cups whole-wheat flour; spoon into measuring cup and level to top*
1 cup unprocessed (raw) bran flakes (page 213); store in freezer; don't substitute with flour if you don't have, just omit
2 teaspoons salt or 3 teaspoons kosher salt
2 tablespoons grated orange peel (from 1 large orange) or 1/8 *teaspoon orange oil, optional*
1 cup raisins, soaked in warm water and drained, optional

1. To make the sponge: Sprinkle $\frac{1}{2}$ teaspoon yeast over $\frac{1}{4}$ cup water. Let sit 2 or 3 minutes and whisk to combine. Stir in $\frac{1}{2}$ cup flour. The mixture will be like thick paste. With a rubber spatula, scrape into a mound and cover tightly with plastic wrap. Put in the microwave proofer (page 193) or in a 75- to 85-degree F warm spot for 1 to $1\frac{1}{2}$ hours. Tiny bubbles should begin to appear on the surface, it should smell like yeast with vinegar overtones, and look like thick pudding. If not, discard and start again.

2. Grease the bread pan with vegetable oil spray and set aside. In a large bowl, combine the all-purpose and whole-wheat flours and bran with a spoon, and set aside. (If you use a fork or whisk, bran particles will settle on the bottom of the bowl.)

3. **To mix with a stand mixer:** Sprinkle the yeast over the surface of the warm water in the bowl of a stand mixer. After 2 or 3 minutes, whisk until the yeast has fully absorbed the water.

4. With the paddle attachment, turn the mixer on low speed and drizzle in the honey. Mix in the sponge until incorporated. Slowly add the flour mixture $\frac{1}{2}$ cup at a time. Blend the salt and the orange peel or oil into the second cup before adding. When the mixture is like a very thick paste, switch to the dough hook.

5. Continue to add the remaining flour $\frac{1}{2}$ cup at a time, blending thoroughly after each addition before deciding to add more. When the dough starts to come together, add flour 1 or 2 tablespoons at a time. Take your time and don't rush the process; it is critical that you get the consistency of the dough right.

6. Stop adding flour when the dough pulls away from the side of the bowl and all ingredients are in the dough rather than in the bowl. The dough should be a little tacky and feel like playdough, not sticky, wet, or dry. You may end up needing more or less flour than called for in the recipe. (If there are any dry ingredients remaining, correct the dough with a few drops of water until all is combined; if too wet, add in flour, a tablespoon at a time. Mix before deciding to add more.)

7. **To mix by hand:** Dissolve the yeast in the water in a large bowl; add the honey and the sponge and mix well. Combine and add the dry ingredients as you stir with a wooden spoon, adding only as much flour as necessary to form a rough, shaggy dough.

8. **To use a food processor:** Dissolve the yeast in the water in the food processor bowl. Secure the bowl onto the machine and insert the metal chopping blade (not the plastic dough blade). Add the honey and the sponge and mix well. Combine and add half of the flour mixture and pulse the food processor several times. Continue to add the rest of the flour $\frac{1}{2}$ cup at a time, and pulsing after each addition. The dough will be sticky at first and then begin to form a ball. If it doesn't, add more flour 1 tablespoon at a time, and pulse after each addition until it does. When the dough ball becomes smooth, but is still slightly sticky, stop adding flour.

9. Cover the dough and let it rest for 15 minutes.

10. **Knead** the dough in the mixer on low speed with a dough hook for 5 minutes (8 to 10 minutes by hand; 45 seconds by food processor) until smooth and elastic. Shape the dough into a ball (page 192). Transfer the dough to an oiled bowl and turn the dough to coat all over. Cover in plastic wrap making sure to seal the bowl tightly. Place in the microwave proofer (page 193) or in a 75- to 85-degree F spot for 1 to 1½ hours until doubled in size.

11. When the dough has doubled, punch it down to deflate. If adding raisins, sprinkle them over the surface and knead until distributed throughout—take only about 5 minutes to complete. Shape the dough (page 196). Place it in the greased 9 x 5 x 3-inch bread pan.

12. About 45 minutes before baking, set the oven racks on bottom and middle levels. Place sheet pan on the lower level to deflect the heat and to keep the loaf from burning. Don't fill it with water. Preheat the oven to 500 degrees F.

13. Put the pan in the microwave proofer until the top middle of the dough reaches the rim of the pan, about an hour. Use a razor blade or a very sharp knife (not serrated) to make 2 or 3 diagonal slashes in the top, taking care not to slash the bread on the sides. Immediately place the loaf in the oven and reduce the temperature to 450 degrees F.

14. When the loaf has baked for 20 minutes and has risen completely, lower the oven temperature to 350 degrees F. If the top is browning too fast, make a foil tent over it.

15. Bake for 20 to 30 minutes more until the bread reaches an internal temperature of 190 to 210 degrees F as measured with an instant read thermometer. Remove the loaf from the oven and cool on its side on a wire cake rack for an hour or more before slicing. Slice with a serrated or electric knife. If storing, cool about 2 hours or more before wrapping.

Storage: Because of the sponge, this bread stores well-wrapped at room temperature for about 4 days. For long-term storage, freeze the bread for up to 3 months, well-wrapped and placed in an airtight container, such as a resealable plastic bag.

11

QUICK BREADS

*I read that I can substitute butter and oil
with applesauce. How do I do it?
Why are all the blueberries always on the bottom?
. . . and the rest of the skinny on quick breads.*

FOR MANY OF US, quick breads are already familiar and making them has become a family ritual of sorts. In fact, I think of quick breads as everyday recipes. I like to make freshly baked muffins (a mini version of quick bread loaves), pancakes, or waffles for my family every Sunday, and popovers, scones, or biscuits for a special meal. Every Christmas, along with cookies my kids and I make quick bread loaves to give as gifts. The large and varied family of quick breads also includes fritters and other fried desserts, doughnuts, soda bread, and crepes. Quick breads can be served as is, and also make a perfect pairing with whipped cream and dessert sauces, a simple dusting of confectioners' sugar, or a drizzle of maple syrup and melted butter.

A quick bread's texture derives from the ingredients, leavening, mixing, and baking techniques used, and the taste from added flavorings and ingredients. They're typically made from a batter of commonly found ingredients: unbleached all-purpose flour (with some whole-wheat), sugar (table sugar or honey), eggs, fat (butter, margarine, shortening, oil), some type of liquid (milk, buttermilk, juice, yogurt, sour cream), and salt.

When baked, a quick bread loaf or muffins should have good volume and a rounded, craggy, cracked top. When cut open, it has small, irregularly shaped air holes and a moist crumb; its interior should be without tunnels. When the fat, sugar, and egg content of a recipe is twice that of a quick bread recipe, you have reached the cake level; however, every recipe varies.

Quick breads are called "quick" for two reasons. First, they are "quick-leavened" with one or a combination of carbon dioxide produced by a chemical leavening agent (baking powder, baking soda, or cream of tartar paired with an acid in older recipes),

QUESTION: *What's the difference between yeast breads and quick breads?*

ANSWER: They primarily differ in the way they are leavened and mixed, plus the type of ingredients and method of baking. Yeast breads are made by mixing and kneading all the ingredients together. The dough is leavened with packaged yeast or a sourdough or sponge starter (page 202), and is left to ferment and rise. Kneading is required to develop the dough as yeast breads need high gluten development for proper consistency. Quick breads are so named because the dry and liquid ingredients are each mixed separately, and then mixed together quickly to avoid forming excess gluten, with no kneading or rising time required. They are baked right away, usually with a shorter baking time. Popular quick breads include nut, fruit and vegetable loaves; cornbread (recipe, page 222); muffins (recipe, page 224); biscuits (recipe, page 232); waffles (recipe, page 239); pancakes (recipe, page 241), and many coffee cakes.

ingredients that turn to steam (as in the case of popovers), and heat from the oven. Chemical leaveners begin releasing carbon dioxide gas the moment they are moistened (and baking powder releases carbon dioxide again when heated) for a quick rise in the oven, versus yeasted breads that require fermenting for a couple of hours or even days in a sourdough starter to develop their flavor and volume. Because of this, quick breads derive their flavor and texture from their other ingredients rather than fermented yeast. (However, some quick bread recipes such as waffles and pancakes may contain yeast along with chemical leaveners for added leavening and flavor.) Second, most quick bread recipes are quick to make: line up your ingredients, start the clock, and see if you aren't done in almost an hour!

Of course, there are some persistent challenges that can plague you even when you make seemingly simple quick breads. The best and most reliable way to avoid them is to understand how ingredients interact in quick breads.

Quick breads are generally made from thick dough, drop dough, or poured batter. Dough can range from thick, rolled, and cut with a sharp-edged cutter or knife—such as for biscuits and scones—to a looser drop batter, dropped from a spoon to form irregular rounds or dumplings on a cookie sheet. Pour batters flow, and range from thick to thin. Thick batters for muffins and loaves are baked in molds: loaf pans, muffin tins, and cornstick plaques. Thinner batters for pancakes, waffles, and crepes are too liquid to mold and must be poured directly onto a hot griddle or waffle iron to cook.

THE ALCHEMY OF QUICK BREADS

Whether you're making moist muffins for a bake sale, or whipping up a batch of buttermilk pancakes, you can rely on your ingredients to work together in these recipes in some fairly predictable ways.

SPOTLIGHT ON INGREDIENTS

FLOUR

Unbleached all-purpose flour is generally used in making quick breads. Whole-wheat flour may be substituted for no more than 50 percent of the all-purpose flour in some quick bread recipes, but the muffin or loaf will not rise as high.

I've seen cake or self-rising flour used, primarily in biscuit recipes. Cake flour with less gluten-forming protein is less likely to form tunnels during mixing, will produce a more tender muffin than hard wheat flours, and is often an ingredient in cake-like muffins.

QUESTION: *HELP! I made a muffin recipe and instead of all-purpose, I used whole-wheat flour. Now I have a whole set of door stops! How can I make a muffin with more fiber?*

ANSWER: You can substitute for up to half of the unbleached all-purpose flour. If you use all whole-wheat, you'll end up with doorstops, as you sadly found out. Whole-wheat flour contains more gluten-forming proteins than all-purpose, making the muffins tough and dense. (For cakey muffins that rely upon a light and aerated texture, don't use any whole-wheat flour.) Personally, I don't like adding any whole-wheat flour to quick breads because you always get some heaviness and dryness. But I want more fiber, too. To solve this problem, one day it dawned on me to blend ½ cup of unprocessed (raw) bran flakes per recipe with unbleached all-purpose flour. You get the best of both worlds: the right amount of gluten from using the flour stated in the recipe, as well as more fiber and a delicate, nutty flavor. Unprocessed bran contains 24 grams of fiber per cup while whole-wheat flour has 12 grams of fiber per cup!

QUESTION: *My recipe calls for cornmeal. I saw two types at the grocery store: stone ground and regular. I didn't know which one to buy. Please help!*

ANSWER: Commercial cornmeal is available in fine (including water-ground) or coarse grinds (stone-ground). In my experience, most recipes that simply state "cornmeal" mean fine grind, the standard cornmeal in the grocery store. It gives a lighter texture. You can't easily exchange one for the other because texture and flavor are affected (stone-ground makes the recipe dryer and more coarse), but you can exchange water-ground for blue cornmeal or white cornmeal; both are a little sweeter. Stone-ground is made from yellow or white dried corn, ground slowly to preserve the essential oils.

GRAINS

Cornmeal, bran, oatmeal, spelt, and flaxseed can all play a role in a muffin recipe.

FAT

Fat contributes to tenderness and helps breads stay fresh longer. Butter, margarine, vegetable oil, and vegetable shortening are used to prepare quick bread batters. But-

QUESTION: *My favorite muffin recipe always turns out dry. How do I make it moist? I use an oven thermometer, mix them quickly, measure accurately, and don't overbake. What causes this?*

ANSWER: You probably just have a recipe that makes dry muffins. My trick is to add some vegetable oil with the liquid ingredients in the recipe: start with 1 or 2 tablespoons and add no more than $\frac{1}{4}$ cup total. Don't substitute something else for the oil.

Oil and other liquid fats always stay liquid and never set into a solid form even when the muffins have cooled. Lubrication is a function of oil. The liquid oil coats the flour and other ingredient particles, allowing for a smoother dough, easier mixing, and some mixing tolerance. It also gives the perception of moistness and tenderizes gluten, though not as effectively as solid fat does.

ter contributes flavor to a recipe. Other fats indirectly contribute to the flavor of the product because they act as carriers for flavorings and spices. Melted solid fat (butter, margarine, and vegetable shortening) or vegetable oil is used unless the recipe calls for creaming the solid fat with sugar. Oil does not aerate when creamed with sugar so it does not have air holding properties. Cake muffins made with solid shortening, as opposed to stick butter, generally have a softer crumb and firmer texture. Those made with butter have a richer flavor. Recipes made with oil tend to be more moist.

Solid fats such as butter, margarine, or shortening, remain solid when set. They can melt, but always return to their solid state. When melted, they don't have the same characteristics as oils, so they can't be used instead.

MIXING

There are different mixing techniques used when making quick breads. Each technique gives a different texture and character to a recipe—quick breads can vary

QUESTION: *Why is it easy to overmix a muffin batter?*

ANSWER: "Don't overmix a muffin batter" is one of the cardinal rules of muffin making. (The others are "Don't overbake" and "Remove the muffins from the muffin tin to cool on a wire cake rack.") Wheat flour is made up of particles of protein—glutenin and gliadin—which when mixed with moisture in the recipe produce gluten. When a muffin batter is overmixed, more gluten is formed from the mixing and thus more structure. It will have a tendency to crack but is less likely to do so than a quick bread batter.

If the formula is low in tenderizers—fat and sugar—as in more quick bread-like muffins, it is easy to develop more gluten from overmixing than is desirable, creating a tough, dry, and flavorless muffin. Also, in these batters the flour isn't coated with fat before the liquids are added. Fat acts a "raincoat" and coats the flour before the liquids are added, preventing the formation of gluten. Chemical leaveners are quickly mixed and work effectively with a low to moderate gluten structure.

With a more cake-like muffin, mixing the batter beyond the optimum amount results in a smoother batter; however overmixing causes the air bubbles to deflate and the carbon dioxide to dissipate from the batter. This produces a muffin that is flat, flavorless, and somewhat rubbery. The increase in gluten development also results in tunnels or holes throughout the muffin.

from light and puffy (beignets) to flat and tender (pancakes or crepes) to rough (muffins) to cake-like or even crispy.

QUICK BREAD LOAVES AND MUFFINS:
POINTERS, QUESTIONS, AND RECIPES

Sarah Says: The secret to quick breads is this: Stir ingredients as minimally as possible. Don't overmix. Bake as soon as the batter is in the pan. Take your quick bread out as soon as it is done. You get the picture; be quick.

QUESTION: *In changing a muffin recipe that calls for a regular size muffin pan to a mini-muffin pan or a muffin top pan, how should I change the cooking temperature and time? What about if I want to bake the muffin recipe in a loaf pan?*

ANSWER: Generally keep the baking temperature the same as the recipe because you're still baking the same recipe. However, if the pan you're using is glass or dark nonstick, reduce the oven temperature in the recipe by 25 degrees F.

The baking time will change. Many factors affect baking times: the temperature of the ingredients; whether the pan is shiny or dull; the accuracy of your oven; and the number of pans that are in the oven at once. Since it is impossible to give exact baking times, a good recipe gives a range of time. Check when it starts smelling and looking done. Obviously mini-muffins will bake much faster than regular muffins because they are smaller and shallower. Conversely, if you bake the recipe in a loaf pan the temperature stays the same, but the baking time will lengthen. Make a note of the time on your recipe for future baking.

Muffins are done when they are light or golden brown, feel firm to the touch, and start to come away from the sides of the pan. They should smell delicious. A toothpick or cake tester inserted in the center of a muffin should come out with a few moist crumbs.

Muffins don't require a long baking period, so be sure to preheat the oven to the correct temperature. Here is a chart I made for you to use as a guide.

Baking times are estimates. At an oven temperature of 350 degrees F, generally:

- standard-sized muffins and tops bake in about 20 to 25 minutes;
- mini-muffins bake in 15 to 20 minutes;
- jumbo muffins bake in about 25 to 35 minutes;
- jumbo muffin "tops" bake in about 20 to 25 minutes.

QUESTION: *I want to substitute for the fat in a quick bread loaf recipe with a fruit puree, such as applesauce. How do I do it?*

ANSWER: It's not as easy as advertised! Quick breads and muffins with oil as the fat in the recipe are among the best candidates for substituting fruit purees. When oil is used, the recipe usually does not rely on it for leavening, unlike cake-like recipes in which creaming butter with sugar produces necessary air bubbles. Butter can be reduced only with much work.

The rule I developed is: when a recipe calls for one cup of oil, substitute ¾ cup of unsweetened applesauce. When using fruit purees, substitute ½ cup fruit puree plus ¼ cup unsweetened applesauce. Also add 2 tablespoons vegetable oil for better flavor and mouthfeel. Other adjustments are generally necessary as well:

- the flavors must be increased;
- the leaveners may need adjusting. Since applesauce is acidic, the recipe may need some baking soda;
- acidic buttermilk, a tenderizer much as fat is, could replace milk;
- mixing methods might change from creaming to "muffin method;"
- a high-gluten flour may need to be substituted for a low-gluten one.

In muffins, merely reducing the amount of fat results in a tougher texture because gluten develops more freely. In my recipes, I often substitute flour with lower gluten-forming proteins, such as whole-wheat pastry flour, and adjust other ingredients. Often, another tenderizing agent such as sugar can be added or increased to act in place of the fat.

APPLESAUCE CAKE SQUARES

MAKES ONE 11 x 7 x 2-INCH PAN

I reduced the fat and adjusted other ingredients from the original recipe to make an all-purpose recipe for snacking. Applesauce and oil give a moist texture, and the oil enhances the recipe's flavor. Buttermilk gives a more tender texture, while eggs give a creamy one. I kept the all-purpose flour and whole-wheat instead of softer flour because I like cake squares that have substance.

INGREDIENTS

CAKE
Vegetable oil cooking spray
1½ cups unbleached all-purpose flour
1 cup whole-wheat flour (substitute unbleached all-purpose);
  spoon into dry measuring cup and level to top
1½ teaspoons baking soda
1 teaspoon ground cinnamon
¼ teaspoon salt
1 cup dark brown sugar, packed
¾ cup buttermilk, well shaken
¾ cup unsweetened applesauce; spoon into metal measuring cup and level to top
2 large eggs
2 tablespoons canola oil
2 teaspoons vanilla extract
½ cup walnuts, chopped (page 26)
½ cup raisins

GLAZE (MAKES ABOUT ⅔ CUP)
1 cup confectioners' sugar; spoon into dry measuring cup and level to top
3 tablespoons lemon juice, strained (from 1 lemon)
1 teaspoon grated lemon peel (from 1 lemon)

1. Position a rack in the center of the oven and preheat the oven to 350 degrees F. Spray or coat an 11- by 7- by 2-inch cake pan with vegetable oil.

2. In a medium bowl, whisk together the flours, baking soda, cinnamon, and salt until well combined. Set aside.

3. In another medium bowl, whisk together the brown sugar, buttermilk, apple-

sauce, eggs, oil, and vanilla until well-blended. Make a well in the center of the dry ingredients, and pour in the applesauce mixture. Using a large spoon, stir until almost combined. Add the walnuts and raisins. Stir to combine. Don't overmix; the batter will be lumpy. Spoon the batter into the prepared pan. Gently smooth the top.

4. Bake for 30 to 40 minutes until the top is lightly browned and the cake sounds hollow when tapped. Don't overbake or the cake will be dry. Cool in the pan on a wire cake rack.

5. To make the glaze: Place the confectioners' sugar in a small bowl. Add the lemon juice and peel. Blend with a fork until combined. The consistency should be like corn syrup. If too thick, add a few drops water; if too thin, add a few teaspoonfuls sugar. Dip the tines of a fork in the confectioner's sugar glaze and drizzle over the top of the cake. Allow the glaze to set a few minutes before serving. Serve squares from the pan.

Variations: Pumpkin: Use $\frac{1}{4}$ cup applesauce and $\frac{1}{2}$ cup pumpkin puree instead of $\frac{3}{4}$ cup applesauce. Add an additional $\frac{1}{2}$ teaspoon ground cinnamon, and $\frac{1}{2}$ teaspoon ground nutmeg.

Banana: Use $\frac{1}{4}$ cup applesauce and $\frac{1}{2}$ cup mashed bananas instead of $\frac{3}{4}$ cup applesauce. Use $\frac{1}{2}$ cup currants instead of raisins. And always *mash* bananas with a fork so they retain a little texture, rather than puree them in a blender; otherwise you'll be able to bounce your bread around the room! Use well-ripened bananas, flecked with lots of brown spots, but not blackened.

Carrot Raisin: Add $\frac{1}{2}$ cup shredded carrots.

QUESTION: *I want to make a chocolate muffin, but I can't get it chocolaty enough. Do you have any recipes?*

ANSWER: Whenever I develop chocolate muffins, I can get a good chocolate flavor because the recipe contains a high amount of fat and sugar as in a cake recipe. I like to use both cocoa powder and chocolate squares, adding intensity.

CHOCOLATE MUFFIN TOPS

MAKES 12 MUFFIN TOPS OR MUFFINS

In order to get the optimal chocolate taste, these muffins have more cake-like proportions. They bake with a flatter top than a regular muffin because of it.

INGREDIENTS
Vegetable oil cooking spray
2¼ cups unbleached all-purpose flour; spoon into dry measuring cup and level to top
¼ cup Dutch-process cocoa powder; spoon into dry measuring cup and level to top
2 teaspoons baking powder
½ teaspoon baking soda
½ teaspoon salt
1 cup whole or 2% milk, room temperature
1 cup sugar
⅔ cup vegetable oil; measure in glass measuring cup
2 large eggs, room temperature
2 teaspoons vanilla extract
2 ounces semisweet chocolate, melted and cooled (two 1-ounce squares)

1. Position a rack in the middle of the oven and preheat the oven to 350 degrees F. With vegetable oil spray, grease the insides of 12 muffin top cups (2 tins). Set aside.

2. In a medium bowl, combine the flour, cocoa powder, baking powder, baking soda, and salt. Sift if the cocoa powder is lumpy. Set aside.

3. In a medium bowl, combine the milk, sugar, vegetable oil, eggs, and vanilla extract. With a handheld electric mixer on medium-low speed, combine until the mixture becomes bubbly.

4. Make a well in the center of the flour mixture and pour in the milk mixture. With a few strokes of a spoon, combine the ingredients until just mixed. Stir in the cooled melted chocolate and mix to combine. With the mixer on low, blend the ingredients until smooth, about 20 seconds.

5. Divide the batter evenly among the muffin top tins to rims. Lightly spread as much as you can to the edges.

6. Bake for 20 to 25 minutes until the top of a muffin springs back when lightly

QUESTION: *Is it necessary to put water in the empty cups of a muffin tin, or is it just an old wives' tale? If we should do it, why?*

ANSWER: If one of the tin cavities is empty, fill it half-way with water before baking so it won't smoke in the oven.

pressed with a fingertip. Remove from the oven and let sit for 10 minutes in the pan before removing to a wire cake rack to cool.

JUST RIGHT CORNBREAD
OR MUFFINS

This cornbread recipe is just right! Buttery and moist, it is one of my favorites. My trick is to use canola oil, which gives the perception of moistness, since cornbread can be dry.

INGREDIENTS
Vegetable oil cooking spray
1 cup unbleached all-purpose flour; measure in dry measuring cup and level to top
1 cup yellow cornmeal, water- or fine grind; do not use stone-ground; measure in dry measuring cup and level to top
¼ cup sugar
2 teaspoons baking powder
½ teaspoon salt
1 large egg, room temperature
1 cup milk, room temperature
¼ cup oil
2 tablespoons unsalted butter, melted

1. Position a rack in the middle of the oven and heat the oven to 425 degrees F. Grease an 8-inch square pan or 12 standard muffin cups.

2. Combine the flour, cornmeal, sugar, baking powder, and salt in a medium bowl. Make a well in the center.

3. Mix the egg, milk, and oil in a small bowl. Pour into the well in the dry ingredients and fold lightly with a rubber spatula. Stir until almost combined. Pour the melted butter on top; stir until ingredients are just combined. Pour the batter into the greased pan.

4. Bake for about 20 to 22 minutes (15 to 20 for muffins) until the top is golden brown and lightly cracked, and the edges have pulled away from the side of the pan. It will also sound hollow when tapped, and the top crust is solid. You will hear bubbles popping, but that is ok.

5. Transfer the pan or muffin tin to a wire cake rack for 5 to 10 minutes. Cut the cornbread into squares and serve warm. Unmold the muffins; turn them upright on the rack to cool. Reheat in a 350 degree F oven for 10 to 15 minutes if necessary.

QUESTION: *How can I get my muffins to dome just like in the delis? Should I add more baking powder or baking soda? Why does my muffin crack?*

ANSWER: The answers lie with the recipe and a couple of other factors. First of all, don't add more leaveners to your recipe; otherwise when the muffins bake, you'll find batter oozing from your muffin tin all over your oven!

Muffins low in sugar and fat are more likely to dome and crack than those that have more. Large amounts of sugar and fat keep gluten from forming so cracking and doming are not as likely. However, with a cornbread muffin that has oil and little sugar, it doesn't take much to get a dome and a crack, because that's the nature of that type of muffin.

Batter thickness is a part of it. Thinner batters are less likely to dome. How much you fill the muffins cups will also have an effect: fill them ¾ full with a thick batter and your muffins will dome; fill to the top, and the batter will rise and perhaps spread, if you grease the top of the pan.

Oven heat is important: Preheat the oven to 400 degrees F. Place the filled muffin tin in the center of the oven, close the door, and turn the temperature down to the temperature called for in the recipe. Don't peek until the muffins are almost done so the oven stays nice and hot.

The higher the oven's heat, the faster the leaveners produce gas, making the muffin top puff when first put in the oven. (This is known as oven spring.) If done early in the baking, the exposed batter in direct contact with the oven heat will set at a quicker rate than the interior. If the outside is forced through the initial high heat, the gluten proteins set quickly, making a dome. The higher temperature sets the crust. The later, lower oven temperature bakes the muffin interior without burning the crust.

The net result: when the heat finally does penetrate, the "kick" produced by the leavening and steam will be trapped by the crust which has already set. Voilà: the crust will dome best with a thick batter.

My Cinnamon Raisin Bran Muffins recipe (recipe follows) produces muffins that dome in the way you're looking for.

Variation: Raspberry or Blueberry Cornbread or Muffins: Stir in ½ cup of fresh or frozen raspberries or blueberries to the batter right before baking.

Storage: Store at room temperature for 2 to 3 days; can be frozen.

CINNAMON RAISIN
BRAN MUFFINS

❖

MAKES 12 MUFFINS

If you want muffins that have a nice dome, these are the ones.

INGREDIENTS
Vegetable oil cooking spray
2½ cups unbleached all-purpose flour; spoon into dry measuring cup and level to top
½ cup unprocessed (raw) bran flakes (page 213); spoon into dry measuring cup and level to top
1½ teaspoons baking powder
½ teaspoon baking soda
1 teaspoon ground cinnamon
½ teaspoon salt
¾ cup buttermilk, well shaken; measure in liquid measuring cup
¾ cup vegetable oil; measure in a liquid measuring cup
⅔ cup sugar
2 large eggs
½ cup raisins or dried cranberries

1. Position a rack in the middle of the oven and preheat the oven to 400 degrees F. Spray the muffin tin cups, not the top of the pan, with vegetable oil spray.

2. Combine the flour, bran flakes, baking powder, baking soda, cinnamon, and salt in a medium bowl. Make a well in the center. In another medium bowl, mix the buttermilk, oil, sugar, and eggs. Beat with a wire whisk or handheld electric mixer on low speed until frothy. Pour into the well in the dry ingredients and fold lightly with a rubber spatula. Stir until almost combined. Add the raisins and mix until the batter is combined. Divide evenly among the muffin tin cups.

3. Place the muffin pan in the oven. Immediately turn the heat down to 350 degrees F. Bake for 20 to 25 minutes or until the tops are browned and the middle springs back when touched. Let the muffin pan rest on a wire cake rack for 10 minutes before unmolding the muffins. Turn the muffins upright on the rack to cool.

QUESTION: *I would like to know a way to stop my blueberries or chocolate chips from falling to the bottom of my cake mixture while it bakes. This happens to me all the time and I've tried putting them in flour first. What am I doing wrong? Help!*

ANSWER: Nuts, dried fruit, or chocolate pieces sink during baking because the batter it not thick enough to keep them suspended. This can be caused by the ingredients being too heavy for the batter, so you might try cutting them into smaller pieces. The trick to baking with blueberries is to use older ones for more flavor, not tart or new ones. Frozen blueberries are just perfect for muffins.

LEMON BLUEBERRY CAKE MUFFINS

❖

MAKES 12 MUFFINS

These have a wonderfully tender and cake-like texture from creaming the butter and sugar, just like making a cake. Because of this, though, they don't dome as high as regular muffins.

INGREDIENTS

Vegetable oil cooking spray

1½ cups unbleached all-purpose flour; spoon into dry measuring cup and level to top

2 teaspoons baking powder

½ teaspoon salt

½ cup (1 stick) unsalted butter, room temperature

¾ cup sugar

1 teaspoon lemon extract

¼ teaspoon vanilla extract

2 large eggs, room temperature

½ cup whole or 2% milk, room temperature

½ cup blueberries, washed and dried

1. Position a rack in the middle of the oven and heat the oven to 350 degrees F. Spray the muffin tin cups with vegetable oil spray.

2. Combine the flour, baking powder, and salt in a medium bowl. Set aside.

3. Soften the butter with a handheld electric mixer on low speed. Add the sugar in a steady stream at the side of the bowl. Increase the speed to medium and beat for 5 minutes until light yellow and fluffy (page 39). Add the extracts.

4. With the mixer on low, add the eggs one at a time and beat for 20 seconds after each addition. Without turning off the mixer, add the flour in three equal portions, alternately with the milk in two equal portions, beginning and ending with the flour mixture, in a steady stream at the side of the bowl (page 47). At the end, beat for 1 minute or until smooth. Fold in the blueberries with a large rubber spatula. The batter should be thick and fluffy. Divide the batter evenly in the prepared muffin tin; lightly smooth the tops.

5. Bake for 30 to 40 minutes until well-risen and deep golden brown. Remove the

pan to a wire cake rack and let the muffins sit for about 5 minutes. Remove the muffins from the pan and place on the wire cake rack; let cool thoroughly.

BUILDING A BETTER BISCUIT

If anything makes a home baker panic, it's the thought of making a flaky, light, and tender biscuit from scratch. Questions abound about failed biscuits. "My biscuit isn't flaky. Why?" "Why are my biscuits always so dry?" "My dough is always so sticky that I can't handle it. Please help!" I know it is a lot easier to buy ready-made in a can from the refrigerated section or a bag from the freezer case and to bake them, but there's nothing like a homemade biscuit still warm from the oven. The definition of a perfect biscuit varies depending on cultural background, geographic location, and available ingredients.

Besides baking powder or baking soda, other ingredients include wheat flour (all-purpose, cake, or biscuit), salt, solid fat (butter, margarine, vegetable shortening, or lard—or possibly oil) and liquids (milk, buttermilk, or cream). Biscuit flour, also known as Southern all-purpose flour, sold under the brand name White Lily (*www.whitelily.com*), is a low-gluten flour. Many bakers use it to make the lightest and most mouthwatering biscuits. Sugar is found in some biscuit recipes, making them more cake-like in texture. Biscuits are mixed in certain ways depending on the type you are making, and baked right away in a hot, fast oven—sometimes up to 500 degrees F—and are done within 10 to 15 minutes. They are best when served piping hot.

Biscuit making is as much a technique as a recipe. It is easy to follow the recipe "to the letter" but not quite have the technique needed to master each type. Making a biscuit is much like making pie crust pastry, which requires a quick and light touch, cold ingredients, and a hot oven. When not done "right," a hard, dry "hockey puck" of a biscuit is the result. Making my Old-Fashioned Buttermilk Biscuit recipe (page 232) will help you perfect your biscuit making skills. Don't be upset if your first few batches are lopsided, or don't rise as high as you hoped. It takes practice, but once you have mastered the steps you will be able to bake consistent, flaky, tender biscuits.

No matter what type you bake, getting your recipe to bake with all the attributes of a good biscuit can be a frustrating and elusive task. Undermixed biscuits have a smaller volume and rough, spotted crusts, and the interior isn't as flaky, with a coarse texture. Overmixing the dough causes excessive gluten development, so the biscuits are humped on top, dry, and tough. Poor distribution of the baking powder or soda, the result of not stirring the dry ingredients well enough, can cause yellow specks on the top crust.

No matter what type of biscuit you are making, the general rules are to handle the dough gently, keep the ingredients cold, work quickly, and dust your hands and the dough only with enough flour to make things manageable. The dough should be soft and sticky for a drop biscuit, but less sticky and smoother for a rolled biscuit.

BISCUIT TYPES AND MIXING

There are two main types of baking powder biscuit: rolled and cut, and dropped, each mixed using specific techniques. A third type, the beaten biscuit—not discussed here in detail—is found in the South. The chief differences between biscuit types are the type of fat used, the method of introducing it, and the particular ratio of ingredients—rolled and cut biscuits have less liquid than drop biscuits. Flour plays an important role: the amount of protein in the flour has an influence on flakiness. The higher the protein content (all-purpose), the flakier and tougher the biscuit; the lower the protein level (biscuit or cake flour), the less flaky but more tender the biscuit. The way in which the dough is worked greatly affects the outcome. Biscuits of any type may be sweetened.

The baking powder biscuit comes in a few forms:

Rolled and cut biscuits are one of the most popular baking-powder leavened quick breads. During baking the biscuit should rise to double or triple its original height. The interior should be light, fluffy, and tender, and the crust slightly crusty, even golden brown. Well-prepared biscuits have a flat top and straight sides. Around the sides you will be able to see the flaky layers.

The *drop biscuit* is made from a dough similar to rolled and cut biscuits, but with more liquid for a softer dough that can be dropped by the spoonful onto a baking sheet. Sometimes a liquid fat is used, and is mixed with the liquid ingredients. Oil gives a moister biscuit.

Shortcakes, as for strawberry shortcake, are sweet from added sugar. They can be rolled and cut or dropped. The biscuits are larger and are split or served whole, and filled or topped with sweetened fruit and whipped cream or ice cream. Strawberry shortcake is mentioned in writings from England as far back as the 1500s.

BISCUIT-MAKING TIPS

1. Measure ingredients accurately. Flour is measured by spooning into a measuring cup and leveling off with a straight edge. Sift the flour a couple of times (four is good) after measuring to aerate it. Sifting makes a slightly higher, more tender biscuit.
2. Preheat the oven so it is really hot. Most biscuit recipes say to bake at 425 to 500 degrees F. The high heat helps the leavening get going very quickly, making the biscuit puff before the crust sets.
3. Vegetable shortening or lard should be packed into a dry measuring cup so there are no air pockets. I like to use a small rubber spatula. Cold butter can

be used; make sure it is really cold. It is cut into the flour mixture using a pastry blender, two knives or a fork, or with your fingertips. The result should be pieces the size of peas tossed in a mixture of shaggy dough.

4. Fold the liquid ingredients into the dry ones with a rubber spatula. They can also be stirred with a wooden spoon or a fork. First make a well in the center of the dry ingredients, and pour the liquid into the well. Mix only until they are *just* moistened. Don't overmix. It will lead to dry and tough biscuits.

5. Place the biscuits on an ungreased baking sheet one inch apart for crusty sides, or almost touching for soft sides. For the best results use a heavy-weight light-colored baking sheet, not a dark nonstick sheet.

6. Overbaking does not produce the ideal biscuit. Bake biscuits just until golden brown. Biscuits are best hot from the oven.

7. **Storage:** It is best to enjoy biscuits steaming hot out of the oven because they contain no preservatives to prevent staleness. Biscuits tend to get stale and hard and tasteless in a hurry, but they can be reheated by placing them on an ungreased cookie sheet reheated for about 10 minutes in a 425 degree F oven; watch carefully so they don't burn.

   Biscuits can be frozen, either fully or partially baked. Don't freeze biscuits

QUESTION: *Why are my drop biscuits crumbly?*

ANSWER: Drop biscuits are naturally more crumbly than rolled biscuits because they aren't kneaded. Both dropped and rolled biscuits are less crumbly right after they come out of the oven. Once they've cooled or been stored—even if just for a couple of hours—they dry out a little and get more crumbly. Biscuits will also be more crumbly if the oven temperature is too high or if they've baked too long.

QUESTION: *How is tenderness obtained in rolled biscuits?*

ANSWER: Both cutting in the fat and kneading contribute to flakiness in the dough. However, be careful because too much kneading makes the biscuit tough and dry.

Sarah Says: To keep your biscuits tender, pop your mixing bowl with the measured flour in the freezer for a few minutes before starting, and keep the butter and milk chilled. Also, you should work quickly and avoid overmixing.

for longer than two months. To freeze fully baked biscuits, cool them to room temperature and immediately place them in plastic freezer bags, pressing out as much air as possible. To thaw, let biscuits sit at room temperature about one hour, unwrap, and reheat in an oven. To freeze partially baked biscuits, make the dough and bake only until the biscuit is set but isn't beginning to color. Remove from the oven and cool, then wrap and freeze. When you're ready to bake, preheat the oven to 375 degrees F and finish baking the biscuits from the frozen state until the tops are golden.

To freeze biscuit dough, prepare and cut biscuits according to the recipe directions. However, be aware that they won't rise as high when baked because the leaveners become weaker the longer they are stored. Freeze uncovered on a cookie sheet 1 to 2 hours, then place them in freezer bags or

QUESTION: *My biscuits don't rise very high and aren't very flaky, even though I follow the recipe to the letter.*

ANSWER: Flakiness in biscuits is obtained by the following two steps:

1. Cutting cold plastic fat (butter or shortening) into the flour which results in the fat being subdivided into pea-size pieces. This increases the surface area of the fat and thus more flour can make contact with it.
2. Manipulation of the dough, which involves mixing, kneading, folding, and sometimes rolling the dough into layers of fat and flour, gives a layered crumb. The dough must first be stirred adequately and kneaded sufficiently to develop enough gluten to obtain the desired flaky texture.

stack in rigid containers with a piece of waxed paper between each biscuit. Cover and freeze for up to four weeks. Thaw biscuits unwrapped at room temperature about one hour. Bake in a preheated 425 degree F oven for 20 to 25 minutes.

OLD-FASHIONED BUTTERMILK BISCUITS

MAKES TWELVE 2-INCH BISCUITS

These mile-high biscuits are always a treat. This recipe was adapted from one by Tami Smith, who works for me. She is a pastry chef and an avid baker.

INGREDIENTS

⅓ cup unsalted butter, cold, or vegetable shortening
2 cups unbleached all-purpose flour; spoon into measuring cup and level to top
1 tablespoon sugar
3 teaspoons baking powder
1 teaspoon baking soda
1 teaspoon salt
¾ cup cold half-and-half or whole or 2% milk, plus extra for brushing the tops
of the biscuits

1. Position a rack in the middle of the oven and preheat the oven to 425 degrees F. Use a clean, ungreased baking sheet, or line a baking sheet with parchment paper.

2. Cut the butter into 1-inch cubes and refrigerate it for 30 minutes, or freeze it for 10 minutes until cold. In a medium bowl, combine the flour, sugar, baking powder, baking soda, and salt. Sprinkle the chilled butter over the flour and toss with a spoon. Cut the butter into the dry ingredients with two knives (in a scissor motion) or a pastry blender until the butter pieces are no larger than small peas. With your fingertips press the butter into the flour so it forms large flakes. If the butter becomes greasy, chill until hardened.

3. Drizzle a small amount of the half-and-half over the dry ingredients while tossing with a fork. Repeat until the dough just comes together; it should not be dry. You may need more or less half-and-half. Gently press the dough with your hands and turn it out onto a cool work surface or Silpat baking mat. If the dough is the right consistency, there is no need to flour the work surface; in fact it is better if you don't. Bring the dough together with both hands and knead 30 times, no more. Give the dough a quarter turn each time. The dough will come together when kneaded. Don't add more flour. After kneading the dough will be cohesive and slightly bumpy.

4. Pat or roll out the dough to about ¾-inch thickness. Roll the dough forward to the opposite edge in one movement, not back and forth. Cut with a 2-inch biscuit

cutter with a sharp edge, to make a clean cut. Keep the cuts close to each other to prevent a lot of scraps. (Scraps don't rise as high as the original dough.) Cut straight down through the dough; don't twist. This helps to make a high-rising biscuit. Lift the cut biscuit dough gently with your fingertips, trying not to distort the circle. Place on an ungreased baking sheet. Place close together for softer sides, or place 1 inch apart for crustier biscuits.

5. If you have scraps, stack them on top of each other and roll with a rolling pin. Recut. They will not rise as high as the original biscuits, but they still will be good.

6. Brush the tops with half-and-half. Place the biscuits in the oven and immediately reduce the heat to 350 degrees F. Bake for 12 to 15 minutes until the tops are just lightly browned and the bottoms are a slightly darker color.

7. Remove from the oven and serve warm with butter. Biscuits become stale quickly, so serve them as soon as they cool. Store any leftovers in a resealable plastic bag at room temperature for up to 1 day.

Note: If you want to make larger biscuits, use a 3- or 3½-inch biscuit cutter.

Storage: page 229.

SCONES

Traditional scones are a small quick bread that is buttery, flaky, moist, and tender. Scones are formed into triangles and baked until golden brown on a cookie sheet in the oven or sometimes on a griddle on top of the stove. Julia Child calls them "British biscuits." Recipes are nearly identical to biscuits, except that scones are made from a richer dough with less baking powder and more butter and sugar, making them flakier, more tender, and more buttery, but rising to only double in height, as opposed to two to three times for a biscuit.

When done right, scones should have some height from rising, be lightly browned and a little crisp on the outside, and cooked all the way through on the inside, but still be moist. They should also have a tender, light texture with a pure buttery flavor and just the right amount of add-ins. But, sometimes they don't turn out that way and resemble a lead weight.

The secret of making any good scone is having fresh, cold ingredients, a quick, light hand when mixing, and a hot oven. Ingredients are mixed together in steps, each one taking mere seconds so the dough isn't overmixed. Otherwise you'll get a dry and dense scone that doesn't rise as high and can be used to keep your door propped open. After mixing, the dough should be soft and sticky—in fact it is better to have the dough difficult to handle rather than too dry.

Scones are mixed by one of two methods, depending on the fat used and the desired texture. When solid fat such as stick butter is used, the recipe is mixed by the

QUESTION: *What is a true scone texture? I've had some that are flaky or more cake-like. Please explain.*

ANSWER: Today's scones vary from recipe to recipe, and there is great latitude in what a scone can be. Traditional scones are flaky, while others now are similar to more cake-like shortcake biscuits, with a softer texture. Shortcake biscuits are sometimes made with cake flour instead of all-purpose flour, and less butter and sugar than scones; these differences make them less flaky than scones. Flaky scones are made with all-purpose flour, baking powder (or baking soda with buttermilk or another acidic ingredient), butter, and milk, heavy cream (for cream scones), or sour cream. Adding an egg changes the texture and color of the scones, helps them brown better, and makes them puffier and more cake-like. Sugar adds sweetness and is a tenderize; even a small amount does the trick. While these ingredients are similar to baking powder biscuit dough, scones are richer and sweeter.

"biscuit mixing method," also used with making flaky scones. The fat is cut into the flour and dry ingredients and then the liquid ingredients are mixed in. This is the most common method. When liquid fat such as melted butter or oil is used, the "muffin mixing method" is preferred. That's when the dry ingredients and wet ingredients are each mixed separately, and then combined right before baking. Drop scones are made this way.

To keep your scones flaky pop your mixing bowl with the measured flour into the freezer for a few minutes before starting, and keep the butter, eggs, and milk chilled. Scone dough must be kept cold until it goes into a hot oven. Work quickly and avoid overmixing.

The traditional scone is rolled or patted into a circle (I pat mine into a square) and cut into triangles like a pie. Other shapes can be cut with a cookie cutter. Other recipes have you divide the kneaded dough into twelve or so individual heaps that are placed on a cookie sheet. Make sure you don't get too small—the smaller the scone, the drier the texture when baked.

FLAKY TART RED CHERRY SCONES

Today's trend is to dress up scones with dried fruit, citrus zest, chocolate chips, orange or lemon flavoring, ginger, or poppyseeds, or with herbs, cheese, bacon, and vegetables. The combinations are endless. Adding fresh berries or fruit to a scone recipe doesn't work because the dough is kneaded; kneading squishes the fruit and the dough gets too wet from the juice.

INGREDIENTS
$\frac{1}{2}$ cup (1 stick) unsalted butter, room temperature
2 cups unbleached all-purpose flour; spoon into measuring cup and level to top
$\frac{1}{4}$ cup sugar
2 teaspoons baking powder
$\frac{1}{2}$ teaspoon salt
$\frac{3}{4}$ cup heavy cream, room temperature; measure in liquid measuring cup
$\frac{1}{2}$ cup dried tart red cherries or raisins

1. Position a rack in the middle of the oven and preheat the oven to 400 degrees F.

2. Cut the butter into 1-inch cubes and refrigerate it for 30 minutes or freeze it for 10 minutes to get really cold.

3. In a medium bowl, combine the flour, sugar, baking powder, and salt. Sprinkle the chilled butter over the flour and toss with a spoon. Cut the butter into the dry ingredients with two knives (in a scissor motion) or a pastry blender until the butter pieces are no larger than small peas. With your fingertips press the butter into the flour so it forms large flakes. If the butter becomes greasy, chill until hardened. Make a well in the center of the dry ingredients and pour in the cream.

4. With a large spoon, mix in the cream until the dough is just moistened and looks shaggy. Add the cherries. Stir a couple of strokes past shaggy until the dough starts to come together. Place the dough on a lightly floured surface and knead until the dough just holds together.

5. Pat the dough into an 8-inch square, $\frac{1}{2}$-inch thick. Cut it into triangles and bake on an ungreased or parchment paper–lined baking sheet. Bake for 20 minutes until puffy, the edges and the tops lightly browned. A scone should sound hollow

when tapped on top. Take the scones from the oven and cool on a wire cake rack. Serve warm.

Note: For a more cake-like scone, use 1 cup of heavy cream instead of $\frac{3}{4}$ cup and work the dough very lightly.

Storage: Scones are best served the day they are made, ideally warm from the oven, but can be reheated at 350 degrees F for a few minutes. If you have extras, let them cool thoroughly and wrap in plastic wrap, place in an airtight plastic bag or container, and freeze. They'll stay good for about a month. To reheat, let them thaw in their wrapping at room temperature, unwrap, and warm in a 350 degree F oven for 5 minutes.

PANCAKES, WAFFLES, AND CREPES

A piping-hot stack of homemade pancakes or waffles drenched in butter and maple syrup is an all-American breakfast, but can be served at any meal including dessert. A crepe, wrapped around a sweet or savory filling and topped with a sauce, is such a treat. There are hundreds of savory or sweet recipes that range from basic to elaborate.

Pancakes, waffles, and crepes are all quick breads, with crepes having the thinnest batter. Pancakes and waffles are leavened with baking powder, baking soda, or both. Crepes are leavened by eggs that have had air whisked into them. What they have in common is that once the batters are mixed, they must be cooked right away. With pancakes and waffles, the chemical leaveners start releasing carbon dioxide gas, and with crepes, the air bubbles whisked into the eggs and batter will deflate. Care must be taken not to overmix or overbeat the batters. Once the wheat flour is moistened, it produces gluten every time you stir it. It is imperative to just combine the ingredients, otherwise the pancakes and waffles will be tough and dry. With crepes, over-mixing creates too much air in the batter. If that happens large air bubbles will appear during cooking; they will pop and leave craters.

Waffle makers with nonstick grids need to be greased between batches. Spray the plates of your waffle iron with a light coating of vegetable oil spray before you plug it in.

If grids are not nonstick they have not been pretreated, so season them before using for the first time. Brush fat on the grids. Heat until the grids begin to smoke. Bake a waffle to absorb excess fat, and discard it. The waffle iron is ready to use. After baking waffles, wipe the grids gently with a paper towel while they're still warm to remove crumbs. Don't wash the grids or put any water on them. The seasoned grids darken and prevent sticking. However, if the batter begins to stick on the grids wash them with warm suds, rinse, wipe dry, and reseason with unsalted fat.

WHOLE GRAIN WAFFLES

MAKES SIX TO EIGHT 4-INCH-SQUARE WAFFLES

My kids love waffles, so I try to make them as often as I can. Be sure to use a non-stick waffle iron and preheat it until hot. Serve with pure maple syrup and melted butter. I freeze extras so the kids can warm them in a toaster oven when the mood strikes.

INGREDIENTS
Vegetable oil cooking spray
1½ cup unbleached flour; spoon into dry measuring cup and level to top
¼ cup unprocessed (raw) bran flakes (page 213), optional
2 teaspoons baking powder
½ teaspoon salt
1¼ cups whole or 2% milk; measure in liquid measuring cup
2 tablespoons butter, melted and cooled
2 large eggs
2 tablespoon sugar

1. Preheat the oven to 200 degrees F.

2. Spray both sides of the nonstick waffle iron with vegetable oil spray. Preheat the waffle iron. Meanwhile, in a medium bowl, combine the flour, bran, baking powder, and salt until well combined. In another medium bowl, whisk the milk, butter, eggs, and sugar until combined. Make a well in the center of the dry ingredients and pour in the milk mixture. Using a spoon, stir until just combined. The batter will be thick. Don't overmix.

3. Pour 1 cup batter until it comes within 1 inch of the edges. Shut the top. Cook until the waffle batter stops steaming, sometimes just 2 to 3 minutes. Don't lift the cover while cooking. Transfer to a baking sheet and keep warm in the preheated oven while cooking the remaining waffles. Between batches, spray both sides of the waffle iron with oil. Serve hot with maple syrup.

Variations: Buttermilk Waffles: Omit the bran and baking powder and add ¾ teaspoon baking soda. Substitute 1½ cups buttermilk for the milk.

Orange Pecan Waffles: Add the grated peel of 1 orange or ¼ teaspoon orange oil to the wet ingredients. Mix the batter and fold in ¼ cup finely chopped pecans.

QUESTION: *When I put waffle batter on the iron and shut it, my batter never fully fills the iron. How can I make the batter fill it?*

ANSWER: Most waffle irons take 1 cup of batter at a time. Fill a 1-cup dry measuring cup or a ladle with batter. Spread evenly to within one inch of the borders. It will spread more when the top of the waffle iron is closed. Be careful not to overfill the waffle iron, or some of the batter will squeeze out and drip down the sides.

QUESTION: *My waffles had a crispy texture and then lost their crispiness as they cooled. How can I keep them crisp?*

ANSWER: Freshly baked waffles can turn disappointingly soggy. There are two ways to extend the life of waffles.

When you preheat the waffle iron, also preheat the oven to 200 degrees F. Then, as the cooked waffles come off the waffle iron, place them on a wire cake rack on a baking sheet in the oven. Don't stack the waffles or place them directly on the baking sheet, or the hot waffles will "steam" and get mushy. Serve within 15 to 20 minutes.

To revive the waffles' crispiness, toast the waffle for about a minute in a toaster oven set on low.

RISE AND SHINE PANCAKES

MAKES ABOUT EIGHT 4-INCH PANCAKES

Nothing beats a stack of steaming hot pancakes fresh from the griddle.

INGREDIENTS
Vegetable oil cooking spray
1 cup unbleached all-purpose flour
2 teaspoons baking powder
$\frac{1}{8}$ teaspoon salt
$\frac{3}{4}$ cup whole or 2% milk
1 large egg
2 tablespoons sugar
1 tablespoon canola oil

1. Spray a large griddle or skillet with vegetable oil spray. Preheat over medium-high heat until a splash of water sprinkled on the surface turns to tiny droplets which dance and then disappear.

2. In a medium bowl, whisk the flour, baking powder, and salt until well combined.

3. In another medium bowl, whisk the milk, egg, sugar, and oil until combined. Make a well in the center of the dry ingredients, and pour in the milk mixture. Using a spoon, mix until combined.

4. For each pancake, pour $\frac{1}{4}$ cup of the batter onto the hot griddle. Cook until tiny bubbles appear on the top and the edge looks cooked. Turn with a pancake turner and continue cooking until the underside is browned. Spray the griddle between batches.

Variations: Buttermilk Pancakes: These tend to be thicker and very moist on the inside. Instead of milk, use $1\frac{1}{4}$ cups buttermilk. Omit the baking powder and use $\frac{1}{2}$ teaspoon of baking soda. For **Blueberry Buttermilk Pancakes:** Sprinkle 1 tablespoon fresh blueberries or frozen on each pancake right after it is poured onto the griddle. Makes 6 pancakes.

Whole-Wheat Orange Pancakes: Substitute $\frac{1}{2}$ cup whole-wheat flour for $\frac{1}{2}$ cup all-purpose. Add the grated peel of $\frac{1}{2}$ orange or $\frac{1}{4}$ teaspoon pure orange oil and a few gratings of nutmeg to the milk mixture.

QUESTION: *When should I flip my pancakes?*

ANSWER: You must watch for the signs. Turn pancakes when the tops have some tiny bubbles popping and pocking the surface. The edge should look slightly dry. Before you flip, double check underneath to see if the bottom is a medium, golden brown. (If it is browning too quickly, turn down the heat.) Slide a metal spatula or pancake turner under it and take a peek. If it is ready, just slide the spatula all the way under and flip as close to the surface as you can. It is easier to flip pancakes on a griddle because it doesn't have a tall rim. But with a pan, if you work from the middle out, you're going to be ok.

A 4-inch pancake takes anywhere from 2 to 5 minutes for the bottom to cook to a golden brown color. The thinner the batter and the smaller the pancake, the faster it cooks. As the pan gets hotter, pancakes cook more quickly but also burn faster. After flipping, the second side takes a much shorter time to finish—1 or 2 minutes—and never browns as evenly as the first.

ONLINE SOURCES

❖

**MY FAVORITE PLACES TO GET INFORMATION,
INGREDIENTS, AND KITCHEN STUFF:**

http://www.wholefoods.com
http://www.bridgekitchenware.com
http://www.kingarthurflour.com
http://www.sugarcraft.com
http://www.hodgsonmill.com
http://www.williams-sonoma.com
http://www.wilton.com
http://www.candylandcrafts.com
http://www.chefstore.com
http://www.surlatable.com
http://www.chefsresource.com
http://www.clabbergirl.com/products.htm
http://www.whitelily.com

INDEX

baking pans (*cont.*)
    for muffins, 216, 221
    preparing of, 34, 35, 64, 94–95
baking powder, 18
    in cookies, 93
    expiration dates of, 16, 19
    storing of, 16
baking soda, 18
    in cookies, 93
    expiration dates of, 16, 19
    storing of, 16
baklava, 120
    pear, 121–22
balloon whisks, 12
banana cake squares, 219
bar cookies, 90–91, 106–15
    chewy chocolate chip cookie bars, 112–13
    chocolate brownie-cake bars, 110
    double chocolate fudge brownie bars, 108–9
    Florida lime pie bars with a coconut–graham
        cracker crust, 114–15
    slicing of, 106
    storing of, 107
barley flour, 17
Bartlett pears, in baklava, 121–22
batter, for pancakes and waffles, 238, 239, 240,
    241
beaten biscuits, 228
beating, 35
    of egg whites, 22, 23, 26, 36–38, 64
    of egg yolks, 39, 64
bench scrapers, 11, 106
Beranbaum, Rose Levy, 176
biscotti:
    cutting of, 101
    orange mocha chip, 102–3
biscuits, 227–33
    baking tips for, 228–29
    "British," 234
    buttermilk, 232–33
    doneness of, 227
    storing of, 229–30
    types of, 228
bittersweet chocolate, 161, 162
black and white chocolate mousse tart,
    157–59

blending, 35
blends, of chocolate, 163–64
blind baking, *see* pre-baking, of pie crusts
blueberry(ies), 225
    buttermilk pancakes, 241
    cornbread, 223
    crumble pie, 149–50
    lemon cake muffins, 226–27
    muffins, 223
bowls, 8–9
bran:
    cinnamon raisin muffins, 224–25
    in quick breads, 214
bread machines, 180
    kneading dough in, 191
    yeast for, 188
breads, artisan, 196, 205
breads, quick, *see* quick breads
breads, yeast, *see* yeast breads
"British biscuits," 234
broken dough, 126
brown Bettys, 125
brownies, 106–11
    baking techniques for, 109, 111
    cakey vs. chewy, 106–7
    cocoa powder in, 165
    double chocolate fudge, 108–9
    slicing of, 106
    storing of, 107
browning, of cheesecakes, 77
brown sugar, 21–22, 93
    measuring of, 32
    storing of, 16
    in yeast breads, 183
buckles, 125
Bundt cake, almond, 57–59
butter, 19–20
    creaming of, with sugar, 35, 39–40,
        94
    melting of, 15, 188
    phyllo dough and, 120
    salted, 21
    stick form, 31
    storing of, 16
    temperature of, 14–15
    in yeast breads, 182, 188

frosting:
    of butter cake, 50
    orange-honey, for layer cake, 62–63
fructose, 22
fruit:
    banana cake squares, 219
    blueberry buttermilk pancakes, 241
    blueberry cornbread or muffins, 223
    blueberry crumble pie, 149–50
    mixed-up apple pie, 147–48
    in muffins, 225
    pear baklava, 121–22
    pies, 125, 143–54
    purees, in quick breads, 217
    raspberry cornbread or muffins,
      223
    raspberry tart with a cornmeal crust,
      151–52
    as sweetener in yeast breads, 183
    thickeners, for pies, 144–45
    toppings, for cheesecakes, 75
    see also citrus fruit; dried fruit
fudge brownies, 106, 109
    double chocolate, 108–9
fudge sauce, chocolate ganache, 175–76

galettes, 125
ganache, 174
    fudge sauce, 175–76
genoise, 45, 64, 68
German chocolate, 162
glaze:
    for applesauce cake squares, 218–19
    for Priscilla's orange sponge cake, 69–71
gliadin, 17, 18, 205, 215
gluten, 18, 21, 109, 117–18, 127, 128, 150
    in biscuits, 227
    in pancake batter, 238
    in quick breads, 215
    in yeast breads, 181–82, 184, 186, 188, 189,
      190, 196, 197, 205
glutenin, 17, 18, 205, 215
gluten window, 192
graham cracker crusts:
    for cheesecakes, 75
    for chocolate mousse tart, 157–59

grains, in quick breads, 214
granulated sugars, 21–22
grittiness:
    of chocolate, 168–69
    of icing, 56
grocery store breads, 182
grunts, 125

heaping, as technique, 33
heavy cream:
    in cheesecakes, 73
    in ganache, 174, 175–76
    whipped, 24, 25
honey, 21–22, 93
    in buttercakes, 61
    -orange frosted layer cake, 62–63
    in pear baklava, 121–22
    in yeast breads, 183
humidity:
    for baking cheesecakes, 74, 76
    for rising yeast dough, 193–94

ice baths, 159
icebox pies, 125, 153
icing:
    caramel, 56
    for chocolated frosted fudge layer cake,
      177–78
    coconut, 56
    cream cheese, 60–61
    grittiness of, 56
    royal, 22
    seven-minute vanilla bean, 55–56
    spatulas, 11
indirect method, in dough fermentation,
    180
ingredients:
    cookie texture and, 92–94
    measuring of, 29–33
    mixing of, 35–42
    and order of adding, 47
    shelf life of, 15–16
    storing of, 15–16
    temperature of, 14–15
    working with, 13–27
Instant ClearJel, 144

mixers, electric, 9, 191, 204
mixes, cake, 45
mixing:
    of biscuit dough, 227
    bowls, 8
    cookie texture and, 94
    methods of, 35–42
    of pie crust dough, 135
    of quick bread batter, 215–16
    spoons, 9
    of yeast dough, 188–89
molasses, 21–22
    in yeast breads, 183
molded cookies, 91
morsels, chocolate, 163–64
    melting of, 170
mousse tart, chocolate, black and white,
    157–59
muffins, 213–17, 225
    baking tins for, 10, 216, 221
    blueberry, 225
    chocolate, 219, 220–21
    cinnamon raisin bran, 224–25
    corn, 222–23
    doneness of, 216
    lemon blueberry cake, 226–27
    oven temperatures and, 223
    raspberry, 223

Neufchatel, 73
    in chocolate peanut butter cup cheesecake,
        88–89
no crack New York dense and creamy
        cheesecake, 82–84
no-knead yeast batter breads, 181
non-diastatic malt, 184
nonstick pans, 7
nut pies, 125
nuts, 26–27
    storing of, 16
    in whole grain waffles, 239

oat flour, 17
oatmeal:
    in quick breads, 214
    raisin cookies, jumbo, 104–5

offset spatulas, 11
oil, 19–20
    applesauce in place of, 217
    in cakes, 46
old-fashioned buttermilk biscuits, 232–33
olive oil, 19, 20
orange:
    in citrus angel food cake, 66–67
    -honey frosted layer cake, 62–63
    mocha chip biscotti, 102–3
    pecan waffles, 239
    sponge cake, Priscilla's, 69
    whole-wheat pancakes, 241
ovens:
    humid, for cheesecakes, 76–77
    melting chocolate in, 167–68
    preheating of, 33, 42, 199
    shelves in, 33
    temperatures of, 77, 199–200, 216–17,
        223
    thermometers for, 7, 33
    see also microwave ovens
oven spring, 198
overproofing, 198
over-risen dough, 195, 198

pan breads, 180
pancakes, 238, 241–42
panning, of bread dough, 196
paper, on baking pans, 10, 95
parchment paper, 10, 95
pastry, 116–23
    alchemy of, 118–19
    American pie, 126
    choux, 116–17, 123
    pear baklava, 121–22
    phyllo, 117–18, 119–20
    puff, 116, 117
    strudel, 117–18
pâte à choux, 116–17
pâte brisée, 126, 130–34
pâte sablé, 126
pâte sucrée, 126
peach cobbler, 150
peanut butter chocolate cheesecake,
    88–89

storing (*cont.*)

    of pie dough, 139

    of sponge cake, 71

    of vanilla beans, 56

stovetop pies, 125, 153

straight dough method, 180

strainers, 11

strawberry shortcake, 228

strudel dough, 117–18

substitutions:

    for chocolate, 178

    for fat, 217

sugar, 21

    in cheesecakes, 73

    in cookies, 93, 94

    cookies, classic crispy, 100

    in egg foams, 36

    honey used in place of, 61

    in pie crusts, 127

    powdered, 21–22

    storing of, 16

    in yeast breads, 183

sugared dough, 126

summer coating, 164

sweet chestnut flour, 17

sweet chocolate, 161, 162

sweet dough, 118

sweetened condensed milk, 23–24

sweeteners, 21–22

    storing of, 16

    in yeast breads, 183

sweet pie crust, 126

syneresis, 73, 78

syrup, chocolate, 33

table salt, 26

tape measure, as kitchen equipment, 5–6

tapioca, as thickener, 145

tart(s):

    black and white chocolate mousse, 157–59

    definition of, 125

    fruit fillings for, 143–53

    pans, 10

    raspberry, with a cornmeal crust, 151–52

    unmolding of, 152

temperature:

    in fermentation, 185, 186, 187, 188

    of ingredients, 14–15, 16, 94

    of melting chocolate, 171, 172, 173

    of ovens, 7, 33, 77, 199–200, 216–17, 223

tempering, of chocolate, 169, 170–74

"tenderizers/weakeners," 13

10X sugar, 21–22

terms, in measurement, 29–31

texture:

    of cookies, 91–95

    of scones, 234

Theobroma cacao, 160

thermometers, 6–7, 33, 199

thickeners:

    for fruit pies, 144–45

    in lemon meringue pie, 156

timbales, 91

timer, 7

tolerance, in cakes, 45

toppings, for cheesecakes, 75

"tougheners/strengtheners," 13

triticale, 17

ultimate buttercake with seven-minute vanilla bean icing, 53–56

unmolding, 42–43, 49, 58

    of cheesecakes, 79–80

    of tarts, 152

unshortened cakes *see* foam cakes

unsweetened chocolate, 161, 162

"use by" dates, 16, 19, 20

vanilla bean(s):

    icing, seven-minute, ultimate buttercake with, 53–56

    saving seeds of, 56

vegetable oil, 19, 20

vinegar, in fermentation, 206

vital wheat gluten, 184

waffles, 238, 239–40

water:

    in muffin tins, 221

    in pastry dough, 119

    in recipes, 24

seizing of chocolate and, 168–69

in yeast breads, 182

water baths, for cheesecakes, 74, 76–77

waxed paper, 10, 95

weather, cream puffs and, 122

weeping:

in cheesecakes, 78

in custards, 73

in lemon meringue pies, 154

weights, for pre-baking pie crusts, 139, 140

wheat bread, whole grain, from a starter, 208–10

wheat flour, 17–18

in pastry dough, 117–18

in pie crusts, 126–29

in yeast breads, 181–82

whipped cream, 24, 25

whipping, technique of, 36

whisks, 12

white chocolate, 161, 164

chips, in black and white chocolate mousse
tart, 157

White Lily, 227

whites, of eggs, 22, 23, 26, 36–38, 64

white sandwich bread, 202–3

whole grain:

flour, 17

waffles, 239

wheat bread from a starter, 208–10

whole-wheat:

flour, 182

flour, in muffins, 213

orange pancakes, 241

windowpane kneading test, 191–92

yeast, 19

activation and fermentation of, 181, 182–83,
185–88, 205–7

expiration dates on, 16, 20

in quick breads, 212

substituting types of, 20

troubleshooting for, 194

yeast breads, 179–210, 212

additions to, 184

alchemy of, 181–87

baking of, 199–200

cooling of, 200

dough mixing and, 188–89

first rising in, 192–95

freezing of dough for, 198

kneading dough and, 190–92

punching down and, 195–96

second rising in, 197–99

shaping of, 196–97

starters for, 19, 180, 205–7

storing of, 200–201

types of, 180–81

ABOUT SARAH PHILLIPS

❖

Sarah Phillips has spent most of her professional life cooking and baking. She has been an entrepreneur, making both gourmet cookies for Manhattan stores and low-fat mixes carried in national grocery store chains; a recipe developer for the Chicago Metallic Bakeware Company; and the baking expert on iVillage.com. Most recently, she developed the "Ask Sarah" Message Board for Bakers on her website, *www.baking911.com*. Today the website receives more than five million hits every month. *www.baking911.com* has been recommended by the *Los Angeles Times* and in other news media as well as online. Sarah is a member of the Home Bakers Association and has appeared on television.